T0181381

Lecture Notes in Computer Science 10796

Commenced Publication in 1973
Founding and Former Series Editors:
Gerhard Goos, Juris Hartmanis, and Jan van Leeuwen

More information about this series at http://www.springer.com/series/7411

Juan Moreno García-Loygorri
Antonio Pérez-Yuste
César Briso · Marion Berbineau
Alain Pirovano · Jaizki Mendizábal (Eds.)

Communication Technologies for Vehicles

13th International Workshop
Nets4Cars/Nets4Trains/Nets4Aircraft 2018
Madrid, Spain, May 17–18, 2018
Proceedings

 Springer

Editors
Juan Moreno García-Loygorri (iD)
Escuela Técnica Superior de Ingeniería
  de Sistemas de Telecomunicacion
Madrid
Spain

Antonio Pérez-Yuste (iD)
Escuela Técnica Superior de Ingeniería
  de Sistemas de Telecomunicacion
Madrid
Spain

César Briso (iD)
Escuela Técnica Superior de Ingeniería
  de Sistemas de Telecomunicacion
Madrid
Spain

Marion Berbineau
University of Lille
Villeneuve d'Ascq
France

Alain Pirovano
Ecole Nationale de l'Aviation Civile
Toulouse Cedex 4
France

Jaizki Mendizábal (iD)
Ceit-IK4 Asociación Centro Tecnológico
San Sebastián - Donostia
Spain

ISSN 0302-9743   ISSN 1611-3349 (electronic)
Lecture Notes in Computer Science
ISBN 978-3-319-90370-5   ISBN 978-3-319-90371-2 (eBook)
https://doi.org/10.1007/978-3-319-90371-2

Library of Congress Control Number: 2018940151

LNCS Sublibrary: SL5 – Computer Communication Networks and Telecommunications

Printed on acid-free paper

This Springer imprint is published by the registered company Springer International Publishing AG part of Springer Nature
The registered company address is: Gewerbestrasse 11, 6330 Cham, Switzerland

Preface

The Communications Technologies for Vehicles Workshop series provides an international forum on the latest technologies and research in the field of intra- and inter-vehicle communications. It is organized annually to present original research results in all areas related to physical layer, communication protocols and standards, mobility and traffic models, experimental and field operational testing, and performance analysis among others.

First launched by Tsutomu Tsuboi, Alexey Vinel, and Fei Liu in Saint Petersburg, Russia (2009), the Nets4Workshops series (Nets4Cars/Nets4Trains/Nets4Aircraft/Nets4 Spacecrafts) have been held in Newcastle upon Tyne, UK (2010), Oberpfaffenhofen, Germany (2011), Vilnius, Lithuania (2012), Villeneuve d'Ascq, France (2013), Offenburg, Germany (2014 Spring), Saint Petersburg, Russia (2014 Fall), Sousse, Tunisia (2015 Spring), Munich, Germany (2015 Fall), San Sebastian, Spain (2016 Spring), Halmstad, Sweden (2016 Fall), and Toulouse, France (2017 Spring).

These proceedings contain the papers presented at the 13th International Workshop on Communication Technologies for Vehicles Nets4Workshops series (Nets4Cars/ Nets4Trains/Nets4Aircraft/Nets4Spacecrafts 2018), which took place in Madrid, Spain, in May 2018, organized by the Universidad Politécnica de Madrid (Spain).

The call for papers resulted in 17 submissions. Each of them was assigned to the international Technical Program Committee to be reviewed at least by two independent reviewers. The co-chairs of the four Technical Program Committees (Nets4Cars, Nets4Trains, Nets4Spacecrafts, and Nets4Aircraft) selected 17 full papers for publication in these proceedings and presentation at the workshop, five of them for Nets4Cars, seven for Nets4Trains, and five for Nets4Aircraft. In addition, two demonstration papers were also accepted and a keynote speech focused on Nets4Spacecrafts. The order of the papers presented in these proceedings was aligned with the workshop program.

The general co-chairs and the Technical Program Committee co-chairs extend a sincere "thank you" to all the authors who submitted the results of their recent research as well as to all the members of the hard-working comprehensive Technical Program Committee that worked on the reviews.

March 2018

Juan Moreno García-Loygorri
Antonio Pérez-Yuste
César Briso
Marion Berbineau
Alain Pirovano
Jaizki Mendizábal

Organization

General Co-chairs

Antonio Pérez-Yuste   Universidad Politécnica de Madrid, Spain
Marion Berbineau   IFSTTAR, France
César Briso Rodríguez   Universidad Politécnica de Madrid, Spain
Juan Moreno   Universidad Politécnica de Madrid, Spain
   García-Loygorri
Alexey Vinel   Halmstad University, Sweden

TPC Co-chairs (Nets4Trains)

Jaizki Mendizabal   CEIT and Tecnun (University of Navarra), Spain
Juan Moreno   Metro de Madrid S.A./Universidad Politécnica de Madrid,
   Garcia-Loygorri   Spain

TPC Co-chairs (Nets4Aircraft)

David Matolak   University of South Carolina, USA
Pedro Pintó Marín   Hispasat, Spain
Alain Pirovano   ENAC, France
César Briso   Universidad Politécnica de Madrid, Spain
Alexey Vinel   Halmstad University, Sweden

TPC Co-chairs (Nets4Cars)

Antonio Pérez-Yuste   Universidad Politécnica de Madrid, Spain
Mohammed Kassab   ENISO, University of Sousse, Tunisia

Steering Committee

Marion Berbineau   IFSTTAR, France
César Briso Rodríguez   Universidad Politécnica de Madrid, Spain
Jaizki Mendizabal   CEIT and Tecnun (University of Navarra), Spain
Juan Moreno   Universidad Politécnica de Madrid, Spain
   García-Loygorri

Antonio Pérez-Yuste   Universidad Politécnica de Madrid, Spain
Alain Pirovano   ENAC, France
Alexey Vinel   Halmstad University, Sweden

Technical Program Committee

F. José Arqués	Universidad Politécnica de Madrid, Spain
Aitor Arriola	Ikerlan, Spain
Marion Berbineau	IFSTTAR, France
Hervé Bonneville	MERCE, France
César Briso	Universidad Politécnica de Madrid, Spain
César Calvo-Ramírez	Universidad Politécnica de Madrid, Spain
Ana González Plaza	Universidad Politécnica de Madrid, Spain
Cristophe Gransart	IFSTTAR, France
Ke Guan	Beijing Jiaotong University, China
Danping He	Beijing Jiaotong University, China
Mohammed Kassab	ENISO, University of Sousse, Tunisia
Jaizki Mendizabal	CEIT, Spain
Juan Moreno García-Loygorri	Universidad Politécnica de Madrid, Spain
Antonio Pérez-Yuste	Universidad Politécnica de Madrid, Spain
Joshua Puerta	CEIT, Spain
José Manuel Riera	Universidad Politécnica de Madrid, Spain
Stephan Sand	DLR, Germany
Mohammad Soliman	DLR, Germany

Hosting Institution

Universidad Politécnica de Madrid, Spain

Organizing Committee

César Briso Rodríguez	Universidad Politécnica de Madrid, Spain
Juan Moreno García-Loygorri	Universidad Politécnica de Madrid, Spain
Antonio Pérez-Yuste	Universidad Politécnica de Madrid, Spain

Co-organizer and Sponsoring Institution

Hispasat, Spain

Contents

Nets4Aircrafts and UAV

3D Air-X UAV Communications: Challenges and Channel Modeling

David W. Matolak$^{(\boxtimes)}$

University of South Carolina, Columbia, SC 29208, USA
matolak@sc.edu

Abstract. The use of unmanned aerial vehicles (UAVs) is growing rapidly, for an expanding variety of applications. These UAVs range in size from a few centimeters to the size of passenger jet aircraft, and will fly a large assortment of missions that take them from the stratosphere to residential neighborhoods. Control and communications must hence be extremely reliable. In this paper we summarize some key characteristics of UAV communications, describe fundamentals and challenges for reliable UAV communications, some current efforts in the area, and provide a framework for analysis and modeling of a vital component in any UAV communication system: the air-ground channel. Features of this channel are discussed, with example references to the literature. Suggestions for future work in air-ground channel modeling are provided. The conference presentation of this work will include example results.

Keywords: Unmanned aircraft · Drone · Channel modeling

1 Introduction

The use of unmanned aerial vehicles (UAVs), also known as unmanned aircraft systems (UAS) and by the popular term "drones," has been growing rapidly. News on UAVs appears in the popular press daily, with applications also expanding, e.g., [1]. Work on, and use of, these vehicles and their operation and applications spans entities from international organizations such as the International Telecommunications Union (ITU) [2] to individual consumer hobbyists. If projections of the numbers of UAVs aloft in the worldwide airspace come true, thousands of UAVs will be in continuous operation in the skies above the United States alone within the next 10 years [3].

There are multiple ways to classify UAVs [4], and multiple organizations around the globe are preparing for their use in both controlled airspace [5, 6] and uncontrolled or "loosely controlled" airspace [7]. The airspace definitions are generally defined by the International Civil Aviation Organization (ICAO) [8], and are functions of altitude, aircraft size and capabilities, proximity to populated areas, and sometimes local regulations. Airspace definitions can be changed temporarily for reasons of safety or military purposes.

© Springer International Publishing AG, part of Springer Nature 2018
J. Moreno García-Loygorri et al. (Eds.): Nets4Cars 2018/Nets4Trains 2018/Nets4Aircraft 2018, LNCS 10796, pp. 3–15, 2018.
https://doi.org/10.1007/978-3-319-90371-2_1

Operating UAVs requires communications, navigation, and surveillance (CNS), just as for piloted or "manned," i.e., human-occupied aircraft[1]. Yet for UAVs, additional requirements may be imposed. This is because UAVs can have missions that are dramatically different from those of piloted aircraft, and such missions can yield physical differences including UAV flight locations, kinematics (velocities and accelerations, both linear and angular) and momentum, flight duration, and range. Examples include UAVs flying very near or within urban areas, forests, or indoors, UAVs flying at stratospheric altitudes over continental distances continuously over multiple days, as well as UAVs flying rapidly at extremely low altitudes generally considered too close to earth to be safe for human-occupied flights. These differences affect the requirements of UAV CNS systems.

The growth of UAV applications and numbers will impose new demands for more reliable CNS systems for a larger number of aircraft. Safety of human life, then property, are the paramount concerns, but system efficiency and other considerations (e.g., cost) are also germane in CNS system design. New UAV CNS systems will need to be more reliable, adaptive, and rapid than present systems.

In this paper we focus on communications for UAVs. Section 2 provides a brief overview of UAV communications and networking, comparing with other forms of communication systems such as those for terrestrial applications, and for conventional human-occupied aircraft. Some fundamentals and challenges are described, motivating study of the air-ground (AG) channel. This is followed by a short overview of some example recent work on UAV CNS systems. Since an accurate characterization is essential to the design of reliable UAV communication systems, in Sect. 3 we describe the AG channel and its characterization. Section 4 presents suggestions for future work on UAV communications, and Sect. 5 concludes with a summary.

2   UAV Communications and Networking

The topic of UAV communications and networking is both broad and deep, hence our treatment is necessarily a summary one. Such aircraft could of course form networks of UAVs alone (sometimes called swarms) as well as networks of UAVs connected with piloted aircraft [9]. Most such networks ultimately connect to one or more ground stations (GS). For small UAVs the link may be to a single individual. Links through other platforms such as satellites, high-altitude platforms, and mobile earth stations on terrestrial vehicles (e.g., cars, trains) and boats are also possible, and many of these are planned for the future. Many of these types of links are also formed in military communication networks involving aircraft. These sorts of multi-platform aircraft

---

[1] Some organizations, e.g., ICAO, prefer to use the term "remotely piloted aircraft" (RPA) for UAVs, but this term could exclude UAVs whose flights are "pre-programmed" and hence—if considered piloted at all—are piloted only by specifying flight path in advance. Also, RPAs can carry human occupants. In this paper we use the terms UAV and piloted aircraft as two distinct classes, recognizing the imprecision of these designations.

connections are often designated air-X, and in some cases such connections may be established opportunistically [10].

The use of UAVs is being considered, and is taking place at present, for a large number, and growing variety, of applications. Small rotorcraft, whose maneuverability and hovering capabilities are attractive for some applications, are often used, but fixed wing UAVs are used as well. A partial list of applications includes filming, police and public safety surveillance, industrial monitoring, scientific and environmental observation, agriculture, package delivery, civil infrastructure inspection, and the augmentation of terrestrial networks by the addition of a "third dimension" (3D) composed of UAVs aloft. The cellular community has recently been increasing its attention on UAV communications for terrestrial network augmentation with LTE [11, 12]. So-called "smart community" applications are also envisioned [13, 14].

Much prior work used for communications in terrestrial applications and for piloted aviation applications naturally pertains to UAV communications: the same layers of the communications protocol stack are used, but some differences arise. As with commercial piloted aircraft, UAVs can move at velocities larger than those of terrestrial vehicles. As aircraft altitude increases, the communication link range also generally increases. Traditional civil aviation is conservative for safety reasons, and for passenger aircraft, still uses analog voice communications at VHF for pilot to air traffic control. This is changing, but slowly. In order to improve UAV link performance, new techniques are being proposed. This includes physical layer techniques such as multicarrier waveform designs [15, 16], and multiple access layer techniques [17], as well as techniques at the networking layer and above.

The performance of any communication technique depends strongly upon the channels over which signals travel. This is because in many cases the wireless channel is the most significant impediment to communications reliability, as it can be lossy, distorting, and temporally and spatially varying. Because of the importance of communication link reliability to safety, the air-ground (AG) channel for UAVs has seen renewed attention from researchers [18]. In the subsections that follow, we provide a summary of some of the fundamentals and challenges associated with UAV communications, largely at the physical and data link layers, and then highlight some notable recent work on UAVs.

2.1 Fundamentals and Challenges

Two of the first things associated with UAVs are altitude and mobility. Although the altitude of UAVs (especially small ones) can be very low, one of the communications advantages of aircraft is their ability to move above local obstacles. This generally increases the probability of a line of sight (LOS) to any GS, and that reduces channel attenuation (path loss). In cellular-like deployments of UAVs, this can be a disadvantage as well, as interference also propagates far in LOS conditions, and hence must be balanced against desired signal levels [19]. Very low-altitude flight makes some channel characteristics for the UAV similar to terrestrial channels, but such flights introduce other challenges, such as careful and accurate navigation.

Mobility enables UAVs to reach a wider variety of GS locations, but can also present challenges if the UAV must keep moving for aerodynamic (e.g., fixed wing) or other reasons (e.g., mission requirements, winds). Fast moving aircraft can produce larger Doppler shifts that must be tracked by receivers. This may become significant for higher frequency bands that are being proposed: an example is the 5 GHz band that the ITU is considering for UAV use, where with small UAVs traveling up to 100 miles/hour (45 m/sec), Doppler shifts can reach $f_D = v/\lambda = vf/c = 45(5 \times 10^9)/3 \times 10^8 = 745$ Hz. Here λ is wavelength, f frequency, and c the speed of light. This Doppler shift[2] is approximately 5% of the current (15 kHz) subcarrier spacing used in LTE, and requires compensation and tracking. If the Doppler spreads are also appreciable, this could produce significant performance degradation, particularly in multicarrier systems, where the spreads induce inter-subcarrier interference.

Doppler spreads constitute the range of Doppler shifts imposed upon transmitted signals, typically caused by multipath propagation—the multipath components (MPCs) travel longer distances than the LOS component, and arrive at the receiver at different spatial angles. Doppler spread values generally scale with the angular extent of scattering around the GS, since scatterers near UAVs are rare, except for low-altitude flights, or perhaps when a UAV is flying in a large swarm. Even in such low-altitude cases though, the UAV AG channel can be much more rapidly varying than terrestrial channels. Figure 1 illustrates these considerations for a near-airport setting.

Controlling UAV mobility, especially when there is more than a small number of aircraft, can be challenging, even if the UAVs are not flying in swarms. Many aircraft —piloted and UAVs—rely on the Global Positioning System (GPS) or other satellite navigation systems. If this is unavailable for some reason, navigation must be done by other means, using signals transmitted from known geographic locations, or inertial computations, or use of maps and sensors (e.g., radar altimeters). Controlling mobility becomes more difficult as altitude decreases, and must be more precise as UAV flights take place near built-up areas, vegetation, or terrain. Traditional air traffic management (ATM) techniques used for civil piloted aircraft will be insufficient for such cases; more will be said on this in the next subsection. Small UAVs must also contend with winds and weather, and depending upon frequency band and geometry, these could also impact communication performance, as they can affect UAV location and antenna orientation. Table 1 provides a short list of some of the features distinguishing UAV from terrestrial communications.

2.2   Example Recent Work

As noted, a number of organizations are working on UAV deployments, regulations, and the communications and networking technologies required to safely and reliably operate UAVs. Here we highlight just a few visible efforts.

---

[2] Note that this Doppler shift is the maximum absolute value for a single platform (transmitter or receiver) in motion, which occurs when the platform is directly approaching or receding from the GS. When the flight path is not along this line, f_D is multiplied by $cos(\theta)$, where θ is the angle between velocity vector and LOS line. If both platforms are in motion, the calculation naturally becomes more complicated.

Fig. 1. Illustration of UAVs and piloted aircraft in near-airport environment, emphasizing altitude and mobility (adapted from NASA).

Table 1. Qualitative comparison of characteristics of terrestrial and UAV communications.

Characteristic	Terrestrial (cellular)	UAV
Velocities	Typically small	Potentially very large
Probability of LOS	Typically small	Potentially large
Temporal availability	Very long	• Large for "loitering" fixed-wing aircraft • Very small for rotorcraft
Range	Small-medium	Potentially very large
Mobility management	Well established	Ill-defined

The National Aeronautics and Space Administration (NASA) of the United States has several programs in UAV research. One is UAS in the National Airspace System (NAS) [20], depicted in Fig. 2, and the other is UAS Traffic Management (UTM) [7], depicted in Fig. 3. NASA is generally supporting the US Federal Aviation Administration (FAA); the FAA has designated several UAV test sites across the United States. As indicated in Figs. 1 and 2, the two NASA programs have different objectives. The UAS in the NAS program is targeted at medium and larger size UAVs that would, at least for a portion of their flight, share airspace with piloted aircraft. This program investigated AG channel models (more in the next section), surveillance techniques (often termed "detect and avoid"), and communications and networking requirements at the lower few layers of the communications protocol stack. Several standards were developed by the Radio Technical Commission for Aeronautics (RTCA) [21], and these standards made use of the NASA UAS in the NAS work. The latest work in this program is focusing on high-reliability air-satellite links.

In contrast, the NASA UTM program is aimed at smaller, low-altitude UAVs. This includes UAVs flying in populated areas, for such services as package delivery and law enforcement. A somewhat related effort is Uber's Elevate program [22]. In this project, the company that pioneered the "crowd-source-taxi" service plans to extend this to an

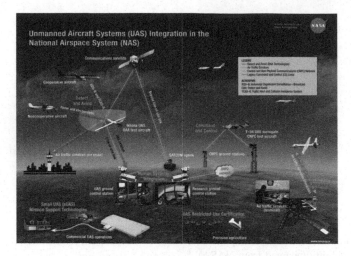

Fig. 2. NASA UAS in the NAS illustration [20].

Fig. 3. NASA UAS traffic management illustration [21].

air passenger service. Their plan is for vertical takeoff and landing aircraft that will initially ferry passengers from one tall building to another, in urban areas. If that proceeds successfully, Uber will extend to other flights within metropolitan areas. These flights will initially be "pre-programmed" and will have a licensed pilot on board as an emergency back-up measure.

The cellular industry has also initiated some research from individual companies [19, 23], and from the cellular industry organization Third Generation Partnership Project (3GPP) [24, 25]. These efforts are aimed at using the cellular standard Long Term Evolution (LTE) for low-altitude UAV connections, and contain some interesting field trial results. This industry's interests are primarily in enlarging their subscriber base. This has been done with the provision of cellular and internet service to airline passengers from companies such as GoGo [26] and SmartSky [27], which essentially employ terrestrial cellular base stations with directional antennas pointed to cover the hemisphere above.

Numerous other efforts, both from individual investigators, and small teams, have also appeared, and the literature is growing rapidly. We cannot be comprehensive here, but note only a few examples: [28, 29, 30]. Interested readers are encouraged to turn to the literature, e.g., [10, 31].

3 Channel Modeling for UAVs

Study of the wireless channel for UAVs has grown in the past several years. This mostly pertains to the AG case, although air-satellite and air-air channels have also seen some attention. All these, and other air-X channels have remaining work to do as well. Here we focus on the AG channel.

As with other types of channels, the AG channel may be classified into categories such as LOS versus non-LOS (NLOS), and by altitude, frequency band, etc. From an engineering perspective, for links through the troposphere from the lower VHF band (>30 MHz) through the EHF band (few hundred GHz), the channel can be modeled as a linear time varying system, hence it is completely characterized by its impulse response (IR) $h(\tau,t)$, or equivalently by the Fourier transform of the IR, the time-varying channel transfer function (TF) $H(f,t)$. There is a rich literature on modeling channels in this way, so we do not cover fundamentals here. See [18, 32, 33, 34].

3.1 AG Channel Model Framework

Figure 4 provides an illustration of the AG channel; worth pointing out is that from the perspective of the channel, the designation of "unmanned" or "piloted" is irrelevant. Note that the structure of the channel model embodied in Fig. 4 is general, and can apply for example to small UAVs. In Fig. 4 we identify five primary components (MPCs) that can exist between a GS and aircraft (and vice-versa, as the channel is reciprocal):

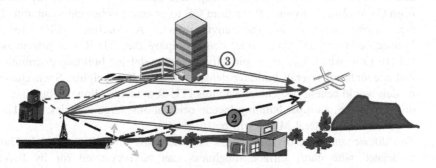

Fig. 4. Illustration of five primary components in the AG channel.

1. The line-of-sight (LOS) component is often, but not always present.
2. The surface component. This may be mostly specular, or, depending on surface roughness, may be substantially suppressed. Spherical earth divergence can also be accounted for (typically only significant at large link distances).
3. Lateral multipath components (MPCs). These emanate from large, electrically smooth objects such as buildings, or smooth hillslopes. Other large objects such as vehicles (land or watercraft, parked aircraft...) may also contribute, depending on the local setting.
4, 5. Diffuse and unresolvable MPCs can be components from rough surface scattering, which can be treated with component #2 (i.e., they have delay very close to that of the primary surface component), or can be from rough obstacle surface scattering, but associated with objects that generate lateral MPCs (#3), or might be components from obstacles very near the GS.

Components four and five can likely be represented as a single type, possibly differentiated according to their source (or according to delay).

Additional comments on these components are as follows:

1. The LOS component if present can be computed from the AG geometry, and from knowledge of the tropospheric refractivity profile. For the simplest level of model(s), at short range, refractivity can be assumed constant. Given link distance, this component is deterministic, and can be computed via the free-space Friis transmission equation.
2. The surface component can be computed from a two-ray model. The curved-earth two-ray (CE2R) model is more accurate than the flat-earth 2R (FE2R) model, but for the simplest model level and short link ranges, the FE2R can be used [37]. The strength of this component must account for surface roughness (e.g., via Rayleigh criterion & Gaussian surface height distribution) and wave divergence (negligible for short ranges). Except for random surface variations, and any randomness (actually, uncertainty) in surface material parameters (permittivity ε and conductivity σ), as with the LOS component, given geometry, this component is also deterministic.
3. For "known" settings where complete environment information is available, the lateral MPCs can be estimated from maps and geometry, essentially ray-tracing from GS to obstacle to aircraft (or from GS to ground to obstacle to aircraft) for the largest objects in the environment. A starting point for a "geometric-stochastic" AG model could employ the ITU-R recommendation P.1410 [36], which has an empirically based model for building distributions that accounts for overall building density and building heights. Such channel models would benefit by generalizing this ITU-R model to allow for buildings of different shape, multiple building façade orientations, large vehicles, etc. Thus, in general these lateral MPCs will be stochastic.
4, 5. The diffuse and unresolvable MPCs are the most difficult to model. Those associated with earth surface roughness can be accounted for by Ricean small-scale fading for conditions where there is a large enough number of these scattered components. Diffuse scattered MPCs from large obstacles might also be treated similarly. Unresolvable MPCs from objects very near the GS, and

from portions of the aircraft itself, might also be "traced." Weak MPCs at delay values not associated with components 1-3 can also be included. Aside from the approximately known delays of some of these MPCs, these components will also be stochastic.

In Table 2 we provide a list of some qualitative comparisons of AG channel characteristics between the terrestrial and UAV cases.

Table 2. Qualitative comparison of channel characteristics relevant to terrestrial and UAV communications.

Characteristic	Terrestrial (cellular)	UAV
Path loss models	Log-distance	Friis, 2-ray, log-distance
Narrowband small scale fading	Typically Rayleigh, occasionally Ricean	Typically Ricean, occasionally Rayleigh
Root-mean square delay spreads	Typically small	Typically small, occasionally very large
Stationary distance	Typically small	Can be large if LOS present
Doppler spreads	Typically small	Can be large if velocity large

3.2 Modeling Considerations

For engineering purposes, models for path loss and narrowband amplitude fading are most essential. If signal bandwidths are large enough, delay dispersion models (i.e., $h(\tau,t)$ or $H(t,f)$) are also required, and if mobility is large enough, Doppler models are also required. The simplest models, such as the single-path LOS model, which can employ the Friis transmission equation, are deterministic, but most often the AG channel is modeled as at least partly stochastic.

Example path loss models for the LOS AG channel (from the NASA UAS in NAS research) appear in [35, 37, 38]. These models take one of two forms: (i) the common log-distance form, or (ii) a quasi-deterministic form represented by a 2-ray model (CE2R or FE2R) plus random MPCs. Airframe shadowing—the attenuation caused by the aircraft itself by blockage of the LOS component—was also modeled in [39]. Small scale fading was modeled as Ricean, with K-factors approximately independent of distance, and at least 12 dB. All these models pertain to the aviation bands near 970 MHz and 5 GHz, but delays and numbers of MPCs should be applicable to frequency ranges beyond these values. Path loss models for urban settings are of great interest, but because of the difficulties of conducting measurement campaigns in these areas, only limited simulation models currently exist, e.g., [40], without experimental validation.

Because of the importance of accurate channel modeling to reliable UAV communications, research on the AG channel is expanding. Current topics of interest for smaller UAVs include low-altitude models [41, 42], vegetation effects [43] and accurate modeling of earth surface reflection [44], antenna pattern effects [45], and multiple-input/multiple-output (MIMO) [46]. Another topic is the estimation of stationarity distance [35], the spatial extent over which channel statistics remain essentially constant.

4 Future Work

As alluded to throughout this paper, there is much remaining work in the area of UAV communications and networking at multiple layers of the communications protocol stack. Other topics such as mobility (air traffic) management, frequency band coordination, and network resilience are also vital.

In terms of the AG channel, suggestions for future work are:

- estimation of stationarity distances as functions of altitude and locations;
- quasi-deterministic adaptive/predictive models [47];
- urban AG path loss and delay dispersion models;
- future large-scale MIMO models, i.e., using entire aircrafts as arrays;
- explicit models for air-X using cars, trains, and boats;
- millimeter wave band (mmWave) short range models.

5 Summary

In this paper we presented a review of communications and networking for unmanned aerial vehicles or UAVs. The rapidly growing use of these aircraft for multiple applications will require more reliable communication links. We described some fundamentals and challenges associated with communications for UAVs, and included a short review of some significant efforts to integrate UAVs into the worldwide air-space and more locally. A framework for air-ground channel modeling was also described, along with a very brief discussion of some practical modeling considerations. Several topics for future work were also presented.

Acknowledgment. The author would like to thank his colleagues Uwe Carsten-Fiebig, Nicolas Schneckenberger, Ismail Guvenc, Wahab Khawaja, Ruoyu Sun, and Hosseinali Jamal for collaborations and discussions that have resulted in contributions to this work.

References

1. CNN Website. http://money.cnn.com/2018/02/15/technology/aerobotics-farm-app-drones/index.html. Accessed 19 Feb 2018
2. International Telecommunications Union: Characteristics of unmanned aircraft systems and spectrum requirements to support their safe operation in non-segregated airspace. ITU-R M.2171, December 2009
3. US Department of Transportation: Unmanned aircraft system (UAS) service demand 2015–2035: literature review and projections of future usage. Technical report, v.1.0, DOT-VNTSC-DoD-13-01, February 2014
4. Templin, F., Sheffield, G., Ballesteros, P.T., Jain, R.: Revolutionary and advanced universal, reliable, always available, cyber secure and affordable communication, navigation, surveillance (CNS) options for all altitudes of UAS operations: UAS CNS architecture concept for controlled air space. NASA SASO RSCAN Program Report, 17 June 2017

5. Radio Technical Commission for Aeronautics (RTCA). www.rtca.org. Accessed 20 Feb 2018
6. Matolak, D.W.: Summary of NASA air-ground channel measurements and models. Appendix Q in Command and Control (C2) Data Link Minimum Operational Performance Standards (MOPS) (Terrestrial), Radio Technical Commission for Aeronautics (RTCA) Inc., 6 May 2016
7. National Aeronautics and Space Administration (NASA): Unmanned aircraft systems traffic management (UTM) program. https://www.utm.arc.nasa.gov/index.shtml. Accessed 22 Feb 2018
8. International Civil Aviation Organization (ICAO). https://www.icao.int/Pages/default.aspx. Accessed 19 Feb 2018
9. Bekmezci, I., Sahingoz, O.K., Temel, S.: Flying ad-hoc networks (FANETs): a survey. Ad Hoc Netw. 11, 1254–1270 (2013)
10. Hayat, S., Yanmaz, E., Muzaffar, R.: Survey on unmanned aerial vehicle networks for civil applications: a communications viewpoint. IEEE Commun. Surv. Tutor. 18(4), 2624–2661 (2016)
11. Lin, X., et al.: The sky is not the limit: LTE for unmanned aerial vehicles. https://arxiv.org/abs/1707.07534. Accessed 27 Feb 2018
12. Van der Bergh, B., Chiumento, A., Pollin, S.: LTE in the sky: trading off propagation benefits with interference costs for aerial nodes. IEEE Commun. Mag. 54(5), 44–50 (2016)
13. Menouar, H., Guvenc, I., Akkaya, K., Uluagac, A.S., Kari, A., Tuncer, A.: UAV-enabled intelligent transportation systems for the smart city: applications and challenges. IEEE Commun. Mag. 55(3), 22–28 (2017)
14. Chandrasekharan, S., et al.: Designing and implementing future aerial communication networks. IEEE Commun. Mag. 54(5), 26–34 (2016)
15. Kakar, J., Marojevic, V.: Waveform and spectrum management for unmanned aerial systems beyond 2025. https://arxiv.org/pdf/1708.01664.pdf. Accessed 27 Feb 2018
16. Jamal, H., Matolak, D.W.: FBMC and LDACS performance for future air to ground communication systems. IEEE Trans. Veh. Technol. 66(6), 5043–5055 (2017)
17. Lyu, J., Zeng, Y., Zhang, R.: Cyclical multiple access in UAV-aided communications: a throughput-delay tradeoff. IEEE Wirel. Commun. Lett. 5(6), 600–603 (2016)
18. Matolak, D.W.: Air-ground channels & models: comprehensive review and considerations for unmanned aircraft systems. In: IEEE Aerospace Conference, Big Sky, MT, 3–10 March 2012
19. Amorim, R., Nguyen, H., Mogensen, P., Kovacs, I.Z., Wigard, J., Sorensen, T.B.: Radio channel modeling for UAV communication over cellular networks. IEEE Wirel. Commun. Lett. 6(4), 514–517 (2017)
20. National Aeronautics and Space Administration (NASA): UAS in the NAS. https://www.nasa.gov/centers/armstrong/programs_projects/UAS_in_the_NAS/index.html. Accessed 27 Feb 2018
21. Radio Technical Commission for Aeronautics: Command and control (C2) data link minimum operational performance standards (MOPS) (Terrestrial). DO-362, 22 September 2016
22. Uber, Inc.: https://www.uber.com/elevate.pdf. Accessed 27 Feb 2018
23. Qualcomm, Inc.: https://www.qualcomm.com/documents/lte-unmanned-aircraft-systems-trial-report. Accessed 27 Feb 2018
24. Third Generation Partnership Project (3GPP): Technical specification group radio access network; study on enhanced LTE support for aerial vehicles (Release 15). 3GPP TR 36.777, V15.0.0, December 2012

25. Third Generation Partnership Project (3GPP): TR 36.777, V15.0.0 Annex H: Field Trials Results on Mobility, December 2012
26. GoGo Business Aviation. https://business.gogoair.com/. Accessed 28 Feb 2018
27. SmartSky Networks. https://www.smartskynetworks.com/. Accessed 28 Feb 2018
28. Khawaja, W., Guvenc, I., Matolak, D.W.: UWB channel sounding and modeling for UAV air-to-ground propagation channels. In: IEEE Globecom, Washington, DC, 4–8 December 2016
29. Yanmaz, E., Kuschnic, R., Bettstetter, C.: Channel measurements over 802.11a-based UAV-to-ground links. In: Proceedings of IEEE Globecom, Wi-UAV Workshop, Houston, TX, December 2011
30. Takizawa, K., Ono, F., Suzuki, M., Tsuji, H., Miura, R.: Measurement on S-band radio propagation characteristics for unmanned aircraft system. In: Proceedings of EuCAP, The Hague, Netherlands, 6–11 April 2014
31. Khawaja, W., Guvenc, I., Matolak, D.W., Fiebig, U.-C., Schneckenberger, N.: A survey of air-to-ground propagation channel modeling for unmanned aerial vehicles, in review. IEEE Commun. Surv. Tutor. December 2017. http://export.arxiv.org/pdf/1801.01656. Accessed 28 Feb 2018
32. Parsons, J.D.: The Mobile Radio Propagation Channel, 2nd edn. Wiley, Chichester (2000)
33. Levis, C.A., Johnson, J.T., Texeira, F.L.: Radio Wave Propagation: Physics and Applications. Wiley, Hoboken (2010)
34. Hlawatsch, F., Matz, G. (eds.): Wireless Communications Over Rapidly Time-Varying Channels. Academic Press, Burlington (2011)
35. Matolak, D.W., Sun, R.: Air-ground channel characterization for unmanned aircraft systems —part I: methods, measurements, and results for over-water settings. IEEE Trans. Veh. Technol. **66**(1), 26–44 (2017). (online 2016)
36. International Telecommunications Union: Propagation data and prediction methods required for the design of terrestrial broadband radio access systems operating in a frequency range from 3 to 60 GHz. Rec. ITU-R P.1410–5, February 2012
37. Sun, R., Matolak, D.W.: Air-ground channel characterization for unmanned aircraft systems —part II: hilly & mountainous settings. IEEE Trans. Veh. Technol. **66**(3), 1913–1925 (2017). (online 2016)
38. Matolak, D.W., Sun, R.: Air-ground channel characterization for unmanned aircraft systems —part III: the suburban and near-urban environments. IEEE Trans. Veh. Technol. **66**(8), 6607–6618 (2017). (online 2016)
39. Matolak, D.W., Sun, R., Rayess, W.: Air-ground channel characterization for unmanned aircraft systems—part IV: airframe shadowing. IEEE Trans. Veh. Technol. **66**(9), 7643–7652 (2017). (online July 2017)
40. Al-Hourani, A., Kandeepan, S., Jamalipour, A.: Modeling air-to-ground path loss for low altitude platforms in urban environments. In: Proceedings of Globecom, Austin, TX, 8–12 December 2014
41. Simunek, M., Perez-Fontan, F., Pechac, P.: The UAV low elevation propagation channel in urban areas: statistical analysis and time series generator. IEEE Trans. Antennas Prop. **61**(7), 3850–3858 (2013)
42. Cai, X., Gonzalez-Plaza, A., Alonso, D., Zhang, L., Briso Rodriguez, C., Yuste, A.P., Yin, X.: Low altitude UAV propagation channel modeling. In: Proceedings of EuCAP, Paris, France, April 2017
43. Kvicera, M., Perez-Fontan, F., Israel, J., Pechac, P.: Modeling scattering from tree canopies for UAV Scenarios. In: Proceedings of EuCAP, Davos, Switzerland, 10–14 April 2016
44. Jost, T., et al.: Ground reflection for low elevations at L- and K-band. In: Proceedings of EuCAP, Davos, Switzerland, 10–14 April 2016

45. Arias, M., et al.: Statistical analysis of the radiation pattern of an antenna mounted on an aircraft. In: Proceedings of EuCAP, Davos, Switzerland, 10–14 April 2016
46. Willink, T.J., Squires, C.C., Colman, G.W.K., Muccio, M.T.: Measurement and characterization of low-altitude air-to-ground MIMO channels. IEEE Trans. Veh. Tech. **65**(4), 2637–2648 (2016)
47. Matolak, D.W., Jamal, H., Sun, R.: Spatial and frequency correlations in two-ray SIMO channels. In: IEEE ICC, Paris, France, 21–25 May 2017

IP Mobility in Aeronautical Communications

Alexandre Tran[1,2], Alain Pirovano[1(✉)], Nicolas Larrieu[1],
Alain Brossard[2], and Stéphane Pelleschi[2]

[1] ENAC, TELECOM/ReSCo, Toulouse, France
{alexandre.tran, alain.pirovano,
nicolas.larrieu}@recherche.enac.fr
[2] Rockwell Collins, Blagnac, France
{alain.brossard,
stephane.pelleschi}@rockwellcollins.com

Abstract. In the sake of modernization, aviation stakeholders decided that the future aviation network infrastructure, in particular for air-ground communication systems, will move towards IP based networks. It has been referred to in the International Civil Aviation Organization as Aeronautical Telecommunication Network/Internet Protocol Suite. Due to the heterogeneous communication environment, it is necessary to support handover between different access technologies and access networks. In this article, we first define the very specific aeronautical communication environment. Our main contribution is a performance assessment of the most deployed network protocols capable of managing IP mobility within the aeronautical environment. We focus our analysis on the Mobile IPv6 protocol and implementation issues of a representative aeronautical network in Omnet++.

Keywords: IP mobility · Air ground communications · MIPv6

1 Introduction

The current aeronautical communication infrastructure for Air Traffic Management (ATM) has to evolve in order to respond to an endless increase in air traffic and to support more stringent data link communications. In this way, aviation stakeholders gathered in several groups such as International Civil Aviation Organization (ICAO), European Organization for Civil Aviation Equipment (EUROCAE), Radio Technical Commission for Aeronautics (RTCA) and Airlines Electronic Engineering Committee (AEEC), are working on a future IP-based Aeronautical Telecommunication Network (ATN/IP). Its goal is to interconnect all the aeronautical subnetworks with the IPv6 protocol.

The aeronautical environment is different from other communication domains (e.g. personal wireless communication in 4G networks or vehicular communications). The two main key problems are the global mobility and the safety-related data which have very stringent quality of services (QoS) requirements. Whereas some solutions have already been proposed in [1], no solution has been taken on yet by the aviation industry.

To handle the node mobility in IPv6, the Internet Engineering Task Force (IETF) has developed Mobile IPv6 (MIPv6) [2]. It allows a seamless communication between

© Springer International Publishing AG, part of Springer Nature 2018
J. Moreno García-Loygorri et al. (Eds.): Nets4Cars 2018/Nets4Trains 2018/Nets4Aircraft 2018, LNCS 10796, pp. 16–26, 2018.
https://doi.org/10.1007/978-3-319-90371-2_2

a mobile node and its correspondent node via a Home Agent (HA). In this article, we investigate MIPv6 for an aeronautical scenario through the xMIPv6 model of the INET framework [3].

The remainder of the paper is organized as follows: Sect. 2 provides an overview of the aeronautical communications environment and its evolution towards IP based networks. Section 3 highlights the need of managing the node mobility under different IP networks and presents some dedicated protocols, with their strengths and flaws. In Sect. 4, we explain our simulation model for MIPv6 in a context of an aeronautical environment. We then analyze the first results and conclude with several suggestions for our simulation model and the IP mobility management in an aeronautical environment.

2 Aeronautical Air Ground Communications and Data Link

2.1 From Analog Voice to Data Link

The first radio transmitter has been invented and tested by AT&T (American Telephone & Telegraph) in 1917, allowing for the first time voice communications between ground personnel and pilots. But, it was only in 1935 that airborne radios were considered reliable and efficient enough to be widely deployed on existing aircraft. These air–ground communication means were proposed in order to increase air safety. From these years, the very high frequency (VHF) band was mainly used for radiotelephony services between pilots and controllers. It has been further augmented with Satellite Communication (SATCOM) since the early 1990s. Hence, voice communications are possible even in oceanic areas where direct communications with VHF ground stations cannot be deployed regarding their range.

Nevertheless, considering the increasing number of aircraft in airspace, the lack of resources makes it necessary to foresee new solutions in order to avoid congestion. Data link (or digital data link) came up as the promising solution. Data link indeed provides the ability to transmit short and relatively simple digital messages between aircraft and ground stations via communication systems. In July 1978, the engineering department at Aeronautical Radio Incorporated (ARINC) introduced a first data link means known as Aircraft Communications Addressing and Reporting System (ACARS). And during the 1980s, air traffic control (ATC) authorities promoted the use of ACARS between controllers and pilots to improve the safety and efficiency of air traffic management. At the beginning of the 1980s, the International Civil Aviation Organization (ICAO) created a special committee known as Future Air Navigation System (FANS), where Boeing and then Airbus developed their products, known as FANS-1/A (Fig. 1).

According to ICAO, four categories of communications are defined in aeronautical telecommunications. Air Traffic Service Communications (ATSCs) and Aeronautical Operational Control (AOC) Communications that are considered as safety related, and Airline Administration Communications (AACs) and Aeronautical Passenger Communications (APCs) that group non-safety-related. Critical communications follow specific international rules defined by ICAO (for example, only some dedicated frequency band can be used) and are based on dedicated systems. These latter must meet very stringent QoS requirements mainly based on transaction time, continuity, availability and integrity. In this paper, our focus will be on critical services (ATSC and AOC).

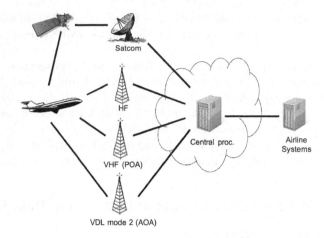

Fig. 1. Air-ground communication systems

Airbus and Boeing worked on a first set of applications using the available technologies for air-ground data communications focusing on oceanic and remote airspaces with no radar coverage and poor high frequency (HF) voice communications. These applications thus addressed communication and surveillance needs for these airspaces. In parallel of the deployment of FANS-1/A, ICAO working groups continued to develop standards for a new aeronautical dedicated network and a set of applications: ATN (Aeronautical Telecommunication Network). In addition to ground–ground applications, ATN also defines air–ground data link applications, similar to those of FANS 1/A with some modifications and enhancements released in FANS-2/B. Besides, ATN defines a global internetwork architecture. As such, it relies on different "real" subnetworks, allowing interconnections between ATN routers. ATN defines a stack of Open Systems Interconnection (OSI) standardized protocols from the network layer up to the application layer. ICAO working groups also developed standards for the underlying air–ground subnetworks: in the VHF and HF bands, and also through satellite. More specifically, several technical choices or protocol stacks were proposed in the VHF band and are called VDL (VHF data link) mode 2 to 4. Thus, considering aeronautical data link communications, in each successive generation, we found a set of application services (FANS), which uses an upper layer architecture based on lower layer architectures and radio systems (HF, VHF, SATCOM, etc.).

2.2 Future Trends

The aviation industry has identified the need to develop new data communication protocols and services to meet the safety and performance requirements of aviation for the year 2020 and beyond. Besides, the aviation industry desires a modern, off-the-shelf, efficient, and robust network infrastructure common to both ATS and AOC safety services. Commercial IP has been identified to be the successor in the long term of the ATN/OSI network infrastructure. It will be referred as Aeronautical Telecommunication Network/Internet Protocol Suite (ATN/IPS), based on IPv6. Indeed, the Internet

Protocol IPv6 is a widespread telecommunications standard in the industry that is maintained and extended by the IETF. It will favor the interconnection between aeronautical domains that have already begun to migrate to IPv6, like for instance ground networks. Also, IPv6 should support a world-wide deployment with enough address space. It will be implemented on both aircraft and ground infrastructure. It is expected to use multiple line-of-sight and beyond-line-of-sight subnetworks such as Inmarsat SwiftBroadband, Iridium Certus, AeroMACS, future SATCOM and L Band Digital Aviation Communication System (LDACS) systems, and VDL Mode 2.

ATN/IPS should benefit for all the actors. Greater communications are expected for airlines compared to ACARS and ATN/OSI, while avionic suppliers and airframe manufacturers will be capable to provide more bandwidth and capabilities by using future data link technologies. The Fig. 2 shows how the ATN/IPS network should be used in the future.

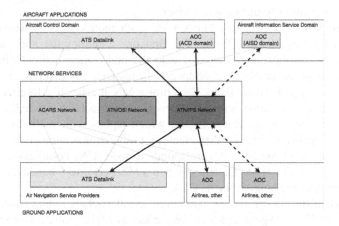

Fig. 2. ATN/IPS implementation (from [4])

3   IP Mobility

The need of being always connected to the Internet has significantly arisen since the last decade. Internet mobility has thus become an attractive research area over the years. Several solutions have been proposed to provide a seamless communication for an end user while on the move and changing his access network to the Internet. The process of switching onto different networks is called handover. The handover process is either horizontal or vertical, depending on whether it switches to the same network technology or a different one. A handover is efficient if the user does not perceive any interruption. The main difficulty is related to the fact that application sessions are identified with an IP address, so changing network access and thus IP address may result in application sessions being broken. Therefore, a handover mechanism that keeps the IP address will be transparent to the application layer.

3.1   Mobility Main Principles and MIPv6 Protocol

Several solutions based on different layers can deal with the mobility in IP networks [1]. The more adapted solution to the aeronautical environment according to [1] is based on the network layer. Indeed, providing a solution above the network layer is not suited for a deployment in an aeronautical environment as it should be implemented on all the existing end systems. Besides, considering the aircraft as a mobile network, it makes more sense to manage the mobility issue at the network layer to avoid doing it for each running application. More details on other possibilities to handle the mobility in IP networks are presented in [1].

In the context of IPv6, the IETF has developed an extension to deal with the mobile nodes (MNs) in the network layer which is Mobile IPv6 (MIPv6) [2]. It provides an efficient and scalable mechanism to handle the node mobility in IP networks. Indeed, it allows mobile nodes to move and change their point of attachment without changing their IP address. Therefore, this mechanism is transparent to the upper layers and allows sessions continuity during a handover.

To do so, MIPv6 uses 2 IP addresses for each mobile node: a Home Address (HoA) and a Care-of-Address (CoA). The first one identifies the node in its home network and the second one allows to locate the node when it moves to a foreign network. The association of the 2 addresses is realized by an entity in the home network called the Home Agent (HA). Each time a MN attaches to a foreign network, it performs a binding association between its new CoA and its HoA by sending a Binding Update (BU) message to its Home Agent, which replies with a Binding Acknowledgement (BA) message. The HA then creates a bi-directional tunnel to forward traffic to the new location of the MN. A correspondent node (CN) communicates with the mobile node by using its HoA. Therefore, when a MN performs a handover to a new IP network, it remains transparent for its CNs.

This mechanism allows session continuity as all packets coming from CNs are captured by the Home Agent and then forwarded to MNs. However, it introduces a triangular routing because packets sent by the mobile node are forwarded by standard IP routes. To solve this issue, MIPv6 allows MNs to perform route optimization (RO) with their CNs. Route Optimization is carried out after a binding association. MN creates a secure bi-directional tunnel with its CNs so that packets are exchanged directly through this tunnel.

3.2   MIPv6 Enhancements

Whereas MIPv6 can provide session continuity during a handover phase, its mechanism is not well adapted in specific environments such as in aviation, or for some specific applications which require very constraint requirements. For instance, very long links have a direct impact on the handover delay and thus introduce a long period during which the mobile node is unreachable. In the following, some enhancements to MIPv6 are described in order to mitigate these issues.

HMIPv6 (Hierarchical MIPv6). HMIPv6 is introduced in [5] as an extension to MIPv6 and IPv6 Neighbor Discovery protocol (NDP). It helps reducing the signaling traffic during the handover phase for local mobility case thanks to a new entity called the mobility anchor point (MAP). It works as a local HA for a MN. HMIPv6 separates the global network into different MAP domains, each one controlled by one or several MAPs (see Fig. 3). A MAP domain is different from a network domain. HMIPv6 introduces 2 addresses to manage the local mobility of a node: the regional care-of-address (RCoA) and the local care-of-address (LCoA). The first one (RCoA) is used to realize the binding with the HA and the CN, if the route optimization procedure is triggered. MN obtains a new RCoA whenever it moves to another MAP domain and attaches to a new MAP. Meanwhile, the second one (LCoA) is used as a binding with the RCoA in the MAP domain. This process allows the MAP to forward packets destined to a MN in its current location through the tunnel created between the RCoA and the LCoA. Besides, HMIPv6 makes the local mobility in a MAP domain transparent to the HA and the CN as the RCoA is not updated.

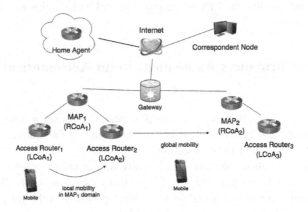

Fig. 3. Mobility management in HMIPv6

In consequence, HMIPv6 is more suitable for local mobility but presents some drawbacks in dealing with global mobility because MNs need to get 2 different IP addresses instead of only 1 with MIPv6.

FMIPv6 (Fast Handovers for MIPv6). FMIPv6, described in [6, 7] as a further enhancement to MIPv6, is a protocol that helps reducing the handover latency and the packet loss during a handover in MIPv6. FMIPv6 makes it possible by introducing a fast binding between MN's previous access router (PAR) and MN's next access router (NAR). This tunnel is created before the binding with the HA. To do so, during the discovery phase, all the access routers must share information about their network prefix so that MN can configure the new CoA accordingly. With this tunnel, data may be tunneled to the new access router even during the handover phase.

By introducing some complexity at the network level, FMIPv6 is more effective than MIPv6 during a handover as it allows to mitigate the negative effects such as handover latency and packet loss.

PMIPv6 (Proxy MIPv6). PMIPv6 [8] is a network-based mobility management. Unlike the previous protocols which are host-based approaches, the node mobility is handled by access routers in the network. Its main interest is to reduce drastically the amount of signaling for the mobile node as it is no more involved in the process. Like HMIPv6, PMIPv6 provides mobility support within a domain called a PMIP domain. As long as the MN moves within the domain, the network has to track the location of MN, which keeps its IP address.

PMIPv6 introduces 2 new entities to manage the node mobility: the mobile access gateway (MAG) and the local mobility anchor (LMA). The MAG realizes the mobility-related signaling on behalf of the MN using its access links. It is responsible for detecting the movement of the nodes in the domain and for executing binding registration with the corresponding LMA. The LMA manages the routes for all mobile nodes in the domain. More information about the whole process are developed in [7, 8, 9].

In consequence, whereas similar to HMIPv6, PMIPv6 seems to be more appealing because it does not involve the MN in the process, and hence helps to reduce signaling traffic seen by the MN.

4   MIPv6 Performances Assessment in an Aeronautical Context

During a flight, an aircraft will be covered successively and/or simultaneously by several air-ground subnetworks belonging to different administrative domains (AN-SPs and ACSPs) depending on its location.

In the current aviation network, an aircraft has a unique identifier (its ICAO address) by which it is reachable at any times. But moving towards different IP networks, the aircraft must obtain an IP address corresponding to the air-ground subnetwork in use in order to maintain its reachability. Consequently, an IP mobility mechanism is required to maintain the ongoing sessions with the aircraft whenever it changes its point of attachment to the air-ground network. Session continuity must be carefully taken into consideration during the process. Indeed, it should not break the ongoing sessions while performing the handover. However, a session in a TCP/IP stack is broken as soon as the IP address is changed.

As a first step of our research work, we decided to perform an evaluation of MIPv6 in a ATN/IPS representative network that will serve as a reference for our future proposal. Indeed, the aeronautical network infrastructure is not like a common ground network equipped with 4G, due to its limited air-ground link capacity coupled with very demanding requirements of ATS applications running on top of that. Therefore, metrics such as packet loss, handover delay, and signaling traffic must be carefully investigated.

A previous work has already been carried out in [10] to evaluate MIPv6 for ATN/IPS. It highlights the fact that handover delay can be very long in particular scenarios.

Our simulation environment is based on Omnet++ [11], a discrete event simulator adapted for wireless communication and its IPv6 framework INET. Omnet++ is based on a modular architecture, thus make it simple to use existing modules and to develop our own ones. The INET framework provides a xMIPv6 module which simulates the standard MIPv6 protocol described in [2]. For now, the xMIPv6 module was tested in a simple scenario.

4.1   Simulation Scenario, Parameters and Hypothesis

Links Modeling and MIPv6 Module. As we do not intend to perform an analysis on link technologies, we have implemented a simple wireless NIC (Network Interface Controller) on each node and router. The wireless NIC uses the well-known CSMA (Carrier Sense Multiple Access) protocol at the MAC (Medium Access Control) layer as in some existing air-ground systems like VDL mode 2, and an ideal physical channel free of errors (bit error, collision…). Hence, base stations have been omitted as the mobile nodes communicate directly with routers equipped with a wireless NIC. In doing so, it allows us to focus only on network layer mechanisms. Besides, movement detection at the network layer is performed when MNs receive an Router Advertisement (RA) announcing a new network prefix. The RFC 6275 recommends to set the RA periodicity between 30 ms and 70 ms. This value seems very low in our context. As it is a source of signaling traffic, the value has been increased up to 300 ms. A further analysis on the impact of this parameter will be investigated. Besides, route optimization has been removed from the MIPv6 module because ATS traffic may not be forwarded by other non-certified providers.

Ground Network. For a first step in our simulation, a simple handover between 2 access routers has been tested out, with one representing the HA for the mobile node, as shown in Fig. 4. It's a realistic scenario if we consider a continental scenario like in Europe where connectivity to the ground network is provided by two Aeronautical Communication Service Providers (ACSPs): Rockwell Collins IMS (formerly ARINC) and SITA. Meanwhile, delay between those routers are modeled based on the guaranteed maximum delay between the 2 ACSPs [10]. For ATS services, the communication end point is an ATSU (Air Traffic Services Unit), which depends on the location

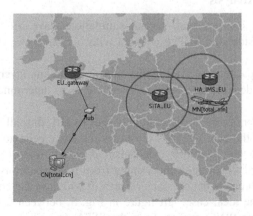

Fig. 4. Simulation scenario

of the aircraft. For now, the application layer integrates a PING application which sends ICMP (Internet Control Message Protocol) messages periodically.

Scenario. We consider one aircraft during its en-route phase at a cruise speed of 220 mps. It is first covered by IMS ground stations which is its HA and flies to a region covered only by SITA ones. The overlapping area, corresponding to the area where the aircraft has an access to both IMS and SITA, is about 50 km long.

As the IdealRadioMedium module is used to simulate the wireless medium, there is no link mechanism to associate the aircraft with only one access router on a dedicated channel. Therefore, when the aircraft goes through the overlapping area, it will receive both network prefixes of IMS and SITA. The MIPv6 module running on the aircraft will thus try to attach to both access networks successively as it will continue to receive RAs even after performing a binding with its new CoA. This phenomenon is known as the ping pong effect. A handover manager is therefore necessary to avoid this effect.

Handover Manager at L2. We thus decide to integrate a handover manager at the layer 2. It is an intermediate layer between the link layer and the network layer. Its role is to filter incoming packets at the network layer of aircraft. Its filtering is based on a predefined priority list of ground stations. When it receives a beacon from a ground station, it checks whether this ground station has a greater priority than the current ground station in use. While this is a static and simple mechanism, it can be easily adapted in the future to a more dynamical decision process by modifying the priority list accordingly. To implement our handover algorithm, layer 2 beacons using MAC addresses have been added. They are sent every 300 ms by each access router with their respective MAC address and their ground station ID. RA messages of the MIPv6 module cannot be used for this purpose because our handover manager is run under the network layer, thus it does not manipulate IP addresses. Another more complex solution has been standardized in IEEE 802.21 [12], referred as Media Independent Handover (MIH) to manage efficiently the handover between different wired and wireless networks. Unfortunately, it is not yet developed for Omnet++ and is not our primary concern, that is why another approach has been taken.

4.2   Results and Analysis

In order to validate our proposal, several simulations have been run using MIPv6 mechanism on one side, and MIPv6 coupled with our handover manager on another side.

Figure 5 shows packets received by the aircraft at the link layer. By inspecting the size of packets, we deduce their type, thus helping us to determine the impact of our system on MIPv6.

Before a handover occurs, the aircraft only sees its HA, thus all the PING packets it receives come from the HA. Figure 5 illustrates the same behavior in both cases (for t < 224 s), therefore our handover mechanism does not impact this phase. It only induced an additional signaling traffic coming from router beacons.

When the aircraft enters the overlapping area, it will have the choice between the 2 access routers. In the ideal case, left figure in Fig. 5, between 220 s and 430 s, the aircraft receives some PING packets from the SITA ground station, highlighting the

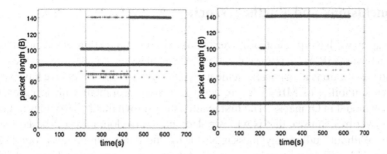

Fig. 5. Packets received by the aircraft in an ideal case on the left, and with our manager on the right

ping pong effect. Those packets are longer (140 bytes instead of 100 bytes) than those sending by the HA because of the additional header corresponding to the tunneling mechanism. Whereas using our handover mechanism, right figure in Fig. 5, the aircraft only receives PING packets of size 140 bytes, thus coming from the SITA station. Indeed, as soon as the aircraft detects the SITA ground station, it creates the binding and maintains it because SITA ground station gets a greater priority, as expected.

More interesting is the number of packet loss at the application layer in both case shown in Fig. 6. With our handover manager, although there are still some lost packets, the number of loss is significantly reduced when the aircraft is covered by the 2 access networks (between 220 s and 430 s).

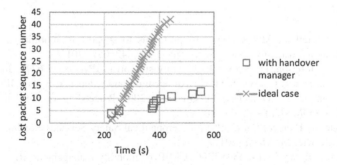

Fig. 6. Packet loss in both scenarios

These first results validate our handover mechanism proposal. While being very elementary, it allows us to handle IP mobility effectively with MIPv6. Nevertheless, the long handover delay mentioned in [10] and the number of messages exchanged during the handover by the aircraft may prevent from meeting the stringent requirements for performance of the ATS traffic. From the IP solutions introduced earlier, PMIPv6 seems to be a good candidate to overcome these issues as the signaling traffic on the air-ground link will be significantly lower.

5 Conclusions and Further Work

In this paper, we have presented the aeronautical communication environment and its evolution towards IP-based communications. We then focus our attention on the mobility issue and the solutions to manage it at the network layer. As a first step, we have started to assess the suitability of MIPv6 for an aeronautical environment with a representative simulation model in Omnet++. The first results have shown that MIPv6 does not provide any handover mechanism, that is why we decided to develop a layer 2-based handover manager. Without adding any messages during the handover process, our handover manager avoids MIPv6 protocol to be affected by the ping pong effect during a handover.

Further works have already been identified. They can be separated into 2 axes. Firstly, enhancements to our model are possible through (a) a more realistic application layer simulating an ATS traffic, (b) a modeling of other air-ground access networks like SATCOM that will helps us to test transatlantic flight scenarios representative of vertical handover scenarios and (c) generating exogenous traffic by integrating several flights in our scenario or by adding external traffic in access routers to measure their impact on the handover procedure in MIPv6. Secondly, a contribution to IP mobility in Omnet++ has been pinpointed. Indeed, in our aeronautical context, MIPv6 seems to present some drawbacks in terms of signaling and handover delay. PMIPv6 may offer better performances regarding these criteria, but it is not yet implement in any Omnet++ framework. Nevertheless, none of these solutions has been designed to be implemented on a very specific environment such as civil aviation, therefore we may adapt PMIPv6 to our scenarios.

References

1. Bauer, C., Zitterbart, M.: A survey of protocols to support IP mobility in aeronautical communications. IEEE Commun. Surv. Tutor. **13**, 642–657 (2011)
2. Perkings, C., Johnson, D., Arkko, J.: Mobility support in IPv6. RFC 6275, July 2011
3. Yousaf, F.Z., Bauer, C., Wietfield, C.: An accurate and extensible mobile IPv6 (xMIPv6) simulation model for Omnet++. In: Omnet++ 2008 Proceeding of the 1st International Workshop on OMNET++ (2008)
4. AEEC: Internet Protocol Suite (IPS) for Aeronautical Safety Services Roadmap Document. SAE ITC, Bowie, Maryland (2017)
5. Soliman, H.: Hierarchical mobile IPv6 (HMIPv6) mobility management. RFC 5380 (2008)
6. Koodli, R.: Mobile IPv6 fast handovers. RFC 5568 (2009)
7. Li, D., Li, Z.: Optimization and enhancement of MIPv6 in ATN. In: Aeronautical Telecommunications Network: Advances, Challenges, and Modeling. CRC Press, Boca Raton (2015)
8. Gundavelli, S., Leung, K., Devarapalli, V., Chowdhurry, K.: Proxy mobile IPv6. RFC5213 (2008)
9. Soto, I., Bernados, C.J., et al.: PMIPv6: a network-based localized mobility management solution. Internet Protoc. J. **13**, 2–16 (2010)
10. Bauer, C., Ayaz, S.: A thorough investigation of mobile IPv6 for the aeronautical environment. In: IEEE Vehicular Technology Conference-Fall Proceedings, pp. 1–5 (2008)
11. Vargas, A., et al.: The Omnet++ discrete event simulator (2005). https://www.omnetpp.org/
12. De La Oliva, A., Banchs, A., et al.: An overview of IEEE 802.21: media-independent handover services. IEEE Wirel. Commun. **15** (2008)

Routing in Wireless Sensor Networks for Surveillance of Airport Surface Area

Juliette Garcia, Alain Pirovano$^{(\boxtimes)}$, and Mickaël Royer

ENAC/TELECOM/ReSCo, Toulouse, France
{juliette.garcia,alain.pirovano,
mickael.royer}@recherche.enac.fr

Abstract. The surveillance of airport surface area is a crucial operation for the safety of passengers and the airport itself. Even if this method has shown its limits, today the airports keep employing visual inspection. Some technology radar based systems are available but they are still very expensive and do not cover exhaustively the needs. In this paper, we present the first part of a research work that aims to propose a surface surveillance method based on wireless sensor networks (WSN). To the best of our knowledge, this is an unexplored alternative. However, considering their low cost and their ability to ensure surveillance in other domains like agriculture, WSNs surely represent an interesting solution in airports. Our research focuses on the definition of a suitable routing protocol for WSN in the context of airport surface surveillance. We present in this article some properties about the context of airport surveillance and then a brief description and classification of the most popular routing protocols for WSN. Finally we identify a routing protocol for WSN that, as the most suitable for the considered context, could be used as reference in the next steps of our research works.

Keywords: WSN · Routing protocols · Airport Surface Area Surveillance

1 Introduction

A WSN is a collection of spatially dispersed devices equipped with sensors, which are strategically deployed to monitor the environment. Sensors periodically gather and transfer data via wireless communication to a central node where data are collected and processed. The central node is known as the sink. WSNs have recently been employed in a variety of applications, including road traffic control, home automation, battlefield surveillance, environment monitoring, among several others. One of the characteristics of WSNs, that have made them popular in the last years, is that sensors are cheap and can be easily deployed with very low impact on their environment. In addition, sensor nodes can be deployed in short time and the network topology can be easily modified, tailored or scaled. Even, under inclement weather conditions these allow high precision of data gathering. In WSN applications, the area of interest is often larger than the communication range of the sensor nodes. Therefore, to reach the sink, a sensor may use other ones as relays. The path to the sink that each data package should follow is defined by a routing protocol. This set of rules is a core element in the functioning of any WSN. If the routing protocol is properly designed, data will arrive to the destination on time and sensors will be efficiently used. Otherwise, various undesired

© Springer International Publishing AG, part of Springer Nature 2018
J. Moreno García-Loygorri et al. (Eds.): Nets4Cars 2018/Nets4Trains 2018/Nets4Aircraft 2018, LNCS 10796, pp. 27–38, 2018.
https://doi.org/10.1007/978-3-319-90371-2_3

phenomena such as excessive delays, unnecessary energy consumption and excessive data replication, may appear. Unfortunately, the construction of an effective routing protocol for WSN is by no means an easy task due to the inherent complexities of this type of networks and the number of properties and parameters that have to be taken into account. A suitable management of network resources (e.g., sensor nodes storage capacity, processing capability and energy), and a proper schedule for data transfer in case of segmented networks, are just some of the main challenges.

In this paper, we emphasize on the selection of suitable routing protocols for WSN for Airport Surface Area Surveillance (ASAS). To the best of our knowledge, this subject has not been addressed in the literature. Our main purpose at this point is to identify one or some routing protocols that are the most appropriate for application in ASAS. To do so, we study some popular routing protocols found in the literature and we classify them according to a set of criteria that allows us to determine which ones are more suitable for the application in airports. The Fig. 1 shows an example of the application we will investigate.

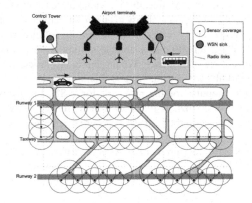

Fig. 1. Airport Surface Area Surveillance WSN-based

The rest of the paper is organized as follows: Firstly Sect. 2 delves into the concept and application of Airport Surface Area Surveillance. Then, we state and explain which types of data have to be collected and the properties of our environment. Section 3 provides a brief review of most popular routing protocols for WSN and their classification. Section 4 discusses the most suitable routing protocols for WSN applied to ASAS. Finally, Sect. 5 concludes the paper and gives some potentials further steps in this research work.

2   Airport Surface Area Surveillance (ASAS)

2.1   Overview and Principles

The airport surface area surveillance is a crucial aspect for the safety of passengers and the preservation of airports integrity. It encompasses a set of strategies used to monitor and control operations in both, movement areas (taxiways and runways) and non-movement areas (aprons and aircraft parking spots). ASAS procedures in movement areas are oriented to accident prevention and short term decision making (e.g. detect and remove objects from the runway). And procedures in non-movement areas focus on short term, less critical decision making (e.g. detect excessive noise levels and intervene).

Some unfortunate past events have put in evidence the need for rigorous ASAS procedures. Along the history, the presence of objects in the runways has caused major economic and human losses associated to minor and fatal aircraft accidents. One of the most popular ones was the Air France Concorde 4590 Flight accident occurred in 2000. During the taking off, one of the tires of the aircraft serving the flight exploded and the aircraft got fire. Two minutes after, the aircraft crashed. An exhaustive investigation revealed that the accident was attributed to a titanium piece (about 3 cm wide and 43 cm long) that had fallen off in the runway from a plane that took off some minutes previously.

Nevertheless, airports continue performing regular self-inspections proceeded by ground personnel that go over the runway. The objective is to ensure that these areas are free from FOD (Foreign Object Damage), animals, and so on [1]. However, even full-conscious, reasoning humans are prone to errors due to fatigue, limited visibility among other factors that can prevent them to locate a FOD for instance. In addition, visual inspections are time consuming and no take-offs or landings can be conducted in parallel. Thus, only a few daily inspections are the typical mark for airports adopting the visual method. Alternative technology-based methods have emerged in recent years. They offer the possibility of conducting more accurate and frequent inspections. However, these technologies have only received the attention of a few major airports in the world, due to their cost. The system based on WSN, that we seek to propose, aims to provide the advantages of the automated, technology-based methods, at an affordable cost.

2.2 Interviews with Airport Managers and Air Traffic Controllers

We have conducted interviews with some actors (airport manager and controllers) that could be the future users of our solution. After a short presentation of our project, during the interviews we seek to determine: (i) the way ASAS are currently being conducted, (ii) expected improvements in ASAS by adoption of WSNs, and (iii) main types of relevant data for ASAS (attributes of interest to be measured). This section is devoted to the discussion of the information collected during the interviews regarding the aspects mentioned above.

How ASAS is Currently Being Conducted. According to the interviewees, nowadays ASAS is mainly and more exclusively done by visual inspection. One of the main limitations of this practice is that airport regular operations (landings, take-offs, taxiing, etc.) need to be stopped during inspections. But with the continuous increasing air traffic, the inspections must be performed as quickly as possible but with effectiveness. In addition, gathered data may contain errors (for instance, due to human fatigue). A few alternative technologies in contrast to visual inspection have emerged in the recent years. Most of them focused on automated runway scanning (ARS) [1]. These technologies use millimeter wave radars to continuously scan runway surfaces and their installation requires a relatively heavy work. The interviewees stated those alternatives are in most cases unacceptable due to their high cost. On the other hand, an interview disclosed by [1] in 2011 to 50 airports around the world concluded that only 6% of airports in the sample were implementing continuous surface surveillance using technology-based methods. The study also suggested the high cost of such technologies as a potential reason for the low statistic.

Expected Improvements of ASAS by Adoption of WSN. Most expectations, from the application of WSN for ASAS, point to three major angles:

– Precision and accuracy: WSNs are expected to enhance the quality of data gathered through the strategic deployment of high precision sensors near critical sensing spots. This way, imprecisions in the data associated to human factors and inaccuracies resulting from lack of closeness during data gathering, could be virtually eradicated.
– Knowledge on spatial components of attributes: WSNs will allow the transition from one/a few to multiple sensing spots. This is expected to dramatically improve the awareness about conditions in airport surface area. Environmental data could be translated into surface or temperature plots, providing traffic controllers with wide spatial information about attributes of interest through an intuitive display for instance.
– Natural coupling with airport operations: WSNs are intended to integrate gently with the daily functioning of airports. Sensing will be conducted by a collection of small devices. These could be conveniently located at several points while keeping closeness to the critical sensing spots, without perturbing regular operations. On the other hand, as explained later the dedicated WSN will certainly result in several segmented ones. Hence, each segmented WSN could opportunistically use airport ground vehicles/personnel as data mules, exploiting their regular displacements to transmit information among isolated parts of the network. It has also to be underline here that as our solution will be based on wireless links and autonomous sensors and therefore its installation and deployment are expected to be easy.

Main Types of Relevant Data for ASAS. The interviewing process also gave us the possibility to list the most relevant type of data that could be monitored with WSNs (see Table 1). The list includes several environmental conditions related to temperature, noise, pollution and visibility that may be considered as non critical. The list includes another subclass of type of data that are sensitive and critical for the safety. Some of these which may justify a brief explanation for the sake of clarity. Taxiway flow rate refers to the number of aircraft that make use of each taxiway during a day of operation. Similarly, apron visit rate and aircraft parking spot visit rate refer to the number of aircraft that make use of each apron and parking spot during a day of operation, respectively. We may also define the state of runway safety lights, which will be a binary variable indicating if each safety light is properly functioning or not, and taxiway misselection, that will indicate if some aircraft went through the wrong taxiway. As critical data we consider also those related with detection of FOD, animals, and intrusion.

Table 1. Attributes of interest for the airports

Attribute	Critical	Non-critical
Numerical		
Pavement temperature	x	x
Noise	x	x
Pollution (NO_2, CO, SO_2)		x
Water/snow height	x	x
Taxiway flow rate		x
Apron visit rate		x
Aircraft parking spot visit rate		x
Categorical		
Presence of animals/foreign object	x	
State of runway safety lights	x	
State of the road	x	x
Taxiway misselection	x	x

Hence, we classified each attribute in the table as critical and non-critical. The classification of attributes in these categories provides insights on the required particularities of the routing protocol for this application. We will go deeper into this in Sect. 4.

2.3   Environment and Network Properties

Finally, some last points that may be important to define a suitable routing protocol are related to the network topology and its properties. As shown in the Fig. 1, two main recurring properties can be stated. Firstly, considering the wide area of an airport, the WSNs should be segmented in several subnetworks. In these cases, a recommended method, to ensure the reachability between each segmented WSN and the sink, is based on the use of vehicles as data mules. These latter will collect data and bring them to the sink. In airport, the data mule role could be played by the existing vehicle or even the arriving aircraft in an opportunistic way. Secondly, as the infrastructure of a typical airport shows geometric shapes, the WSNs topologies are expected to have this same property.

3   Routing Protocols in WSN

This section is devoted to describe some popular routing protocols used in WSN and propose a classification intended to select an appropriated routing protocol for a given application.

3.1   Overview of Popular Routing Protocols for WSN

Before describing some routing protocols, we detail two simple strategies for forwarding data that do not require a routing algorithm. For that reason, these strategies, in our criterion, are not considered as protocols. These are flooding and gossiping strategy.

Flooding Strategy. This is the first strategy created to transfer information between the sensor nodes and the sink. A sensor, every time it senses data, transmits it to all its neighbor nodes and, in turn, these neighbors transmit it to its neighbor nodes, until data reach the destination [2]. It has three critical drawbacks:

- Implosion: which occurs when a node receives duplicated or redundant data. The Fig. 2(a) shows this problem. Here, node A floods its data (a) to its neighbors B and C. In turn, these nodes send a copy of it on to its common neighbor D. As result, it produces resource wastes by sending redundant data to the same node.
- Overlap: which occurs when two sensors sense an overlapping spatial region. The Fig. 2(b) illustrates that sensor A and B cover an overlapping geographic region, named z2. When these sensors flood their data to node C, C will receive duplicated data of z2 region. Again, this strategy produces redundant data and then resource wastes.
- Resource blindness: this strategy does not consider the available energy in each node for taking decisions. The non-consideration of energy resources may lead to wrong or unfeasible decisions in the routing process.

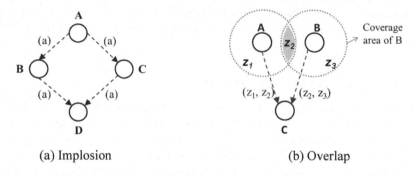

(a) Implosion   (b) Overlap

Fig. 2. Drawbacks in flooding strategy

Gossiping Strategy. It is a slightly enhanced version of flooding. Instead of sending data to all its neighbors, a sensor node sends data to only one randomly selected neighbor node, which selects another random neighbor node, until the data reach the destination [2]. This strategy reduces the implosion problem. However, this could lead to increase the latency to forward the data to the sink.

The following protocols improve the drawbacks of the previous strategies:

SPIN (Sensor Protocols for Information via Negotiation). It is a family of protocols that aims to overcome the problems of implosion, overlap and resource blindness presented in flooding strategy [2].

To overcome implosion problem SPIN adopts a negotiation process. For that, it uses three types of messages: advertisement (ADV), request (REQ) and data (DATA). A node, which collects data, will send an ADV to all its neighbors with meta-data fields which describe the collected information. Their neighbors will specify with a REQ if they are interested in this data. Only the neighbors which confirm their interest for the information will receive the data. This prevents a node from receiving redundant information.

On the other hand, to overcome overlap problem, SPIN uses meta-data descriptors which precise in particular the portion of the region that it collects. Thus, if a node notices, in the received ADV, that it has already received data from a certain part of a region, it indicates in REQ in which parts it is interested.

Finally, this protocol allows the sensor nodes to check their resources before data transmission. Using it, the nodes may be aware of its available energy to make suitable decisions.

Directed Diffusion. In this protocol, the sink is the one who makes information queries. Sensors whose features match with a query will be called sources of information and only these ones can send data. This protocol seeks to determine a single path between the sink and the sources of information [2]. The protocol operates in three stages:

- Spreading interests: the sink sends an interest message to each of its neighbors and these resend it only to its neighbors that have not received it yet. This message specifies a set of the attributes that are of interest to the sink.
- Set up gradients: each node, that receives the interest, stores a gradient that contains the previous node which sent to it the interest and its own data rate. The nodes that never receive an interest will have a null gradient. The source sends the data to all the neighbors with a gradient different than null (possibly it sends along multiple paths), toward the sink.
- Path reinforcement: after the sink starts receiving data, it selects the path with low delay based in the data rate of each sensor node. Once a single path is chosen, the sink requests data at a higher rate.

GEAR (Geographic and Energy Aware Routing). It is an improvement of Directed Diffusion protocol. The main idea is to use geographic information (e.g. provided by GPS) to restrict the number of interests sent in Directed Diffusion to a certain region rather than to send interests to the whole network [3].

Rumor Routing. It is another variation of Directed Diffusion and is mainly used in the cases in which geographic routing techniques are not applicable. Directed Diffusion floods the query to the entire network. However, in some cases the sink requires a bit amount of data and thus the use of flooding is unnecessary. An alternative is to flood the events. For that, once an event occurs, a package (called agent) is sent to "spread rumors about the location of the source". While it is moving, it builds the shortest path to such event. Then, when the sink requests information about the event, its query moves blindly through the network until it stumbles upon a sensor node visited by the agent. The query can take advantage of the path provided by the agent that will drive to the source of information for the shortest path. Once the query arrives to the source, data is sent using the path used by the query [2].

LEACH (Low-Energy Adaptive Clustering Hierarchy). This protocol uses an aggregation strategy, the setup of groups of sensors (cluster) for reducing the redundant information that arrives to the sink [2]. To build these clusters, it works in rounds. Each round consists of two stages:

- Setup stage: in this stage, some random cluster heads (CH) are selected. The CHs are the only nodes that can receive, aggregate and send information to the sink. The remaining nodes must seek the closer CH and join to its cluster.
- Transmission stage: the sensor nodes send collected data to its corresponding CH. And finally, the CHs send aggregated data to the sink. This way, the route created for each node is always composed of 2 hops. The first hop is the selected CH and the second hop is the sink.

PEGASIS (Power Efficient Gathering in Sensor Information Systems). In this protocol, nodes are organized into a chain, using a greedy algorithm. So that, each node sends to and receives from only one of its neighbors. In each round, a random node, called leader, is selected. Then, sensor nodes sense data and send it to its closer neighbor and, in turn, this latter forwards it to its closer neighbor, until the data can reach a leader node. The leader node aggregates data and send it to the sink [4]. This protocol seeks that all the nodes become leader, at least one time, to balance their energy.

TEEN (Threshold Sensitive Energy Efficient Sensor Network Protocol). This protocol is based on cluster formation. It uses a hierarchical structure similar to LEACH, but it proposes an additional level between the CHs and the sink, named second level of CH. This second level aims to extend network coverage. Thus, the route is composed by 3 hops. The first hop is the first level CH, the second one is the second level CH and third one is the sink.

On the other hand, this protocol was one of the first protocols, for WSN, performed for data transfer based on events [4]. This means that sensor nodes send only when a sensed attribute overpasses a given threshold. This protocol manages two thresholds:

- Hard threshold (HT): this is the minimum value beyond which the node sends data to its CH.
- Soft threshold (ST): once the HT is reached, it is possible to test it. This is a change in the value of the sensed attribute which triggers the sending of data from sensor nodes to its CH.   Therefore, HT aims to reduce the number of transmissions by sending only data in the range of the interest and ST aims to reduce the number of transmissions by avoiding sending non-significant changes. This protocol is suitable for time-critical applications. However it is not suitable for applications where periodic reports are needed because user may not get any data if thresholds are not reached.

APTEEN (Adaptive Threshold Sensitive Energy Efficient Network Protocol). This protocol is an extension of TEEN. It considers the transfer of information not only based on events that exceed limits but also periodically. For that, this protocol handles a variable that counts the time. If the elapsed time exceeds a fixed duration, the sensors, even if the sensed data has not exceeded a threshold, must send it. In this way, data is collected periodically and based on events [4].

RPL (Routing Protocol for Low-Power and Lossy Networks). This protocol is the only one which is standardized by the IETF (Internet Engineering Task Force) group. It organizes the WSN as a Directed Acyclic Graph (DAG) rooted at the sink. A DAG is a directed graph with no cycles.

This protocol is supported in the exchange of local messages. The objective function of each node is a measure of its cost to reach the sink. The route to the nodes is built starting from the sink. The sink sends a local message to its neighbors to join the DAG. Each node compares the current value of its objective function with the value of the objective function currently used. If this is convenient for the node, it chooses it as his parent, that is, the next hop to reach to the sink. The neighbor nodes will repeat this process until all the nodes are attached to the DAG. The resulting graph minimizes the cost of routes from sink to all the nodes [5]. This way, the sensor nodes can send data to sink by just forwarding the packet to its immediate parent.

3.2   Classification of Routing Protocols for WSN

To determine the suitable routing protocols for a given application, we classify the solutions according to relevant properties which can be split into two categories:

– Linked to the Context: properties which are directly associated to the specific context and constrain the routing solution. The context contains some characteristics associated with the network and with the handling of the required data.
– Linked to the Algorithm: properties independent to the context, which has to be fixed during the design of the algorithm to optimize the efficiency of the solution.

Linked to the Context

Data Collect Mode. It defines when each node should send data to the sink. It can be:

– Periodic: sensor nodes send data to the sink at a fixed rate.
– Event-based: the system works based on a set of predefined target events, such as the exceeding of a given threshold in a sensed attribute. Sending information only occurs when a target event occurs.
– Query-based: the system uses requests of information generated by the sink.   Each time a query is generated, relevant sensor nodes react and send the requested information.
– Hybrid: the system combines some of the three rules described above.

Topology of the Network. In our classification, it states if every node is able to communicate with any other node or not. Depending of the terrain and the location of data which has to be collected, a network can be:

– Fully connected: every node is able to communicate with each other via direct or multi-hop communication.
– Segmented: some nodes are not able to communicate with other nodes in the network.

Maximum Number of Hops. This refers to the maximum number of hops allowed between any node and the sink. Sometimes, the size and the geometric configuration of the terrain may enforce a known or unknown number of hops to transfer data from some nodes to the sink. According to it, the number of hops can be:

- Limited: the route is composed of a fixed number of hops to reach the sink.
- Unlimited: the route can be composed of any number of hops to reach the sink.

Linked to the Algorithm

Redundancy Control Mechanism. Sensed information is often replicated in two ways: (i) implosion and (ii) overlap (see Flooding strategy in Sect. 3.1). Redundancy control mechanisms are strategies to reduce the amount and impacts of information redundancy.

- Data centric: collected information is temporarily stored in sensors as named data. When information is sent, it is tagged with details about the sensor node that collected it and some attributes related to the data such as the time of measurement. As the messages travel through the network, sensor nodes cross reference the tag of each incoming message with the tags of the data that they already know, and they reject all redundant message.
- Aggregation: some nodes, strategically located over the network, get the responsibility of aggregating information and eliminating redundancies.
- Position centric: when a sensor node has something to transfer, instead of sharing the information with all the neighbors, it builds a route based on its spatial location. This mechanism is often applied in networks with mobile sensor nodes, where locations are determined by GPS.

Route Generation Scheme. It defines when the routes are computed. It can be:

- Proactive: all routes are computed before they are required and then, they are periodically updated.
- Reactive: routes are computed each time a sensor node needs to send data to the sink.
- Hybrid: uses a combination of the proactive and reactive schemes.

Performance Metric. It is the objective to be optimized in the construction of the routes. Most common ones are:

- Latency: time elapsed from the sending of message by a sensor node to its delivery at the sink.
- Energy: amount of energy invested in the transfer.

Table 2 contains the protocols, described in Sect. 3.1, categorized according the classification proposed in this section. In this table, the property P1 corresponds to data collect mode, P2 to topology of the network, P3 to maximum number of hops, P4 to redundancy control mechanism, P5 to route generation scheme and P6 to performance metric.

Table 2. Classification of routing protocols

Routing protocol	Linked to the context			Linked to the algorithm		
	P1	P2	P3	P4	P5	P6
SPIN	P	Fc	Unlim	Dc	Re	Energy
Directed diffusion	Q	Fc	Unlim	Dc	Re	Delay
EAR	Q	Fc	Unlim	Lc	Re	Delay
Rumor routing	Q, E	Fc	Unlim	Dc	Hybrid	Delay
LEACH	P	Fc	Two	Agg	Pro	Energy
PEGASIS	P	Fc	Unlim	Agg	Pro	Energy
TEEN	E	Fc	Three	Dc, Agg	Re	Energy
APTEEN	P, E	Fc	Three	Dc, Agg	Pro, Re	Energy
RPL	P	Fc	Unlim	Dc	Pro	Hops, delay

P: periodic, Q: query-based, E: event-based, Fc: full connected, Unlim: Unlimited, Dc: data-centric, Agg: aggregation, Lc: location-centric, Re: reactive, Pro: proactive

4 Suitable Routing Protocols for WSN Dedicated to Airport Surface Area Surveillance

Up to now, we have highlighted the concept of ASAS in Sect. 2 and introduced some popular routing protocols in Sect. 3. This section is dedicated to select one or some routing protocols that seem suitable for the ASAS context at this point of the study. To achieve this objective, we use the classification introduced earlier and the special features of ASAS problematic.

Data Collect Mode. Based on the information provided in Table 1, two types of data collect mode are required for an airport surveillance case:

– Event-based: presence of animals/intruders, pavement temperature, state of runway safety lights and all the attributes categorized as critical.
– Periodic: pollution, pavement temperature, taxiways flow rate. All the routing protocols which are not exclusively based on query comply with this constraint.

Network Topology. As explained in Sect. 2.3, a WSN deployed for the surveil- lance of an airport should be segmented in subnetworks. This implies the use of data mules or mobile sinks. So far, none of the reviewed protocols has been designed for this kind of topology. Nevertheless, some additional improvements have already been developed to incorporate the use of data mules in the routing protocols. These developments have been carried out by RPL [6] or LEACH [7].

Maximum Number of Hops. The geometry of an airport platform implies some specific constraints for the WSN. For instance, some groups of nodes will follow runways, meaning that the topology will be linear. Thus, some paths between the sensor nodes and the data mules might contain a lot of hops. Therefore, only solutions that support unlimited number of hops can work in this context.

According to this, there is not a reviewed routing protocol that fits to all the properties of the ASAS case. However, some of them are close, particularly RPL that complies with the data collect mode, unlimited number of hops and can be enhanced to support data mules or mobile sinks. Moreover, RPL is the only protocol that has been standardized and indeed it is often used as reference by the research community. That's why, we start studying more deeply RPL as a potential solution of routing protocol in the context of ASAS based on WSN.

5 Conclusions and Further Works

In this paper, we provided a brief description of what is being done in the ASAS and the potential benefits of WSN applied in ASAS. We also provided a description and classification of the most popular routing protocols for WSN available in the literature. Our classification allowed us to identify that RPL is a routing protocol with potential to be implemented for ASAS, but that requires important changes. The main obstacle for implementation of RPL is that it is not suitable for segmented networks, which may often be the case of WSNs in airports. At this point, we will continue reviewing the state of the art about the use of data mule in WSN and work in RPL improvements to make it totally suitable for the ASAS case in WSN.

References

1. Daniel Prather, C.: Current Airport Inspection Practices Regarding FOD (Foreign Object Debris/Damage), vol. 26. Transportation Research Board, Washington, D.C. (2011)
2. Akkaya, K., Younis, M.: A survey on routing protocols for wireless sensor networks. Ad Hoc Netw. 3(3), 325–349 (2005)
3. Yu, Y., Govindan, R., Estrin, D.: Geographical and energy aware routing: a recursive data dissemination protocol for wireless sensor networks (2001)
4. Singh, S.K., Singh, M.P., Singh, D.K.: A survey of energy-efficient hierarchical cluster-based routing in wireless sensor networks. Int. J. Adv. Netw. Appl. (IJANA) 2(02), 570–580 (2010)
5. Accettura, N., Grieco, L.A., Boggia, G., Camarda, P.: Performance analysis of the RPL routing protocol. In: 2011 IEEE International Conference on Mechatronics (ICM), pp. 767–772. IEEE (2011)
6. Safdar, V., Bashir, F., Hamid, Z., Afzal, H., Pyun, J.Y.: A hybrid routing protocol for wireless sensor networks with mobile sinks. In: 2012 7th International Symposium on Wireless and Pervasive Computing (ISWPC), pp. 1–5. IEEE (2012)
7. Mottaghi, S., Zahabi, M.R.: Optimizing leach clustering algorithm with mobile sink and rendezvous nodes. AEU-Int. J. Electron. Commun. 69(2), 507–514 (2015)

Reverberation Time in Vehicular Cabins

Ana González-Plaza$^{(\boxtimes)}$, César Briso, César Calvo-Ramírez,
and Juan Moreno García-Loygorri

Departamento de Teoría de la Señal y Comunicaciones,
ETSIS Telecomunicación, Universidad Politécnica de Madrid, Madrid, Spain
gonzalezplaza.ana@gmail.com, cesarrasec4@gmail.com,
{cesar.briso,juan.moreno.garcia-loygorri}@upm.es

Abstract. This paper research is focused on the reverberation time produced inside cabins where the influence of windows on wide-band signals is substantial. This kind of scenarios are important for the new generations of wireless communications since high-density scenarios with high-traffic demand are one of the keys environments. The study presents a preliminary measurement campaign in a close-room of wideband signals in the frequency range between 1.7 to 6 GHz. Based on the measured s21 parameter, the power delay profile has been obtained in order to analyze the diffuse scattering produced inside this particular environment.

Keywords: Diffuse scattering · Indoor · Propagation · Reverberation time
Room electromagnetics · Wideband measurements

1 Introduction

The new generations of wireless communication systems aim to provide high data rates for high-density scenarios. Train, aircraft and bus cabins are one of the most acknowledged high-density scenarios, where the density of people is of units of persons per meter square.

Cabins and indoor rooms are particular propagation environments that must be particularly analyzed. They are composed of seats, handholds, different kind of furniture and windows whose effect produces the dispersion of the signal. For that reason, the use of determinist methods such as Ray Tracing may not be accurate enough to analyze this kind of environments [1].

Reverberation time provides a representation of the essential features of the diffuse scattering. It can be applied to closed-room propagation environments. This model considers a first-arriving LOS signal, whereas multiple reflections and scattering give rise to a tail with exponential decay, as similarly occurs in acoustics [2].

The room electromagnetics theory has been previously applied for analyzing different indoor scenarios such as offices [3], aircraft cabins [4] or tunnels and stations [5]. In the present study, we consider a general room which is mainly built by concrete, brick and cement walls with glass windows and in each of the positions has a line-of-sight condition (LoS). Shortly, more measurements will be performed in train cabins.

© Springer International Publishing AG, part of Springer Nature 2018
J. Moreno García-Loygorri et al. (Eds.): Nets4Cars 2018/Nets4Trains 2018/Nets4Aircraft 2018, LNCS 10796, pp. 39–43, 2018.
https://doi.org/10.1007/978-3-319-90371-2_4

This study investigates the power delay profile (PDP) in vehicular cabins in order to clarify which is the effect of the windows on wideband signals. The aim is to model the reverberation time produced in this particular environment.

This document is organized as follows: Sect. 2 presents the concept of reverberation time and the theory on which it is based on; in Sect. 3, the measurement campaigned is explained, bringing details regarding the set-up parameters and the closed-room; Sect. 4 provides the results obtained from the measurements; finally, this work is concluded Sect. 5, where some remarks are highlighted.

2 Reverberation Time

Electromagnetic waves are reflected in two different ways accordingly to the geometry of elements. This is a coherent component when the reflection is produced in planar structures, and in a non-coherent scatter when there are random objects and rough surfaces inside the room [2].

In the first case, the walls are planar structures which can be computed by the Fresnel reflection coefficients. Ray tracing is a popular method to characterize this kind of situations. In the second case, scatters produce reflections of the electromagnetic waves in all directions.

Vehicular cabins are composed of seats, handholds, and furniture that cannot be modelled by ray-tracing techniques due to the complexity and the computational load that it might result.

The theory of room electromagnetics allows analyzing the influence of diffuse scattering on the wave propagation. It is derived from the theory of room acoustics, widely exploited in acoustics. (A detailed explanation of it can be found in [6, 7].)

This theory can be applied to electromagnetic waves adjusting the mathematical results, although it should be noted that this connection between the acoustic and electromagnetic waves is not physical since the nature of the waves is completely different.

Besides, acoustic waves are longitudinal, contrary to electromagnetic waves that are transverse and present polarization effect; nevertheless, vertical and horizontal polarizations are represented equally in the diffuse field [1].

This theory relies on the Lambertian reflectance. It consists of the reflection of the wave in an ideal surface (Lambertian surface) in which the incident energy is equally spread in all directions [4]. For that reason, this method should be used exclusively when the randomness of the environment is large enough to assume that the non-coherent scatter dominates over the coherent component. In other words, an empty room with perfectly smooth walls will not be characterized properly using this method.

In the time domain, the energy, W, with initial energy, W_0, leads to an exponential decay of power with a decay constant produced by the multiple scattering [1].

$$W = W_0 e^{-t/\tau} \tag{1}$$

This constant decay is called the reverberation time, τ.

$$\tau = \frac{4V}{cA} = \frac{4V}{cA'\eta} \tag{2}$$

where V and A are the volume and total surface area of the room; A' is the effective area; c is the speed of light; η is the absorption coefficient of the walls, which is directly related to the reflection coefficient, ρ.

$$\rho = 1 - \eta \tag{3}$$

Equation (2) is the same than Sabine's equation [6], used in acoustics.

3   Measurement Set-Up

The environment for the measurement campaign was an indoor lab where different kind of furniture, chairs, etcetera can be found.

The measurements were performed using a Rohde Schwarz ZVL Vector Network Analyzer (VNA). We measure the scatter parameter s_{21} connecting the transmitter to port 1 and the receiver to port 2 in the frequency range between 1.7 and 6 GHz with 4001 measuring points. This provides an approximation of the channel transfer function from which we can obtain the PDP.

Figure 1 shows a schema of the room where the measurement campaign was performed. Its dimensions are 5.6 m × 6 m + 2.6 m × 3.2 m. The transmitter (Tx) is in a fixed position at point Tx. The receiver (Rx) moves along different positions P1, P2, P3. Both the height of the transmitting and the receiving antenna was 1.2 m over the floor.

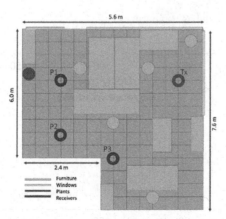

Fig. 1. Closed-room schema. Fixed position of the transmitter in Tx; moving receiver in positions P1, P2 and P3; in light green, positions of the windows; and in dark green and yellow, different items in the room. (Color figure online)

The antennas used were monopoles MGRM-WHF with 5 dBi gain [8], which are designed to be used in the frequency range 1.7–6 GHz.

4   Results

The objective is to analyze the difference in the reverberation time whenever there is an open room or a close one in order to analyze the effect of the windows.

The reverberation time is derived from the PDP measuring the slope of the tail, s. This value is in dB/ns following this relationship:

$$\tau = -\frac{10 \log_{10} e}{s} \tag{4}$$

As the goal is to obtain the effect of the windows over the reverberation time, two experiments have been carried on: in the first one, all the windows are completely cleared; in the second one, the windows have been covered with metallic blinds. Figure 2 describes the PDP in both situations, where P1, P2, P3 are referred to the points in Fig. 1. In case of the cleared windows, the slope, s, is −0.2377 dB/ns which corresponds to a reverberation time of 18.3 ns; for the covered window, the slope is −*dB/ns which corresponds to a reverberation time of 20 ns. A summary of these parameters is enumerated in Table 1.

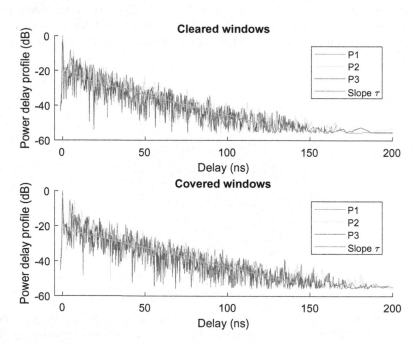

Fig. 2. Resulted power delay profile with cleared windows on the top and covered windows by metallic blinds on the bottom. The results are shown for the three different positions and the reverberation time in both cases.

Table 1. Summary of the results.

	Slope	Reverberation time
Open room	−0.2377 dB/ns	18.3 ns
Closed room	−0.2176 dB/ns	20.0 ns

These results show that, as room electromagnetics theory states, the tail of the PDP is the same independently of the position where the samples are taken. The reverberation time depends on the environment when the environment is dominated by dispersive scatters. We can assume that the diffuse field has spread uniformly in the room since the PDP for the same experiment have the same decay and this decay changes when the experiment varies.

Besides, when the windows are covered the decay of the PDP is slower in comparison to when they are cleared. This is reasonable since the signal is enclosed in the room and, as a result, it takes more time to be extinguished.

5 Conclusions

This study provides some results regarding how the PDP varies according to the windows in a room. This analysis has been made using a simple method, called reverberation time. It has been proven that, when the randomness of the environment is large enough to assume that the diffuse scatter dominates, the decay of the PDP remains the same independently of the location in the room. Besides, it is clear that the decay is greater (i.e., the PDP is extinguished faster) when there are windows in the room. As future work, this measurement campaign will be carried out inside trains to obtain the effect of people and windows on the power delay profile.

References

1. Franek, O., Andersen, J.B., Pedersen, G.F.: Diffuse scattering model of indoor wideband propagation. IEEE Trans. Antennas Propag. **59**(8), 3006–3012 (2011)
2. Andersen, J.B., Nielsen, J.O., Pedersen, G.F., Bauch, G., Herdin, J.M.: Room electromagnetics. IEEE Antennas Propag. Mag. **49**(2), 27–33 (2007)
3. Andersen, J.B., Nielsen, J.O., Herdin, G.B.M.: The large office environment - measurement and modeling of the wideband radio channel. In: The 17th Annual IEEE International Symposium on Personal, Indoor and Mobile Radio Communications (PIMRC 2006), Helsinki (2006)
4. Andersen, J.B., Chee, K.L., Jacob, M., Pedersen, G.F.: Reverberation and absorption in an aircraft cabin with the impact of passengers. IEEE Trans. Antennas Propag. **60**(5), 2472–2480 (2012)
5. Zhang, L., Briso, C., Fernandez, J.R.O., Alonso, J.I., Rodríguez, C., García-Loygorri, J.M., Guan, K.: Delay spread and electromagnetic reverberation in subway tunnels and stations. IEEE Antennas Wirel. Propag. Lett. **15**, 585–588 (2016)
6. Kuttruff, H.: Room Acoustics. CRC Press, Boca Raton (2016)
7. Grant, L.: Diffuse and specular characteristics of leaf reflectance. Remote Sens. Environ. **22**(2), 309–322 (1987)
8. Mobile Mark: Monopole MGRM-WHF. https://www.mobilemark.com/product/magnet-mount-wideband-1700-6000-mhz-mobile-wimax-antenna-for-public-safety-applications/

A Deterministic Two-Ray Model for Wideband Air Ground Channel Characterization

Cesar Calvo-Ramirez[✉], Cesar Briso, Ana Gonzalez-Plaza, and Juan Moreno Garcia-Loygorri

Technical University of Madrid, ETSI Sistemas de Telecomunicacion, C/Nikola Tesla, S/N, 28031 Madrid, Spain
cesarrasec4@gmail.com, gonzalezplaza.ana@gmail.com, {cesar.briso, juan.moreno.garcia-loygorri}@upm.es
http://www.upm.es

Abstract. A two-path deterministic model is developed with an analytical dispersion delay computed solution for two common types of flight. From the results, it is deduced that an optimal antenna for the payload communication link in the Ground Station for flat environments should be a λ/4 linear monopole with a ground plane and vertical polarization at a height as close as possible to the ground.

Keywords: UAV · Ground station · Antenna · Two-ray model
Wideband communication · RMS delay spread · Air-ground channel

1 Introduction

Due to the current growth of the Unmanned Aerial Vehicles UAV, new applications and uses of these devices are created, such as in the agronomy and surveillance sectors [1]. Generally, these applications require flown in rural and semiurban flat areas. Also, the UAV aircraft usually have a payload communication link with a Ground Station (GS), which nowadays this link need more and more capacities and speed. Nevertheless, the maximum throughput is limited by the channel capabilities and one of the most relevant facts that deteriorate the link Air-Ground (AG) in rural environments is specular ground reflexion. The two-ray model [2] or curved-Earth [3] propose a long-distance simplification (>10 m) which does not apply to these conditions because it is likely that UAV can be found less than 10 m away.

The aim of this paper is to determine some general specifications to take into account in GS antenna design regarding two-ray model and angles of arrival (AoA). Two common flight trajectories will be analysed: vertical and horizontal flight.

2 Wideband Model

Focusing on flat environments such as rural, desert, sea… where these scenarios are characteristic for having a low number of multipath components [4]. It can be assumed that one of the most relevant components for modeling is the specular reflection caused by the ground.

© Springer International Publishing AG, part of Springer Nature 2018
J. Moreno García-Loygorri et al. (Eds.): Nets4Cars 2018/Nets4Trains 2018/Nets4Aircraft 2018, LNCS 10796, pp. 44–49, 2018.
https://doi.org/10.1007/978-3-319-90371-2_5

The impulse response of the channel [5] will be used in this analysis to determine the delay dispersion with the rms delay spread parameter.

Firstly, from the geometry of the Fig. 1, we obtain: d, distance from the GS to the UAV; θ, angle between the ground and the reflected ray; m, mast height and h, altitude of the UAV. Two path and delays are considered, τ_1 for the Line of Sight (LoS) component and τ_2 for the Non Line of Sight (NLoS) component.

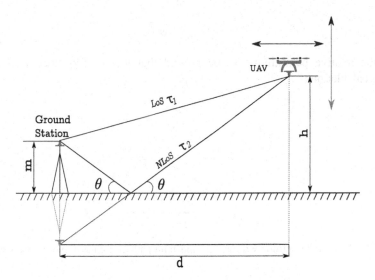

Fig. 1. 2-Ray ground reflection diagram

The difference is taken as τ_g:

$$\tau_g = |\tau_2 - \tau_1| = \frac{1}{c}\sqrt{d^2 + (h - m)^2} - \sqrt{d^2 + (h + m)^2} \tag{1}$$

Also, the θ angle as:

$$\theta = \tan^{-1}\left(\frac{h + m}{d}\right) \tag{2}$$

Then the channel impulse response model is defined by the expression:

$$h(\tau) = \delta(\tau) + \Gamma(\theta) \cdot e^{j2\pi f_c \tau_g} \delta(\tau - \tau_g) \tag{3}$$

In (3) are not considered propagation losses because their effect is negligible for the of the dispersion analysis. f_c variable is the carrier frequency, usually at C band for the payload; $\delta(\tau)$ dirac delta and $\Gamma(\theta)$ is the ground reflection coefficient given by the expression:

$$\Gamma(\theta) = \frac{\sin(\theta) - \rho}{\sin(\theta) + \rho} \tag{4}$$

Where ρ depends on the polarization as:

$$\rho_v = \frac{\sqrt{\varepsilon - \cos^2\theta}}{\varepsilon} \tag{5}$$

$$\rho_h = \sqrt{\varepsilon - \cos^2\theta} \tag{6}$$

ε is the relative permittivity of the ground that we will consider as 5 for the following calculations.

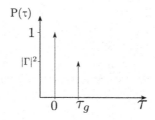

Fig. 2. Power delay profile with the ground multipath component and the LoS ray

Given the model of the (3) equation, we developed the RMS Delay Spread parameter [2] that provides information about the delay dispersion rather important for ultra wideband signals.

$$\sigma_\tau = \frac{\tau_g |\Gamma|}{1 + \Gamma^2} \tag{7}$$

3 Setup

Two configurations are proposed. On the one hand, a horizontal flight at a constant height of 10 m, which simulates one of the most common trajectories of flight with UAV, for a distance range from 10 m to 200 m distance. On the other hand, a vertical flight from 0 to 120 m height at a distance to the GS of 50 m. That simulates a common UAV takeoff and landing trajectory. For both flights, 4 proposals of mast height are analyzed at 1 m, 1.5 m, 2 m and 3 m for each of two polarizations.

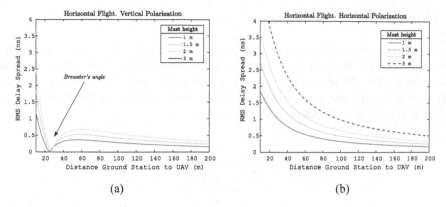

Fig. 3. RMS delay spread for horizontal flight with (a) Vertical polarization, (b) Horizontal polarization

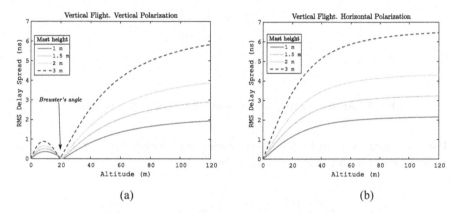

Fig. 4. RMS delay spread for vertical flight with (a) Vertical polarization, (b) Horizontal polarization

4 Results

After computing the Eq. (7) with the conditions of the Sect. 3 it allows us to analyze the dispersion.

In Fig. 3 we see that in horizontal flights the results of RMS delay spread for the comparison of vertical and horizontal polarization shows that are better in vertical for the existence of the Brewster's angle. Although, at long-distances, there is practically no difference. For vertical flights, worse results are obtained at higher altitudes. See Fig. 4.

Regarding the height of the masts, the highest will be provide more coverage but, if is possible, but the shortest had the best results of dispersion and consequently, bandwidth. Therefore, if possible, use the shorter mast.

5 Ground Station Antenna

To consider an optimal antenna for the payload links to the UAV, we must analyze the arrival angle AoA. Taking both the AoA of the LoS component and the NLoS, ground reflect component. We see in Figs. 5 and 6 that the components LoS and NLoS arrives with approximately equal angles respect to the horizontal direction. The mast height is negligible in all cases. Therefore it is set at 1.5 m.

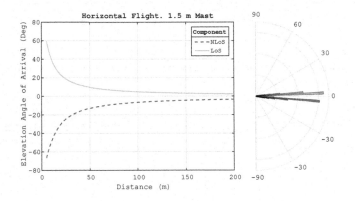

Fig. 5. Angles of arrival for horizontal flight with 1.5 m of mast

For a distance of 10 m to 200 m the angles are between 60° and 4° with more relevance at lower angles in long distances. See Fig. 5.

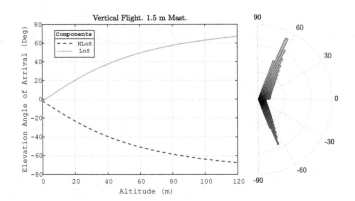

Fig. 6. Angles of arrival for vertical flight with 1.5 m of mast

At a distance of 50 m and 10 m altitude, there is an AoA of ± 10° and increasing the height to 120 m means reaching an angle of ± 67°.

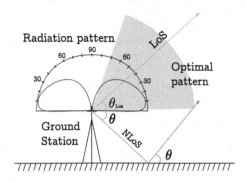

Fig. 7. Radiation pattern for ground station antenna

Taking this into account, the use of a GS antenna with linear and vertical polarization is proposed as in Fig. 7. $\lambda/4$ ground plane monopole antenna or discone to form the pattern proposed. The radiation pattern should favour the angles above, but close, to the horizontal and avoid the angles below the horizontal.

6   Conclusions

The AoA and the delay dispersion with RMS delay spread parameter are analyzed and the results show that the optimum antenna design could be a linear vertical $\lambda/4$ monopole with a ground plane or a discone antenna. The mast high should be the minimum possible despite the loss of coverage to decrease the dispersion.

References

1. Ascending Technologies. http://www.asctec.de/en/uav-uas-drone-applications/uav-precision-agriculture/
2. Rappaport, T.S.: Wireless Communications: Principles and Practice. Prentice-Hall PTR, Upper Saddle River New Jersey (2002)
3. Matolak, D., Sun, R.: Air-ground channel measurements and modeling for UAS. IEEE Aerosp. Electron. Syst. Mag. **29**(11), 30–35 (2014)
4. Matolak, D.W., Sun, R.: Initial results for air-ground channel measurements and modeling for unmanned aircraft systems: over-sea. In: 2014 IEEE Aerospace Conference, Big Sky, MT, pp. 1–15 (2014)
5. Molisch, A.F.: Wireless Communications. Wiley-IEEE Press, Hoboken (2010)

Nets4Trains

Defining an Adaptable Communications System for All Railways

Ben Allen[1], Benedikt Eschbach[2], Marion Berbineau[3,4(✉)], and Michael Mikulandra[5]

[1] Network Rail, 2nd Floor, One Eversholt Street, London NW1 2DN, UK
[2] DB Netz AG, Mainzer Landstrasse 199, 60326 Frankfurt am Main, Germany
[3] University of Lille, Ifsttar, Cosys, 59650 Villeneuve d'Ascq, France
marion.berbineau@ifsttar.fr
[4] Railenium, 59650 Villeneuve d'Ascq, France
[5] Kapsch CarrierCom Deutschland GmbH, Frankfurter Straße 120-126, 63263 Neu-Isenburg, Germany

Keywords: Shift2Rail · X2Rail-1 · Adaptable communication system
GSM-R · LTE · 5G · Radio technology

Acronyms

3GPP	3rd Generation Partnership Project
ASCI	Advanced speech call items
CAPEX	Capital Expenditure
CBTC	Communication-Based Train Control
CCA	Cross cutting activities
EIRENE	European Integrated Railway Radio Enhanced Network
ERTMS	European Rail Traffic Management System
ETCS	European Train Control System
ETSI	European Telecommunications Standard Institute
FRMCS	Future Rail Mobile Communications System
GSM-R	GSM for Railways
IP	Innovation Program
IM	Infrastructure Manager
JU	Joint Undertaking
MORANE	Mobile Radio for Railways Networks in Europe
MVNO	Mobile Virtual Network Operator
NGTC	Next Generation Train Control
OPEX	Operational Expenditure
QoS	Quality of Service
RAN	Radio Access Network
RAT	Radio Access Technology
S2R	Shift2Rail
SERA	Single European Railway Area
SLA	Service Level Agreement
TCMS	Train Control & Management System
TETRA	Terrestrial Trunked Radio
UIC	Union Internationale des Chemins de Fer

© Springer International Publishing AG, part of Springer Nature 2018
J. Moreno García-Loygorri et al. (Eds.): Nets4Cars 2018/Nets4Trains 2018/Nets4Aircraft 2018, LNCS 10796, pp. 53–55, 2018.
https://doi.org/10.1007/978-3-319-90371-2_6

1   Adaptable Communication System in the X2Rail-1 Project of the European Shift2Rail Joint Undertaking

Telecommunication services have become an integral part of the railway transport environment for train control and protection applications as well as voice communication. With the introduction of ERTMS, GSM-R [1] was defined as communication system for mainline railway and foundation for interoperable train operation. At the same time, other railway domains have utilized alternative technologies to satisfy communication requirements linked to their environments, for example Wi-Fi-based systems in combination with TETRA for urban rail.

With new emerging railway applications, advances in telecommunication technology and the expected obsolescence of deployed infrastructure, the railway sector is in the process of assessing and defining a future unified communication system to address existing and new operational requirements for all railway domains, including metro, urban/suburban, mainline/highspeed, regional and freight lines.

Within Innovation Program 2 (IP2) of the European Shift2Rail Joint Undertaking, a Technology Demonstrator (TD) "adaptable communications for all railways" activity was initiated to bring together key stakeholders, to investigate the future communication needs, define and specify key functions and finally develop prototypes and integrated demonstrators to prove the feasibility and capabilities of an adaptable communication subsystem for railways [2].

A key aspect of the future adaptable communication system will be the support of multiple access technologies, including but not limited to LTE, 5G, Wi-Fi or SatCom, combined with bearer independence to address availability, resiliency, performance, capacity, security, safety and maintainability requirements of existing and new railway applications. Moreover, the adaptable communication system allows vertical, cross technology handover between different mobile heterogeneous networks and could enable in the use of public networks in place of or in conjunction with dedicated networks. The communication system will also provide common and standard interfaces towards applications and manages all communication needs for onboard equipment as well as for other users or applications. An important consideration is the ability to smoothly migrate the legacy communication systems towards the future communication system as well as ensuring the support of emerging and future technologies without impacting or interfering with deployed applications and services.

The first project within IP2 is named X2Rail-1 [3], which focused to:

- collect, assess and qualify user and system requirements from users and stakeholders, including railway operators, infrastructure managers, regulatory groups and related associations as well as the inputs from other Shift2Rail projects;
- undertake business model analysis with the aim to explore new operating and deployment models ranging from dedicated and hybrid networks to "network-as-a-service" approaches;
- specify the architecture, subsystems and functions needed to enable an adaptable communication system and
- assess key criteria and create guidelines for the selection of an appropriate communication technologies or radio network candidates.

A key benefit of the program is the close collaboration and ongoing exchange of requirements, guidelines, architectural considerations and impact assessments across all related Shift2Rail technical demonstrator activities, which include but is not limited to:

- Automatic Train Operation (ATO) over ETCS,
- Moving Block,
- Zero on-site testing,
- Smart wayside objects,
- Cyber security,
- Fail Safe Train Positioning,
- On-board train integrity,
- Formal methods,
- Traffic Management evolution,
- Virtual coupling and
- Onboard train control & management system (TCMS);

The Key Note presentation will start with an introduction of the project objectives in the light of the goals of the Shift2Rail Joint Undertaking [4]. The second part will summarize the first public project deliverables and outline the interim results from the business model analysis task, the communication system specification task and the technology selection guideline task. Furthermore an outlook towards the upcoming prototype development will be given including some early view of expected tasks in the future member calls linked to the annual working plan 2018. The presentation will conclude with highlighting the targeted improvements, an impact assessment and overall benefits of the future adaptable communication systems for the different railway domains.

References

1. UIC: GSM-R specifications. 21 December 2015. http://uic.org/gsm-r#EIRENE-Specifications
2. Shift2Rail IP2. https://shift2rail.org/research-development/ip2/
3. http://projects.shift2rail.org/s2r_ip2_n.aspx?p=X2RAIL-1
4. https://shift2rail.org/wp-content/uploads/2013/07/S2R-JU-GB_Decision-N-15-2015-MAAP. pdf

Survey of Environmental Effects in Railway Communications

Nerea Fernandez[1,2], Saioa Arrizabalaga[1,2], Javier Añorga[1,2],
Jon Goya[1,2], Iñigo Adín[1,2], and Jaizki Mendizabal[1,2(✉)]

[1] Ceit, Manuel Lardizabal 15, 20018 Donostia / San Sebastián, Spain
{nfernandez, sarrizabalaga, jabenito, jgoya, iadin,
jmendizabal}@ceit.es
[2] Universidad de Navarra, Tecnun,
Manuel Lardizabal 13, 20018 Donostia / San Sebastián, Spain

Abstract. In order to identify the different external impairments that could exist in the railway environment. A survey of these effects is presented with the aim of identifying the different phenomena that could affect to the communication channel. On one hand, common effects linked to the signal transmission over a wireless communication channel are analysed. On the other hand, as GSM-R is the current communication technology employed in ERTMS, the disturbances interfering it have been studied. Finally, some solutions to mitigate these effects are listed, in this case, focused in handover solutions.

Keywords: GSM-R · Railway · Communication channel · Disturbances
External influences · Environment

1 Introduction

Current railway operation relies on the communication between train and trackside is needed for a correct railway operation. This communication is currently implemented in different ways. If ERTMS is taken as an example, two mechanisms are deployed: the first one, by using balises installed on the track, which give the information when the train passes over each of them and, the other one by a wireless continuous transmission technology by means of GSM-R. This last one allows a continuous and bidirectional communication between the track and the train [1] unlike the balises which only offer unidirectional communication.

The quality and performance of this communication depends, among others, on the communication channel. This communication channel can be damaged by external impairments causing a worse performance than the ideal communication channel.

This paper outlines the objective of identifying these external influences both, the ones related with the different environments where a train could travel through and other phenomena linked to the wireless transmission that could appear, in order to identify the effect on the communication channel. Moreover, the nature of data sent through this communication channel differs depending on the application. This means that, not all of them have the same requirements to perform properly. This is because the undesired effects that influence the channel causes different impact depending on the application itself.

© Springer International Publishing AG, part of Springer Nature 2018
J. Moreno García-Loygorri et al. (Eds.): Nets4Cars 2018/Nets4Trains 2018/Nets4Aircraft 2018, LNCS 10796, pp. 56–67, 2018.
https://doi.org/10.1007/978-3-319-90371-2_7

This paper is structured as follows.

- Section 2 shows the different applications that coexist in the railway environment.
- Section 3 explains the state of art of effects affecting to wireless communications.
- Section 4 shows some different possible existing solutions to mitigate handover.
- Finally, Sect. 5 presents the conclusions.

2 Applications in Railway Environment

According to [2], where the future communications of railways is being defined, different applications from the point of view of the communication have been listed. The classification proposed by [2] related to the different applications that send data through the communication channel is the following one:

- Critical voice and video: require availability, high reliability with low latency and setup time, including at high speed of mobility.
- Critical data: reliability and availability.
- Non-critical applications (non-critical voice, non-critical data, passenger connectivity, etc.).

The diagram represented in the Fig. 1 depicts how the disturbances affecting the channel could influence, as well, the application to the point of no longer being useful for the destination by the time the information arrives.

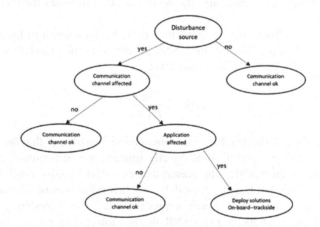

Fig. 1. External influences affecting applications

As the Fig. 1 shows, if the application is affected due to bad performance of the channel new solutions should be needed to be deployed to mitigate the disturbance error source. However, if the application or the communication channel are not affected, then normally the performance will be correct without applying anything else. The aim of improving the communication is to obtain a correct functionality for both, communication channel and service performance.

3 Main Environments and Phenomena in Railway Communications

Railway environment can be considered demanding according to the communications. The communication channel can be affected by different external influences. Some of these impairments are the following ones: weather conditions, environment scenarios, speed of train and electromagnetic disturbances.

This section shows the state of art of the different phenomena affecting the communication channel. This state of art can be shown separately from two points of view: the phenomena that affect all the possible communication channels (no matter the technology) and those that affect to one specific technology, in this case GSM-R.

3.1 Weather Conditions

The communication channel attenuation can be affected by different weather conditions. These conditions depend on the climate peculiarities of the rail corridor region in terms of, e.g., rain characteristics such as statistics of exceeded rainfall rate or raindrop size. However, not only the attenuation caused by precipitation (rain in the previous example) causes impairments in the channel but also other phenomena such as attenuation due to atmospheric gases or due to solid particles in the atmosphere.

According to ITU-R recommendations [3, 4], estimations for attenuations due to different propagation effects in terrestrial line-of-sight systems by radio wave propagation can be calculated. But these recommendations are not the only source to obtain them. The study in [5] evaluates also the performance of different methods to estimate the attenuation.

The weather conditions have a direct impact in the attenuation of the signals so, in turn in the SNR (Signal to Noise Ratio). SNR is defined as the ratio between the power of the signal and the power of the noise level.

$$SNR = \frac{Psignal}{Pnoise} \tag{1}$$

In turn, the SNR is affected due to this attenuation considering that the power of the required signal can be reduced. SNR directly impacts the performance of a wireless communication. A higher SNR value means that the target signal strength is stronger in relation to the noise levels (e.g. caused by no favorable weather conditions). This allows higher data rates and fewer retransmissions, hence resulting in a better throughput. On the contrary, a lower SNR implies lower data rates, which decreases throughput. Therefore, in the railway environments, when the train is close to the base station, the impact of the external influences could be less invasive. This is because thanks to good coverage in the stations, the signal gets the highest values, then the same noise affects less than when the power of signal is worse in other environments.

Consequently, if the SNR is low, the signal that will arrive to the destination could be corrupted, that is, packet error will be present. The worst case respecting to the SNR is when the signal is so attenuated that the receiver is not able to detect it ending in packet loss; the destination will not receive the packet (Fig. 2).

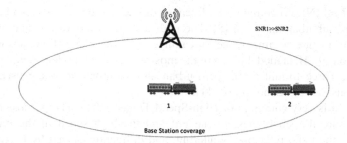

Fig. 2. SNR diagram for the same noise level

Additionally, the weather conditions do not only affect to terrestrial line-of-sight but also to, e.g., WDM-FSO (Wave Division Multiple-Free Space Optics). Some studies about the different weather conditions affecting this last optical system have been developed as referenced in [6].

3.2 Environment Scenarios

The operating train can traverse diverse types of rail corridors and in the same way, the rail corridor can be composed by different scenarios. Depending on this, the characteristics of the communication channel is diversely affected. The Fig. 3 lists the different scenarios identified:

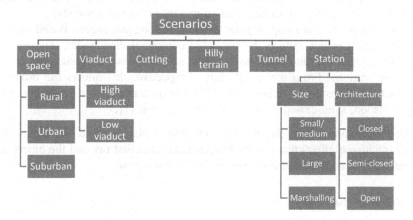

Fig. 3. Different environment scenarios [7]

Below, the explanation of each scenario described in the Fig. 3 is presented:

1. Open space or plain scenario: large cells and continuous coverage where the link between the fixed transmitter and moving receiver normally has a dominant line-of-sight (LoS) component. However, after a certain distance, called breakpoint distance, the impact of the sparse scatters will be noticed at the receiver represented

by non-LoS (NLoS) components. Because of that, the open space can be classified in urban, suburban and rural [8]. The path loss (that implies attenuation) in these scenarios is due to free space spreading, scattering, reflection, absorption and diffraction [9]. Hata model is one of the most widely used models in mobile wireless systems. Three formulas for open, urban and suburban areas are used and their definitions can be found in [10, 11].

2. Viaduct: it is very common for High-Speed Trains (HST). The purpose of viaducts is to ensure the smoothness of the rail and the high speed of the train. In this scenario, the radio reflection, scattering, and diffraction caused by nearby scatters, such as trees and buildings, can also reduce the wanted signal significantly. The viaduct height and relative Base Station (BS) height have great influence on the received signal. Because of the relatively high altitude of the viaduct in comparison with the surrounding terrain, the LoS component is dominant in this scenario.

3. Cutting: this scenario is widely used for HST construction to ensure the smoothness of the rail and help to achieve a high speed of the train when passing through hills. The propagation of radio waveforms in this scenario is significantly affected by the steep walls on both sides.

4. Hilly terrain: the surrounding environment is densely scattered with objects distributed irregularly and non-uniformly. With high-altitude transmitting antennas and low-altitude obstacles, the LoS component is observable and can be detected along the entire railway. However, multipath components scattered/reflected from the surrounding obstacles cause serious constructive or destructive effects on the received signal and, therefore, affect the channel's fading characteristics.

5. Tunnel: represents an environment where HST passes through tunnels, with different lengths ranging from hundreds of meters to several kilometers.

6. Station: where the train stops regularly to load/unload passengers. Based on the size of the station, which reflects the estimated communication traffic, station scenario can be categorized into small to medium size stations, large stations, and marshalling stations. From the architecture perspective, this affects the propagation characteristics inside the station, three HST station scenarios can be recognized, i.e., open station, semi-closed station, and closed station [7].

The propagation effects due to these different scenarios could be summarized in scatters (multipath effect) that causes delay between the first ray and the others and in attenuations that could cause no coverage in the worst case.

3.3   Speed of the Train

The speed of the train could have an impact in the communication channel; but lower in speed range below 250 km/h as in the high-speed range up to 500 km/h [7, 13].

HST wireless communication systems have to overcome many challenges resulting from the high speed of the train, which can easily exceed 250 km/h such as large Doppler spreads, fast travel through diverse scenarios and fast handover [7].

Doppler effect. Unlike traditional environments, Doppler effect becomes another pivotal factor degrading system performance, which increases randomness of received signal [12].

The variation of the reception frequency is generated by Doppler effect as a result of transmitter and receiver movement. The Doppler effect is worse in presence of higher relative speed between the transmitter and the receiver, and therefore it affects to the communication mostly at high speed [13].

When a HST travels at a speed of around 500 km/h, the wireless channels suffer from a high Doppler shift and it increases the difficulty of the channel estimation [14].

The concept of the Doppler effect is related to the velocity of mobile device and angle between reception radio wave and the moving direction. If variation of received frequency occurs, it is possible to recognize a variation factor of carrier frequency as a loss of received signal without compensation for Doppler effect. So, a loss of received signal supposes a loss in the information of the train [13].

Due to the influence that this effect causes to the communication channel, many researchers have tried some approaches, such as [15, 16].

Handover. The handover is a crucial factor to maintain high reliability and availability of mobile communication. The handover addressed in this paper, refers to the horizontal handover. This type of handover uses the same technology and consists in changing the connection from one base station to another base station.

When the train speed is low (under 100 km/h), latency incurred in each procedure of the handover process is not too severe to influence the continuity of wireless communication. However, when the train speed increases (high-speed railway) where shorter handover latency is required, the traditional handover scheme which has been adopted in the GSM network could no longer guarantee high quality performance and results in higher probability of handover failure as a consequence [17].

Handover execution time delay can be divided into two parts, one is the time required to activate the target channel cell, and the other is the time for Mobile Station (MS) to leave the original channel and adjust to the new one [18]. The last one is the key referring to the handover; this time determines the quantity of packets that could be dropped (so, it entails packet loss impairment).

From the information and work from the literature, it could be concluded that because of the Doppler effect and handover, packet loss could be produced.

3.4 Electromagnetic Disturbances

EM interferences could damage the performance of the communication channel [20]. These interferences could be generated by different sources, such as the devices of the train, the train itself or external devices. They can affect differently depending on the current technology of the communication channel (GSM-R, LTE-R).

GSM-R ensures voice and data transmissions between trains and control centers, and, also, between trains. As any radio equipment, it is exposed to electromagnetic.

The concept of the Doppler effect is related to the velocity of mobile device and angle between reception radio wave and the moving direction. If variation of received frequency occurs, it is possible to recognize a variation factor of carrier frequency as a loss of received signal without compensation for Doppler effect. So, a loss of received signal supposes a loss in the information of the train [13].

(EM) disturbances present in the railway environment. Therefore, the quality of GSM-R transmissions can be degraded. Then, it is important to evaluate and predict the effect of these disturbances in order to avoid any loss of train operational capacity [19].

References to the EM disturbances in the GSM-R technology, as it is the current railway communication technology used in ERTMS, and in LTE-R are compiled in this work. This could be taken as an example for other communication technologies.

According to the interferences with GSM-R communications, two main potential sources concerning the EM noise can be distinguished:

- The first type of noise is the transient EM noise, which is produced by the sliding contact between the catenary and the pantograph.
- The second one is the public GSM communications that the adjacent channels to the GSM-R frequency bands use; can produce EM noise on the GSM-R channels. Similarly, same scenario is replicated in E-GSM.
- The third type is the public LTE communications and the LTE-R adjacent frequency bands. This case is the same problematic as in the second type but in different frequency bands.

On-site Analysis of Electromagnetic Disturbances in GSM-R. The GSM-R antennas, fixed on train's roofs, receive signals coming from base stations. But, at the same time, numerous interference signals are also received. In particular, the main source of these interferences is the transient EM disturbances produced by the loss of contact between catenary and pantograph. These electromagnetic disturbances produce sparks and create radiated transient signals (noise level) similar to frequency bands of GSM-R [21].

On one hand, an important parameter to define the impact of the disturbances on the GSM-R transmission is the occurrence of the transient. According to measurement results from reference [22], the time interval between consecutive transients heavily depends on the operating conditions such as speed of train, nature crossed areas, etc. Indeed, in rural areas and at low speed, only a few transients were detected, whereas in urban areas and high speed, they were constantly detecting transients. However, these transient noises are very brief and their impact on the quality of GSM-R transmissions will mainly depend on their recurrences [21]. If few transients appear, the quality of the transmission will only be slightly deteriorated.

On the other hand, another parameter is the probability that a transient interferes in a GSM-R communication channel. It can be estimated using the following approximations:

- The duration of a transient is very short in comparison with the duration of one bit (3.7 ms) [23], and can be approximated by a punctual event.
- The transients produce high levels of interference in the GSM-R band affecting the SNR.

When the transient occurs, it produces an arbitrary decision on a bit inside the burst [23]. Nevertheless, this phenomenon does not affect to all the railway systems. This only affects to electrified lines, since according to [25], the electromagnetic environment for the non-electric regional railway line does not show any interference that could impact the wireless communications.

Coexistence of Public Network and GSM-R Network (Possible Disturbances).
Some of the disturbances affecting the wireless communication channel come from the
public mobile network. The interference between GSM-R and other public networks
increases because both railway and public operators want to have good coverage along
the rail tracks. Instead of cooperating in network planning, railway and public operators
fight for the coverage [26]. In the following paragraphs, some cases related to GSM-R
are explained.

When public GSM base stations are located in vicinity of railway lines and transmit
over carrier frequencies adjacent to GSM-R frequency bands, then GSM-R signals can be
disturbed [21]. It explains that the frequency band studied includes the downlink band of
GSM-R but also the first channel of the down-link band of public GSM [24], that is,
down-link frequency bands of both GSM-R and public GSM are adjacent as Fig. 4 shows.

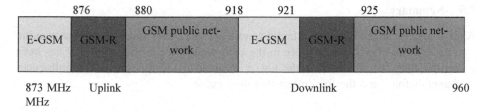

Fig. 4. Frequency of GSM, GSM-R and E-GSM

Theoretically, such interference can be avoided if public operators do not use
frequency bands adjacent to those of GSM-R for the areas close to rail tracks; however,
this is not well implemented in practice [26]. These two channels are then separated by
a frequency band, which can be not enough to prevent from mutual disturbances as the
reference [21] demonstrates. So, public GSM base station signals play a significant role
in intermodulation and/or blocking type interference [27].

The interference could result in severe impairments over voice and data communications as well as packet loss over several hundred meters of track.

This concept does not only appear in GSM public network. In this way, strong
wideband signals (UMTS, LTE) from public network generate intermodulation products inside GSM-R MS receivers, covering the entire GSM-R band and therefore
increasing the probability of interfering with the serving channel of a GSM-R [27]. As
well, the Universal Mobile Telecommunications System (UMTS) 900, which employs
the so-called GSM-Extended (GSM-E) frequency bands, can also induce a residual
noise on the GSM-R channels at the end of the GSM-R frequency bands [21].

The high spectral density of a GSM signal in combination with wideband
UMTS/LTE signals result in a high probability of interference on GSM-R. The current
generation of approved, ETSI compliant GSM-R receivers cannot handle strong signals
from public mobile network operating in nearby frequency bands. In real world
deployments, several strong public mobile network signals are to be expected in the
925–960 MHz band, resulting in high composite receive powers, and a high probability
of blocking and/or intermodulation products falling in the GSM-R band [27].

Theoretical Analysis of Electromagnetic Disturbances in LTE-R: Coexistence of Public Safety Network and LTE-R Network. In some countries, the LTE public safety network uses the frequency band of 700 MHz and also, the LTE-R network is assigned to the same frequency band.

So, the main challenge is to eliminate the radio interference, especially from adjacent LTE public safety network to LTE based wireless train control on the same frequency band in order to get a system faultless and with continuous connection to train control system [28]. The problematic in LTE and LTE-R is the same as the GSM public network with GSM-R [28].

From the results obtained in this work, it could be stated that the EM disturbances could cause packet error (e.g. the transient noises) or the loss of packets (permanent noises as GSM public network).

3.5 Summary

After analyzing all the different external conditions that could affect the communication channel and the effects that produce in the communication, a brief summary has been done. The diagram presented in the Fig. 5 summarizes all the causes (the influences explained before) and the final effect that they cause.

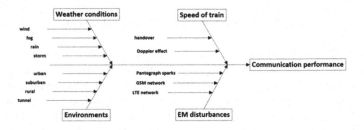

Fig. 5. Causes and effect diagram

The network parameters that are affected by the different external influences (causes) are defined below:

- Delay is understood as the time between the first arrived ray and the others referring to the delay caused by the multipath propagation and not to the delay in the own communication channel.
- Packet error is defined as the error that the transient disturbances can cause in the original signal. This error can be corrected in the destination.
- Packet loss is defined as the error that permanent disturbances can cause in the original signal, so the desired signal would arrive as noise to the destination without any chances of recovering it. In terms of information, packets with the corresponding message do not arrive to the destination.
- Bandwidth (BW): is used as a synonym for data transfer rate, the amount of data that can be carried from one point to another in a given time period.
- Coverage: the geographical area covered by the network of a service provider.

As a summary of all the topics addressed before, the Table 1 shows the relation between the different phenomena and the network parameters (as impairments in the communication channel):

Table 1. Relation between phenomena and network parameters

	Effects	Delay	Packet loss	Packet error	BW	Coverage
Weather conditions	Attenuation	x	x	x		x
Environment scenarios	Attenuation	x	x			x
Speed of the train	Multipath	x	x			
	Handover		x			
	Doppler		x			
EM disturbances	Signal interference		x	x		
Technology					x	

4   Possible Solutions

In the previous section, some external disturbances have been exposed with the corresponding impairments that could appear in the communication channel. Some of these effects could be mitigated if some solutions are applied. There are some solutions that reduce the effects of the disturbances. As example three techniques to reduce the effect in the handover are described as follows:

- Fast handover based on CI (Cell Identity) and TA (Time Advance): fast handover algorithms based on (CI, TA) coordinates method and dynamic threshold to improve the speed of handover is proposed in [18].
- An enhanced handover strategy for GSM-R Technology: handover algorithm by applying a newly proposed technique that changes the handover margin or threshold according to the train speed [29].
- Innovative handover scheme based on dual-antenna technology for GSM-R: turns the handover process to be a soft handover which means that the communication between BS and MS will no longer disconnect during the process [17].

All these improvements could help to reduce the network parameter of packet loss; less time disconnection in handover supposes less time that the train is disconnected to the network. Further details are included in the following subsections.

5   Conclusions

The railway communications can be affected by different external influences e.g. signal interferences, without forgetting, the environment where the train passes through (tunnels, open space, etc.). The different disturbances, affecting the channel, could come from different sources such as the train itself (EM disturbances or the speed of the train) and weather conditions as the different environment where the rail corridor is located. These different influences could cause the modification of the same parameters in the communication channel such as delay or packet error. The result of this disturbances in the channel could be a worse communication channel than the ideal one (only free space losses) which, in the worst case (a large tunnel, for instance), could lead in a channel that could be impossible to transmit through. In addition, depending on the performance of the channel, the applications can be useful for the correct operation of the train or, on the opposite, useless.

Because of the important influences that these interferences could cause in the impairments of the channel, these problems have been analysed. Although these external influences have been addressed individually in this paper, the combination of them in the same scenario is possible (e.g. weather conditions and cutting scenario).

Due to the impact of these influence in the channel, at least, a number of solutions have been theoretically deployed in order to mitigate their impact in the channel. Moreover, the solutions have to mitigate the communication channel impairments until the applications reach the corresponding requirements. Since these solutions do not mitigate/reduce all the undesired effects in the channel (ideal case both channel and applications); there is room for research for further solutions by using other's algorithms and mitigation strategies.

References

1. Theeg, G., Vlasenko, S.: Railway Signalling & Interlocking (2009). ISBN 978-3-7771-0394-5
2. Allen, B., et al.: "Deliverable D3.1 User & System Requirements (Telecommunications)." X2Rail-1: Start-up activities for Advanced Signalling and Automation Systems
3. ITU-R Recommendation P.530-13: Propagation data and prediction methods required for the design of terrestrial line-of-sight systems. ITU (2009)
4. ITU-R Recommendation P.838-3: Specific attenuation model for rain for use in prediction methods. ITU (2005)
5. Andrade, F.J.A., et al.: Evaluation of ITU-R rain attenuation prediction methods for terrestrial links. In: Microwave and Optoelectronics Conference (IMOC), 2015 SBMO/IEEE MTT-S International (2015)
6. Biswas, S.K., et al.: Estimation of link range and bit rate for 16 channel WDM-FSO considering atmospheric turbulence and pointing error under various weather conditions. In: International Conference on Electrical, Computer and Communication Engineering (ECCE), 16–18 February 2017, Cox's Bazar, Bangladesh (2017)
7. Wang, C.-X., et al.: Channel measurements and models for high-speed train communication systems: a survey. IEEE Commun. Surv. Tutor. 18(2), 974–987 (2016). (Second quarter)
8. Pekka, K.: WINNER II channel models—Part II radio channel measurement and analysis results. IST-4-027756, WINNER II D1.1.2, v1.0, September 2007
9. Banimelhem, O., Al-Zu'bi, M.M., Al Salameh, M.S.: Hata path loss model tuning for cellular networks in Irbid City. In: 2015 IEEE International Conference on Computer and Information Technology; Ubiquitous Computing and Communications; Dependable, Autonomic and Secure Computing; Pervasive Intelligence and Computing (2015)

10. Hata, M.: Empirical formula for propagation loss in land mobile radio services. IEEE Trans. Veh. Technol. **29**(3), 317–325 (1980)
11. Lu, J., Zhu, G., Ai, B.: Radio propagation measurements and modeling in railway viaduct area. In: 6th International Conference on Wireless Communications Networking and Mobile Computing (WiCOM) (2010)
12. Liu, Q.-Y., Wang, M., Zhong, Z.-D.: Statistics of capacity analysis in high speed railway communication systems. Tamkang J. Sci. Eng. **14**(3), 209–215 (2011)
13. Bok, J., Ryu, H.-G.: Path loss model considering doppler shift for high speed railroad communication. In: 16th International Conference on Advanced   Communication Technology (ICACT) (2014)
14. Fan, D., Zhong, Z., Wang, G., Gao, F.: Doppler shift estimation for high-speed railway wireless communication systems with large-scale linear antennas. In: 2015 International Workshop on High Mobility Wireless Communications (HMWC) (2015)
15. Qin, T., Jin, D., Zheng, G., Wang, J.: A novel doppler effect testing approach for highspeed railway wireless communication systems. In: International   Conference on Electronics, Communications and Control (ICECC) (2011)
16. Liu, T., et al.: Doppler shift estimation for high-speed railway scenario. In: 2016 IEEE 83rd Vehicular Technology Conference (VTC Spring) (2016)
17. Du, P., et al.: A dual-antenna based handover scheme for GSM-R network. In: 2012 International Conference on Wireless Communications and Signal Processing (WCSP) (2012)
18. Sun, T., Zhou, K., Luo, X., Huang, Y.: Research on the fast handover algorithms of GSM-R for high-speed railway. In: 2015 International Conference on Network and Information Systems for Computers (2015)
19. Dudoyer, S., et al.: Classification of transient EM noises depending on their effect on the quality of GSM-R reception. IEEE Trans. Electromagn. Compat. **55**(5), 867–874 (2013)
20. del Portillo, J., et al.: Characterization of the EM environment of railway spot communication systems. In: IEEE EMC Conference Detroit, Michigan, August 2008
21. Hammi, T., Slimen, N.B., Deniau, V., Rioult, J., Dudoyer, S.: Comparison between GSM-R coverage level and EM noise level in railway environment. In: 2009 9th International Conference on Intelligent Transport Systems Telecommunications (ITST)   (2009)
22. Dudoyer, S., et al.: Study of the susceptibility of the GSM-R communications face to the electromagnetic interferences of the rail environment. IEEE Trans. Electromagn. Compat. **54** (3), 667–676 (2012)
23. Boschetti, G., Mariscotti, A., Deniau, V.: Pantograph arc transients occurrence and GSM-R characteristics. In: Conference Paper, January 2011
24. Dudoyer, S., et al.: Testing of the GSM-R system against electromagnetic disturbances present in the railway environment. In: 9th International Conference on Intelligent Transport Systems Telecommunications (ITST) (2009)
25. Mendizabal, J., et al.: On-board electromagnetic interference field-test and evaluation of a non-electrified   railway   regional   line.   In: 12th   International   Workshop, Nets4Cars/Nets4Trains/Nets4Aircraft 2017, Toulouse, France, 4–5 May 2017
26. He, R., Ai, B., et al.: High-speed railway communications from GSM-R to LTE-R. IEEE Veh. Technol. Mag. **11**, 49–58 (2016)
27. UIC O-8736-2.0: Assessment report on GSM-R current and future radio environment. In: UIC, 07-2014
28. Choi, J.-K., et al.: Challenges of LTE high-speed railway network to coexist with LTE public safety network. In: 17th International Conference on Advanced Communication Technology (ICACT) (2015)
29. Bhattacharya, S., et al.: An enhanced handover strategy for GSM-R technology. In: Third International Conference on Computer and Communication Technology (ICCCT) (2012)

LTE-Based Wireless Broadband Train to Ground Network Performance in Metro Deployments

Haibin Wu[1], Xiang Zhang[1], Lei Xie[1], Julian Andrade[1(✉)],
Shupeng Xu[2], and Xue Yang[2]

[1] Huawei Technologies, Shenzhen, China
{alvin.wuhaibin,zhangxiang4,lei.xie,
julian.andrade}@huawei.com
[2] Zhengzhou Metro Co. Ltd., Zhengzhou, China
xspl969@qq.com, 1169501706@qq.com

Abstract. This paper presents the performance testing of a train to ground communications network deployed in an underground environment and based on 3GPP LTE wireless technology. A fully operational project was deployed in *Zhengzhou, China* in 2016, LTE Node-B have been installed in the tunnel, LTE terminals are deployed onboard in the train, working in 1785–1805 MHz band, with 10 MHz + 5 MHz dual-carrier configuration, a full test was executed and completed in Q3 2016, the feasibility and performance of LTE solution was verified and accepted. During the testing the train was moving among six stations with 7.6 km distance, the signal level received by the train wireless terminals, the throughput achieved between train and ground nodes, as well as the E-E latency are measured in the performance test.

Keywords: LTE-M · Throughput
Signal-to-interference-plus-noise ratio (SINR) · Tunnel · Metro

1 Introduction

Railways and metros are quickly adopting the latest developments on telecommunication technologies in order to enhance safety, improve operation efficiency and provide a better service to passengers. Train to ground communication systems based on reliable and high capacity wireless technologies allow the deployment of advanced railway services like automated train control systems, real time onboard video surveillance, real time rolling stock monitoring, remote train diagnostics, onboard Internet access for passengers, etc.

From 2014 to 2016, while LTE was deployed globally as a mature 4G network technology, China Association of Metros started the analysis, pilot test and commercial trial of LTE based train to ground communications network, and finalized the LTE as industry standard for China Metro in 2016, which is named as LTE-M.

The LTE specification provides downlink peak rates of 300 Mbit/s, uplink peak rates of 75 Mbit/s and QoS provisions permitting a transfer latency of less than 5 ms in the radio

© Springer International Publishing AG, part of Springer Nature 2018
J. Moreno García-Loygorri et al. (Eds.): Nets4Cars 2018/Nets4Trains 2018/Nets4Aircraft 2018, LNCS 10796, pp. 68–78, 2018.
https://doi.org/10.1007/978-3-319-90371-2_8

access network. LTE has the ability to manage fast-moving mobiles and supports multi-cast and broadcast streams. LTE supports scalable carrier bandwidths, from 1.4 MHz to 20 MHz and supports both frequency division duplexing (FDD) and time-division duplexing (TDD). Performance of LTE in metro scenarios was studied in [1].

In China LTE-M is based on 1.8 GHz spectrum (1785–1805 MHz), which is allocated for Metro/Energy/Airport usage by China Ministry of Industry and Information Technology, in most case the Metro applies 2 * 5 MHz to build a dual carrier TDD-LTE based network, some case 10 MHz + 5 MHz is deployed.

To assess the performance of train to ground networks based on LTE, Huawei has deployed a commercial wireless network in Zhengzhou Metro (Line-2) based on 10 MHz + 5 MHz dual carrier configuration [2]. In this commercial trial we have tested and measured radio coverage, throughput and latency. This paper describes the deployed network and the testing with measurement results.

2 Network

The commercial trial network provides LTE coverage for Line-2 of Zhengzhou Metro, covers the 7.6 km distance tunnel from Erligang station to Nansihuan station, totally 6 stations.

The RF radiating system was based on leaky cables. Two leaky cables were used in order to take advantage of MIMO. Both leaky cables were shared by the two networks A and B. Radio units were located along the test route with distances 600 m–1300 m.

The networking structure is shown in Fig. 1.

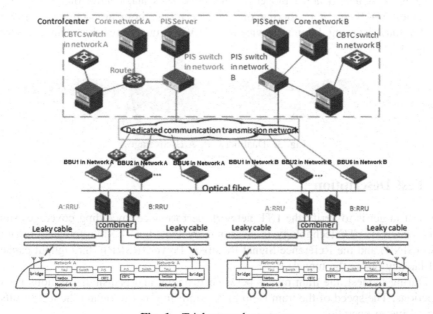

Fig. 1. Trial network structure

The LTE network is integrated into the Metro Communication System, which is a standard LTE network structure, including 6 LTE Node-Bs (Base Stations), Core Network, OMC (Operation and Maintenance Center), with necessary IP networking equipment (Router and Switch). The LTE network is connected with Metro signaling system, PIS and CCTV.

LTE terminal devices include Train Access Unit (TAU), Netbox, Antennas and Switch, are installed in driver's cabins which are located in the headstock and tailstock.

For reliability design, LTE network is deployed with a dual system, which is called A + B redundancy networking. Network A is based on 1795–1805 MHz with 10 MHz spectrum band, serving the CBTC, PIS, CCTV and Train status monitoring. Network B is based on 1790–1795 with 5 MHz band, providing CBTC service only. Frequency use is shown in Fig. 2.

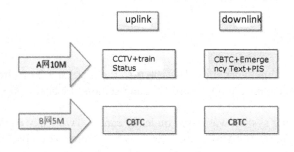

Fig. 2. The dual system design

Network A and B are deployed in the same sites and central office, with same coverage. A + B are not working on standby mode, both are active and running synchronously serving different service needs. A + B dual network coverage is shown in Fig. 3:

Fig. 3. Dual network A/B coverage

3   Test Description

The test target is to verify the LTE network performance, including coverage (signal level which in LTE technology is measured by the Signal-to-interference-plus-noise ratio (SINR) and the Reference Signal Received Power (RSRP)), throughput capacity and latency inside the tunnel.

During the test, the train moves between Erligang and Nansihuan stations in both directions. The speed of the train is up to 50 km/h in order to obtain the test results in normal metro operation.

The coverage test was measured by the received signal power from the train TAU. The train TAU periodically measures the RSRP/SINR from the trackside RRUs by collecting the cell reference signals. The TAU internally converts the measured RSRP to dBm.

Data traffic between the train TAU and trackside RRUs was generated by iPerf, which is a tool located in central office to send UDP packets simulating passenger information traffic. Saturation UDP traffic was sent by the transmitter, and the throughput measured at the receiver provided the network capacity. Therefore, the total UDP throughput represents the available speed of the LTE wireless link.

Transmission latency between the train TAU and application server was generated with IxChariot, which is a tool emulating UDP loop packets. The UDP packets were sent by the train TAU, while the application server received the packets and sent a confirmation packet to the TAU, thus the E-E latency is calculated: half of the round trip latency equals one way transmission latency.

4 Test Results

4.1 Coverage Measurements Results

Figure 4 shows the received RSRP values in the network A, tested by train embedded TAU along the test route. The maximum value is −61 dBm, the minimum value is −103 dBm.

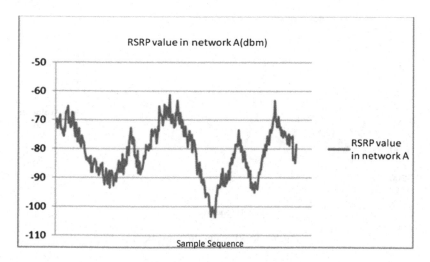

Fig. 4. RSRP value in network A

Figure 5 shows the received SINR values in the network A, tested by train embedded TAU along the test route. The maximum value is 40 dB, the minimum value is 0 dB.

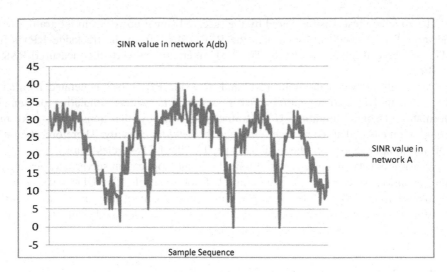

Fig. 5. SINR value in network A

Figure 6 shows the received RSRP values in the network B, tested by train embedded TAU along the test route. The maximum value is −56 dBm, the minimum value is −101 dBm.

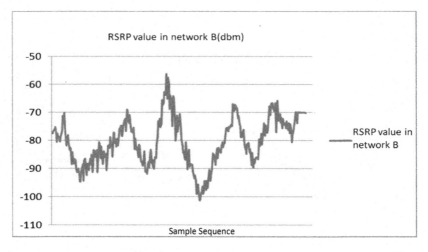

Fig. 6. RSRP value in network B

Figure 7 shows the received SINR values in the network B, tested by train embedded TAU along the test route. The maximum value is 41 dB, the minimum value is 0 dB.

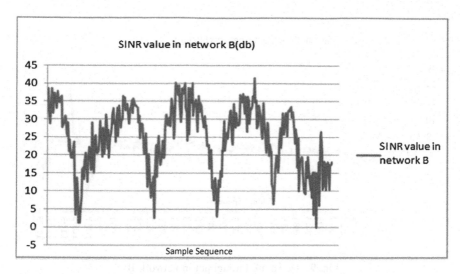

Fig. 7. SINR value in network B

4.2 Throughput Results

UDP Traffic was sent by Iperf in downlink throughput tests. 20 Mbps traffic was loaded in Network A, and 10 Mbps traffic was loaded in network B.

Figure 8 shows the downlink throughput values in the network A, tested by train embedded TAU along the test route. The statistical downlink average throughput is 19.3 Mbps.

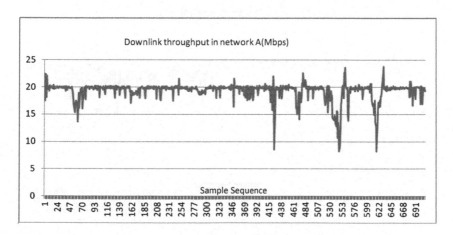

Fig. 8. Downlink throughput in network A

Figure 9 shows the downlink throughput values in the network B, tested by train embedded TAU along the test route. The statistical downlink average throughput is 7.8 Mbps.

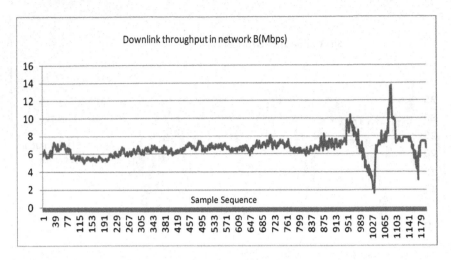

Fig. 9. Downlink throughput in network B

UDP Traffic was sent by Iperf in uplink throughput tests. 10 Mbps traffic was loaded in Network A, and 5 Mbps traffic was loaded in network B.

Figure 10 shows the uplink throughput values in the network A, tested by train embedded TAU along the test route. The statistical uplink average throughput is 6.65 Mbps.

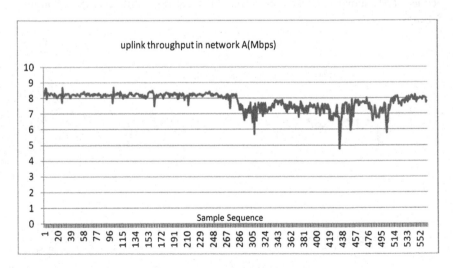

Fig. 10. Uplink throughput in network A

Figure 11 shows the uplink throughput values in the network B, tested by train embedded TAU along the test route. The statistical uplink average throughput is 3.98 Mbps.

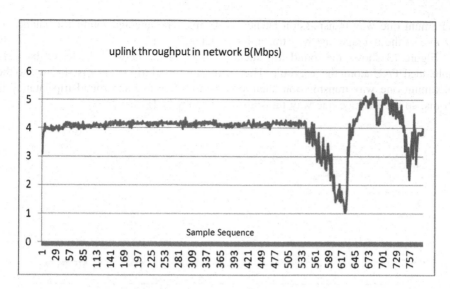

Fig. 11. Uplink throughput in network B

4.3 Network Latency

UDP Traffic was sent by Ixchariot in network latency tests, with 100 kbps packet rate and 200 kbyte packet length. The round trip latency was recorded and one way transmission latency was calculated.

Figure 12 shows the round trip latency values in the network A, tested by train embedded TAU along the test route. The maximum round trip latency is 86 ms, so the

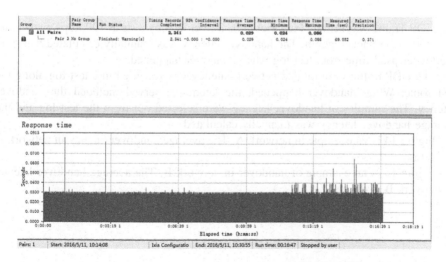

Fig. 12. Round trip latency value in network A

maximum one way transmission latency is 43 ms. The average round trip latency is 29 ms, so the average one way transmission latency is 15 ms.

Figure 13 shows the round trip latency values in the network B, tested by train embedded TAU along the test route. The maximum round trip latency is 108 ms, so the maximum one way transmission latency is 54 ms. The average round trip latency is 36 ms, so the average one way transmission latency is 18 ms.

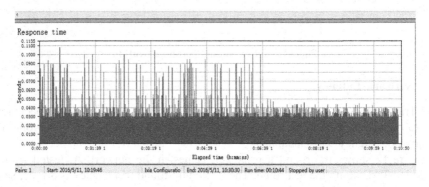

Fig. 13. Round trip latency value in network B

UDP Traffic was sent by Ixchariot in handover latency tests at 100 kbps packet rate and 200 kbyte packet length. The handover latency was manually calculated based on the test elapsed time from test log when handover happened.

The UDP traffic went on and network latency was recorded in a test log along the test route. When handover happened, the latency observed included the handover latency. The samples of handover latency were selected out from the test log and the average handover latency was manually calculated.

Figure 14 is an example in network A. The average handover latency in network A is 31 ms.

Figure 15 is an example of handover in network B. The average handover latency in network B is 43 ms.

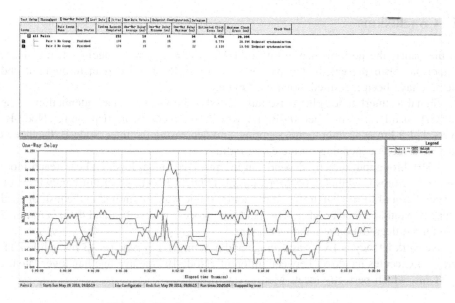

Fig. 14. Handover-latency example in network A

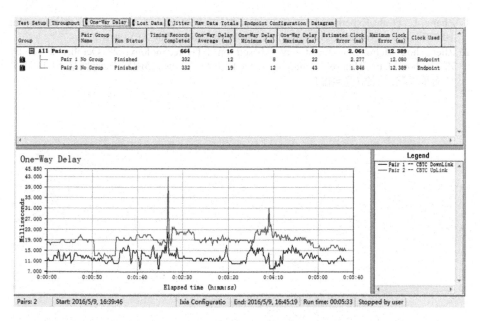

Fig. 15. Handover-latency example in network B

5 Conclusions

In the paper, the performance testing of LTE wireless network deployed in a metro tunnel has been presented. Received signal power level, UDP data throughout and latency have been measured along the tunnel.

Signal-to-interference-plus-noise ratio (SINR) shows that tunnel attenuation in the 1.8 GHz band varies between 0 dB and 40 dB. We recommend deploying eNode-Bs every 1–1.5 km at straight tunnel sections, and decreasing the inter Node-B distance in curved sections depending on the curve radius.

UDP throughput directly depends on the received signal level and can reach more than 19.3 Mbps downlink/6.65 Mbps uplink (TDD 10 MHz spectrum bandwidth) on the condition of fixed UDP traffic. If the actual traffic was not limited in the test, the real capacity would be much higher. The handover process is very fast and there is minimal throughput degradation at handover points.

Network latency is 15 ms as average and maxim latency reaches 43 ms, while LTE terminal executes handover between different eNode-Bs, the average handover latency is 31 ms, which perfectly meets Metro system needs.

References

1. Zhang, L., et al.: Experimental evaluation of 4G technologies in metro tunnel scenarios. In: 10th European Conference on Antennas and Propagation (EuCAP) (2016)
2. Zhengzhou Metro Line-2 test report based on LTE technology, 28 October 2016, by Zhengzhou Metro, Huawei Technologies, UCD, CASCO etc. 郑州地铁2号线基于LTE技术综合承载测试报告(签字盖章)

Technologies Evaluation for Freight Train's Wireless Backbone

Francisco Parrilla[1]($\boxtimes$), Marina Alonso[1], David Batista[1],
Adrián Alberdi[1], Jon Goya[2,3], Gorka de Miguel[2,3],
and Jaizki Mendizabal[2,3]($\boxtimes$) ⓘ

[1] Indra, Transportation, Mar Egeo, 4, 28830 San Fernando de Henares,
Madrid, Spain
{fparrilla,malonsoh,dbatista,aalberdi}@indra.es
[2] Ceit, Manuel Lardizabal 15, 20018 Donostia/San Sebastián, Spain
{jgoya,gdmiguel,jmendizabal}@ceit.es
[3] Universidad de Navarra, Tecnun, Manuel Lardizabal 13,
20018 Donostia/San Sebastián, Spain

Abstract. The current low modal share of intra-EU rail freight transport is partly due to limitations of operational and technical nature, which impact the overall capacity and performance of the sector. In order to overcome these issues, Shift2Rail set a specific Innovation Programme 5 (IP5) focused on Technologies for Sustainable & Attractive European Rail Freight. In this context, the FR8RAIL project, is working on the "Development of Functional Requirements for Sustainable and Attractive European Rail". To overcome these limitations, among other technical areas, the communications of the freight train is involved. This paper deals with the analysis of the and mainly with the evaluation of the technologies currently available. This will lead to the definition of the future freight train communication as an outcome of FR8RAIL project that will positively contribute to and support the Shift2Rail goals to strengthen the role of the freight rail transport.

Keywords: Railway · Wireless backbone · Communication · Freight

1 Introduction

The modal share of intra-EU rail freight transport is less than 20% of the freight transport sector even though rail freight services in EU are not newcomers in the sector. The current rail freight situation is not only due to the existence of legal barriers restricting competition (including the track access regime, taxation, etc.), but also due to limitations of operational and technical nature, which impact the overall capacity and performance.

EU's Transport White Paper sets ambitious objectives to develop rail freight the: almost doubling the use of rail freight compared to 2005, achieving a shift of 30% of road freight over 300 km to modes such as rail or waterborne transport by 2030, and of more than 50% by 2050. Therefore, with the aim of reaching these objectives, freight services need to be improved in terms of cost competitiveness and reliability.

© Springer International Publishing AG, part of Springer Nature 2018
J. Moreno García-Loygorri et al. (Eds.): Nets4Cars 2018/Nets4Trains 2018/Nets4Aircraft 2018, LNCS 10796, pp. 79–91, 2018.
https://doi.org/10.1007/978-3-319-90371-2_9

Then, rail freight will be in a position to offer a cost-effective, attractive service that will compete with the congested road network.

In order to overcome these issues, Shift2Rail set a specific Innovation Programme 5 (IP5) focused on Technologies for Sustainable & Attractive European Rail Freight. In this context, the FR8RAIL project, composed of 18 European partners, is working on the "Development of Functional Requirements for Sustainable and Attractive European Rail" aiming at achieving among others, 100% availability of rail freight transportation information to logistic chain information system that is linked to the WP3. The objective of WP3 is the development of telematics technologies (including HW, SW and algorithms), which will provide essential input information for different applications such as condition based and predictive maintenance, logistic services, traffic management, real time network management and intelligent gate terminals.

The development comprises a wagon On-Board Unit (wOBU), different modules of a wagon and cargo monitoring system for maintenance and logistic purposes, systems for on board and wayside communication. The wOBU will be the basis for being able to implement applications, such as automatic train set-up functionalities as well as a technical solution to provide information about the train to the Traffic Management System (TMS). Therefore, one of the objectives is the choice of a suitable train wireless communication backbone infrastructure.

This paper is structured as follows.

- Section 2 shows the railway freight needs.
- Section 3 presents the scope of the communication technologies evaluation.
- Section 4 includes a comparison of the technologies available.
- Section 5 presents successful implementation cases in railway environment.
- Finally, Sect. 6 presents conclusions.

2   Railway Freight Needs

This section includes a brief explanation of the state of art of the Railway Freight Operation and the freight wagons including:

- Description of technical and functional specifications of the subsystem
- Analysis of specific loading units
- Analysis of the rolling stock
- Analysis of the transport systems in EU
- Analysis of current freight wagon technologies.

2.1   Operation and Traffic Management Subsystem

The Technical Specification for Interoperability (TSI) relating to the operation and traffic management subsystem defines the Railway Freight Operation [1]. These specifications of freight operation are composed of specifications relating to staff, specifications relating to trains and specifications relating to train operation:

- Specs. relating to staff: procedures included in the "Driver's Rule Book" and in the "Book of Forms and Communication Principles" in order to ensure safety-related communication between infrastructure manager's staff and train crews.
- Specs relating to trains: Rules might differ between freight trains crossing a border between members of EU and for those not crossing the border. Train composition covers the operational speed of the train and the fulfillment of the constraints of the route. Dangerous goods transportation shall be supervised by the railway undertaking taking into account the provisions specified in [2].
- Specs relating to train operation: in degraded and emergency operation, drivers should be duly informed.

2.2   Characteristics of Loading Units

First of all, there are several factors which influence the size of a load unit, like maximum size of individual items, the available space on rail wagons, etc. The Centre for Railway Technology describes in [3] two different types of loading units:

- Rolling bins are loading units which dimensions do not exceed 1040 × 920 × 1435 mm (W × D × H) with capacity for 500 kg. This kind of loading unit allows manual handling and it is possible to coupled together several bins in order to make load/unload operations more efficient.
- Air Cargo loading units do not have a standardized dimension. Unlike rolling bins, air Cargo loading units are not equipped with wheels. Rolling floors are used to make easier the loading unit movement. There are two main types of air cargo loading units: air cargo pallets and air cargo containers.

In order to optimize the loading/unloading operation [3], and the processes attached to the freight route, transhipment methods must be defined for each specific route. All these processes must be reliable, quick, safe and cost-efficient. According to the automation level, transhipment methods can be manual, semi-automated or automated.

2.3   Characteristics of Rolling Stock

There are two main types of rolling stock vehicles for high speed rail freight [3].

- Wagons coming from typical freight car constructions, which are designed for speed up to 160–200 km/h. At high speed, the rolling stock performance is limited by the running gear and braking technology.
- Vehicles coming from passenger rolling stock and adapted to carry freight.

An in depth analysis of the State of the Art of the freight wagon working at the maximum standard speed (120 km/h) can be found on the following section.

2.4   Transports Systems in the European Union

In this subsection, different examples of transport systems in European Union [3] are analysed in order to give a first approach about the state of the art of freight operation in several countries.

- Sweden: there are two main uses for freight rail operations: Dedicated mail for the Swedish post office and Express parcel service. The Swedish mail train network consists of a line from Stockholm which bifurcates into three branches to Sundsvall, Gothenburg and Malmö.
- Denmark: the mail trains reach a maximum speed of 140 km/h, which implies that they cannot be considered high-speed (≥ 160 km/h). Each boogie has a loading capacity of 32 tonnes of 63 wheeled mail containers. The railway undertaking (DSB) runs 70 mail trains among seven terminals along Denmark rail network.
- France: TVG Postal manages the freight rail operations in France. At the beginning (1997), the top speed was 160 km/h, but it increased to 200 km/h in the following years. The freight trains consist of BB 22200 locomotives equipped with speed limiters and covered bogie wagons with sliding walls.
- England: the rail plan for England covered an amount of 65 mail trains, from London to Glasgow, Edinburgh, Norwich and Tonbridge. The rail network comprises 45 stations and all terminals are electrified. The kind of load units mainly used are York-container, a universal rolling bin.
- Germany: InterCargo Express (ICGE) express freight trains was introduced by the Deutsche Bahn for intermodal traffic. Each train has a loading capacity of 900 tons and the average speed is about 130 km/h. Load losses occur mainly around the terminals. However, the traffic is high reliability and punctuality. DB Cargo guarantees a punctuality of 94%.

2.5   Freight Wagons

The Technical Specification for Interoperability (TSI) on the Freight Wagon Subsystem [4] sets the basis covered by every Freight Wagon used in European Railways. From this, every country can develop stricter rules to control the Freight Wagons.

Some of the aspects that involve freight wagons are listed as follows:

- Structures and mechanics: The coupler is the mechanical interface between the units conforming a train. The locking system must not need a person standing between both units. and must be able to take the tensions and forces involved on the dragging. The internal lock is the mechanical interface between the elements of a wagon. The internal lock must be able to resist the forces and tensions acting on it during the working state of the system. All these systems must be able to resist the, external or internal, forces involved on the normal operation of the wagon [5]. Toughness is defined as not producing cracks, permanent deformations, or failures. The integrity of the unit must be determinable from the outside of the wagon at a glance. This includes covers, doors, hatches, etc.
- Gauging and track interaction: This refers to the calculation of the designs applied to the rolling stock system, the Freight Wagons in particular. The conformity between the reference profile shall be stablished by the kinematic method described in EN15273-2:2009 [5]. The wagons must be compatible with one or more Train Detection Systems (Track Circuits, Axle Counters, or Loop Equipment). The freight wagon must ensure safe running on twisted tracks. All these must provide the same level of safety at the maximum speed of the line. The axle shall ensure the transmission

of forces and torque in accordance with the area of use. In case the axle allows the gauge variation it shall ensure the safe locking of the wheels and of the corresponding brake equipment. This must be for automatic and manual gauge variations.

- Brake: The function of the train brake system is to ensure that the train can be slowed, stopped or immobilised in a flat area or in a slope. By means of the breaking power the braking power, the available adhesion and some train parameters, the braking performance can be determined. The brake requires 3 functional statuses: (1) Continuous, brake release or application is controlled from a centralized location (loco); (2) Automatic, all units must brake when the control channel from the centralized location applies the brake; and (3) Disengageable, when the wagon is isolated, the brake must be activated. This applies to the Service (speed reducing and stopping) and Parking (immobilization) brakes.

To ensure these minimum braking requirements, the braking equipment must be able to perform an emergency brake without losing braking performance due to thermal or mechanical effects. The Wagon must have a Wheel Slide Protection System (WSP) to control the braking performance during difficult braking (slope, hard conditions). Moreover, there are maintenance rules with technical files that comprise some general documentation, the maintenance design justification and the maintenance description file. The general documentation includes drawings and descriptions of the wagon and its subsystems, requirements related with the maintenance, and configuration files. The maintenance design justification includes precedents, principles and methods used to design the maintenance plan, limits of the Wagon, other important maintenance data, and tests performed on the Wagon. The maintenance description file describes how the maintenance of the Wagon can be conducted, including, tests, corrective and scheduled maintenance activities.

3 Scope of the Wireless Communication Technologies

The purpose of this section is to form a basis for exploring and developing technical means using radio communication technologies in order to enable wireless communication along freight trains. That technical means will be able to provide seamless on-board communications services for sensors, actuators and telematics applications installed on rolling stock and wagons of train compositions. Therefore, it will provide added-value services for both wagon and cargo monitoring applications.

Wireless Sensor Network (WSN) technology will be deeply analysed and specified with special focus on specific requirements taken out from railways freight transport needs, focusing on using low-power communication protocols with required bandwidth for on-board applications.

The aim of the state of the art is to:

- identify available moving and point to point wireless technologies
- characterize them from the point of view of performance and applicability
- describe their advantages and disadvantages for freight application

Based on the analysis, the main goal is to propose the candidates from the listed wireless technologies, which provide smart auto-configuration and self-discovering services to settle those special needs of freight trains, mostly related with dynamic and variable train compositions.

These technologies, which provide sufficient range and fulfil high train speed requirements considered: 350 km/h maximum speed and 27.5 m maximum wagon length.

4 Evaluation of the Wireless Communication Technologies

In this section, the available standard wireless technologies that could satisfy the expected requirements (included in the previous section), are briefly characterized.

The terrestrial technologies available for railway environment are summarized in the following table in order to compare the most important features of each one (Fig. 1).

Technology /Feature	Points	Nodes	Type	Data Rate	Average throughput	Range	Frequency	Spectrum Use	Latency
802.11a/b/g/n/ac	Static	Static	Master/Client Point to multipoint	11-1000 Mbit/s	5-600 Mbits/s	10 -250 m	2,4 / 3,7 / 5,0 GHz	Public	1-10 ms
802.11ah	Static/ slow moving	Moving	Master/Client Point to multipoint	0.65-234 Mbit/s	0.1-100 Mbits/s	100-1000 m	ISM band (868 MHz Europe, 908/916 MHz USA)	Public	20-100 ms
802.11p	Moving	Static/ Moving	Master/Client Point to multipoint	6-108 Mbit/s	>1 Mbit/s	50-300 m	5,850 – 5,925 GHz	Unlicensed	40-200 ms
Bluetooth	Static/ slow moving	Static	Master/Client Point to multipoint	1-10 Mbit/s	0.1-0.5 Mbit/s	10-100 m	2,4 GHz ISM band	Public	10 ms
Zigbee	Static/ slow moving	Static	Master/Client Point to multipoint	20/40 kbit/s (ISM band) 250 kbit/s (2,4 GHz)	1-50 kbit/s	100-1000 m	2,4 GHz band ISM band (868 MHz Europe, 908/916 MHz USA)	Public	10 ms
6LoWPAN	Static/ slow moving	Static	Star Cluster tree Point to multipoint	250 kbps (2.4 GHz) 40 kbps (915 MHz) 20 kbps (868 MHz)	1-50 kbit/s	1-75m	2,4 GHz band ISM band (868 MHz Europe, 908/916 MHz USA)	Public	10 ms
Thread	Static/ slow moving	Static	Master/Client Point to multipoint	250 kbit/s (2,4 GHz)	1-50 kbit/s	10-100 m	2,4 GHz band ISM band (868 MHz Europe, 908/916 MHz USA)	Public	100 ms
WiMAX	Static/ Moving	Static/ Moving	Master/Client Point to multipoint	6-376 Mbit/s	1-50 kbit/s	1000m-50km	2,4 GHz ISM 2,5-2,7 GHz lic. 5,8 GHz unlic. 10,5 GHz lic	Public/ Licensed	50 ms
Z-Wave	Static/ Slow moving	Static	Master/Client Point to multipoint	9.6 kbit/s	0.1-1 kbit/s	30-150 m	ISM band (868 MHz Europe, 908/916 MHz USA)	Public	200 ms
ANT/ANT+	Static/ Slow moving	Static	Master/Client Point to multipoint	20 kbit/s	0.5-200 Hz (8 bytes data)	30-100 m	2,4 GHz band ISM band	Public	10 ms
NB-IoT	Static	Static	Master/Client Point to multipoint	250 kbit/s downlink 20 – 250 kbit/s uplink	1-50 kbit/s	Above 10 km	GSM/LTE	Licensed	1.6-10 s
LoRaWAN	Static	Static	Master/Client Point to multipoint	0.3-50 kbit/s uplink	3-500 bit/s	Up to 20 km	ISM band (868 MHz Europe, 908/916 MHz USA)	Unlicensed	4-120 s
Sigfox	Static	Static	Master/Client Point to multipoint	0.1-1 kbit/s uplink	10-100 bit/s	50 km	ISM band (868 MHz Europe, 908/916 MHz USA)	Licensed	1.6-10 s
Symphony Link	Static	Static	Master/Client Point to multipoint	10-250 kbit/s uplink	0.1-50 kbit/s	Up to 50 km	ISM band (868 MHz Europe, 908/916 MHz USA)	Unlicensed	100 ms – 120 s

Fig. 1. Terrestrial technologies comparison [6–39].

The main satellite technologies in transport environment are summarized in the following table in order to compare the most important features of each one (Fig. 2):

Technology/Feature	Band	GEO/MEO/LEO	Range	Speed	Data rate
GEO-L	L	GEO	300km	130kmh	492kbps
GEO-S	S	GEO	Europe	130kmh	2.2Mbps
IRIDIUM	L+Ka	LEO	Europe	-	1.5-8Mbps
GOOGLE	LTE bands	subLEO	40km	110kmh	50Mbps
Airbus D&S	ISM	LEO	50km	-	0.1-1kbps
Global Xpress	Ka	GEO	World	-	8Mbps

Fig. 2. Satellite Technologies comparison [6–39].

Finally, in the study "On the Performance of IEEE 802.11p and LTE-V2V for the Cooperative Awareness of Connected Vehicles" [40], the following conclusions were extracted:

- Overall, results show that IEEE 802.11p appears robust at limited distances, up to few hundreds of meters. With a beacon frequency of 10 Hz and the given settings, for example, it is proved to support more than 1 vehicle every 10 m with an awareness range up to 250–300 m. At longer distances, the high collision rate due to hidden terminals significantly reduces the communication reliability.
- In the same scenario, with consistent settings, LTE-V2V has been shown to have worse performance at short distance, but to be more reliable when the distance increases. Referring to the same example, 1 vehicle every 10 m could be supported by this technology in the given conditions with an awareness range up to almost 500 m. LTE-V2V thus appears preferable if a larger awareness range is targeted.

5 Successful Implementation Cases in Railway Environment

In this chapter, an analysis of different successful implementation cases will be performed. The following lines will show different real-world railway implementations that proved different technologies trustworthy and applicable for the railway or more general Intelligent Transportation System (ITS). This part can be used, first, as a trustworthiness factor, providing the chosen solution with previous knowledge and trials, and second as a more objective comparison analysis.

Some of the technologies are very new (ANT final specification was performed in 2016) and, due to this, there are no railway physical implementations nowadays. This fact does not mean these technologies are not valid, but that they have not been implemented yet in a railway environment.

5.1   802.11 Family

Based on 802.11 family, Icomera [31] has developed a multi-technology platform to provide broadband Internet access in trains, combining Wi-Fi protocols with satellite technology. First tests of broadband on board trains in the world were performed in Sweden in September 2002.

Furthermore, SNCF, performed, in collaboration with Orange Labs, experimental tests relying on Wi-Fi IEEE 802.11b/g [41]. The tested network was based on four access points located on bridges and pylons, covering an area of 13 km in Vendome, near Tours in France [42].

In [43], an implementation of the IEEE 802.11p physical layer is presented, using the open source ath5 k driver. It conducts and analyzes experiments in both line of sight (LOS) and non-line of sight (NLOS) conditions. The study shows that, in LOS, vehicles can communicate over more than 1 km which, in highway scenarios, can significantly decrease the communication gaps between clusters of vehicles.

The video quality assessment for inter-vehicular streaming [44] presents an emulation-based study to demonstrate to what extent these networks are able to sustain real-time video streaming for vehicle-to-vehicle communication, modeling highways and congested urban road scenarios using Ricean and Rayleigh fading channel models respectively. The results reveal that LTE Direct performs better than 802.11p, which in turn performs better than LTE.

In addition, the control of a platoon using IEEE 802.11p [45] is an active research challenge in the field of vehicular networking and cooperative automated vehicles. A large-scale simulation campaign using Visible Light Communications (VLC) integrated with IEEE 802.11p was performed for platooning. The results of this study show that, although communication delays need to be considered, VLC could improve the safety of the overall system by being coupled with IEEE 802.11p.

5.2   802.15 Family

The ARTEMIS/ECSEL1 project DEWI ("Dependable Embedded Wireless Infrastructure") [46] focusses on the area of wireless sensor/actuator networks and wireless communication. DEWI has a clear focus on short-range technologies and corresponding standards such as Wi-Fi (IEEE 802.11), ZigBee, WirelessHART, ISA100 (IEEE 802.15.4), Bluetooth (IEEE 802.15.1), NFC (ISO 15408 und ISO 14443/ISO 15693), 6LoWPAN/IPv6 (PFC 4919), Z-Wave (ITU-T G.9959), TETRA, TETRAPOL (PMR) or DLNA (UPnP). The Train Integrity Detection System use case was a success in the rail environment. Both, real and laboratory tests were produced. In the laboratory tests, the whole system was tested in a simulated environment on test beds. After the laboratory tests the system was tested, validated and assessed in a real life mock up demonstration on a tourist train controlling the composition of a freight train.

The Train Integrity Monitoring System proposed in DEWI [47] is based on a WSN, which consist of the WSN Nodes (deployed on each wagon), the Coordinator and the Serial Gateway (both deployed on a locomotive). Each WSN Node measurements are send to the Coordinator, which compares the measurements from each node to detect the train integrity. In order to ensure reliable communication between the locomotive and the last wagon of the train, which for freight trains can be as far as ~ 600–750 m, 802.15.4 g, 868 MHz Xbee 868LP radio module is used. It operates in the frequency range from 863 MHz to 870 MHz, with transmit power up to 25 mW (14 dBm) and channel spacing: 100 kHz (max. 30 channels). It can cover a transmission range of up to 8.4 km outdoors, transmit with up to 80 kbps data rate and ensure that in one Xbee network there can be up to 128 nodes (i.e. wagons).

Big companies such as Philips, Siemens or General Electric work in 802.15 protocols. SNCF has interest in 802.15.7 (Li-Fi) for studies in geolocalization products in railway stations.

IONX LLC and the rail freight operator Havelländische Eisenbahn (HVLE) has developed a solution based in 802.15.4 [48]. The solution was deployed on the HVLE freight trains, and IONX provides a low power wireless network. That network, built for IP compatibility based on LoWPAN and 802.15.4e standards, runs the entire length of the train and connect sensors on each wagon to the locomotive.

5.3 WiMAX

A WiMAX solution is used in train connecting the Narita airport to the city center of Tokyo (Narita Express) since October 2009 [41]. Since 2012, the same system equipped the Super Hitachi trains running from Tokyo to Iwaki.

Nomad Digital has develop solutions based on the combination of cellular technologies and WiMAX and it uses this solutions in the Southern Railway of Brighton, the Heathrow Express, the Virgin Trains in UK, and the UTA trains of Utah in US [49].

5.4 Satellite Technologies

Concerning already existing application of GEO satellite based communication, it is worth to mention the "Train Integrated Safety Satellite System (3InSat) Demonstration project", funded by ESA in the ARTES 20 IAP programme [50]. Tests were performed on the RFI lines in Sardinia connecting Cagliari and Olbia (about 300 km) and with a speed up to 130 km/h.

SAFETRIP [51] has explored new opportunities and innovative ITS services to be delivered to passenger cars, trucks and bus drivers. Mobile Satellite System (MSS) from GEO has been retained, in S-band in order to optimize the solutions for antennas. EUTELSAT 10 (previously W2A) in 10°E longitude and the transponder installed by ALCATEL Space at 2,2 GHz was used for the proof of concept.

IRIDIUM is working for its upcoming constellation, Iridium NEXT [52]. Thales Alenia Space has completed the Main Mission Antennas (MMAs), for which one goes on each NEXT satellite. On 2014, Iridium selected Radisys' T-Series Commercial Off-The-Shelf (COTS) platforms to upgrade the ground station infrastructure for NEXT, and support the so-called Certus service. The constellation provides L-band data speeds of up to 1.5 Mbit/s and High-speed Ka-Band service of up to 8 Mbit/s.

GOOGLE has an ambitious project, Loon [53], based on stratospheric airships. The balloons intend to float in the stratosphere, twice as high as airplanes and the weather. GOOGLE enables people to connect to the balloon network directly from their phones and other LTE-enabled devices.

Airbus Defence and Space system [54] will use a dual-mode satellite-terrestrial terminal to switch automatically, with satellite links using a distinct communication protocol and connections to the SIGFOX terrestrial network using the 868 and 915 MHz

Industrial, Scientific and Medical (ISM) bands. The ability to communicate with a satellite in Low Earth Orbit (LEO), over typically 1000 km, has actually been demonstrated early this year in a demo using the Airbus-developed Spot 7 satellite. With LEO, latency can be controlled under 10 ms.

Still, INMARSAT has signed customers on Global Xpress [55], of which one notable capacity buyer is the US government. The US government is particularly interested in global Ka-band and the unique military Ka-band capabilities brought by GX.

5.5   TETRA

Based on the TETRA standard, Indra has deployed an advanced communication network [56] that improves control and security in the railway environment of Buenos Aires. This secure and robust system guarantees the availability of communications by facilitating the transfer of voice and data with neither losses nor delays.

Siemens also offers TETRA radio systems for ETCS for rail projects worldwide (i.e. Warsaw Metro in Poland or Australia rail operators) [57].

TETRA network in Belgium was implemented by the government-owned corporation responsible for providing communications to all Belgian public safety organisations (A.S.T.R.I.D) [58] after the Heysel Stadium disaster in 1985. Due to the establishment of communication in a restricted and priority group mode by the control centre within a small group of users [59], TETRA radio is used in the Brussels public transport company (STIB/MIVB).

6   Conclusions

The status of the Freight Railway, the low density of certain Freight lines and corridors, reduces the possibility of cellular networks to be installed due to the economic impact. The installation costs will overcome most of the benefits of the communications provided later. These constrains for the use of cellular networks in Freight environments do not limit its use on high speed lines or mainlines. The deployment of these systems in other rail environments may be worth for backwards compatibility with old signaling systems (GSM-R). As shown, the new cellular technologies (5G and above) provide the tools needed for connecting point-to-point. These technologies are still under development making its analysis at this point difficult.

Satellite communications, besides the great latency added to the communication have the problem of the shadows in the environment. In certain countries, like Switzerland, the use of satellite communications is nearly impossible due to the mountains and tunnels surrounding the lines and corridors. As shown on the corresponding section, several trials, studies and demonstrators have been carried out. From these studies, no conclusive results were distilled. Satellite communication systems are systems that may proof useful in certain countries or areas and they may be considered as a very situational communication mean.

The low cost of deployment of the receiver devices makes satellite technologies very competitive. This fact in combination with terrestrial technologies as TETRA or other technologies to cover the shadowed areas make the result a very good combined technology solution.

These drawbacks make the point-to-point/point-to-multipoint/adhoc communications the only viable solution. With this, and taking into consideration the specific needs of the Freight railway environments the communication needs can be reduced to only two big cases:

1. The wagon-to-wagon communication. This case implies the use of technologies designed to use point-to-point connections, in short range in a mobile environment. This case is the representation of most Freight lines and corridors.

In this case the most fitting protocols are 802.11p, Zigbee, and ANT/ANT+. This three protocols offer good data rates, in short to medium distances among little devices. The consistency and the infrastructure independency provide them with enough tools to provide a high level of security. The low installation and buy costs of the devices implementing them prove these protocols best suited as well.

2. The V2I/I2 V communication. In this case, we shall consider the use of technologies that allow the use of point-to-multipoint and broadcasting capabilities, in big ranges and static or slowly moving. This case represents most of the shunting yards.

In this case, the most fitting protocol is WiMAX Release 2. This protocol offers big ranges, massive data rates and slowly moving systems. The protocol has the support of a major player that is IEEE. This will give trustworthiness and a level of security for the solution. The installation costs can be reduced below the cost of installation in cellular networks. Although WiMAX is a good solution in terms of cost and features, it is becoming obsolete due to it do not have the support of big companies. The future deployments are pointing towards the use of more modern technologies, as LTE release 14 and 15 or 5G. 5G technologies are not considered in this study because they are in very early stages of the specification for critical communications. Another drawback would be the higher number of 5G devices, since it makes use of higher frequencies, more radio links will be required in order to maintain the coverage.

In combination with other technologies, TETRA could also be explored. As shown recently by Siemens and Indra this technology can be also a solution for the Rail domain. The bigger range provided by the TETRA Mobile Stations could reduce the deployment and installation costs, less radio links will be needed.

To summarize, we must consider two different solutions for two different occasions. IoT (ZigBee, ANT/ANT+) or V2V (802.11p) focused protocols for internal train cases (OBU) and WiMAX, TETRA and LTE technologies for medium and high railway deployments.

References

1. Technical Specification for Interoperability (TSI) relating to the operation and traffic management subsystem. Commission Regulation (EU) 2015/995 of 8 June 2015
2. Directive 2008/68/EC of the European Parliament and of the Council. Inland transport of dangerous goods, 24 September 2008

3. Troche, G.: High-speed rail freight: sub-report in efficient train systems for freight transport. Centre for Railway Technology
4. Wagons - WAG TSI
5. Railway applications - Structural requirements of railway vehicle bodies - Part 2: Freight wagons. EN 12663-2:2010, Regulation No. 22/1997 Sb. - harmonized sphere
6. Parker, T.: Wi-Fi preps for 900 MHz with 802.11ah, 2 September 2013. FierceWirelessTech.com. Accessed 25 June 2014
7. Sun, W., et al.: IEEE 802.11ah: a long range 802.11 WLAN at sub 1 GHz (PDF). J. ICT Stand. 1(1), 83–108 (2013)
8. IEEE 1609 - family of standards for wireless access in vehicular environments (WAVE). U. S. Department of Transportation, 13 April 2013. Accessed 14 Nov 2014
9. Final draft ETSI ES 202 663 V1.1.0 (2009-11). European Telecommunications Standards Institute. Accessed 16 Apr 2013
10. Bilging, B.E., et al.: Performance comparison of IEEE 802.11p and IEEE 802.11b for vehicle-to-vehicle communications in highway, rural, and urban areas (2013)
11. Bluetooth core specification v5.0. www.bluetooth.org
12. Bluetooth radio interface, modulation & channels. Radio-Electronics.com
13. Wang, C., et al.: ZigBee® Network Protocols and Applications
14. Park, S., et al.: IPv6 over Low Power WPAN Security Analysis. IETF. I-D draft-daniel-6lowpan-security-analysis-05, March 2011. Accessed 10 May 2016
15. Introducing thread. SILabs. Accessed 21 Oct 2014
16. Olsson, J.: 6LoWPAN demystified. Texas Instruments (2013)
17. Thread stack fundamentals. Thread Group. Accessed 1 Apr 2017 (2015)
18. WiMAX vs. WiFi, 20 February 2008. Circleid.com. Accessed 18 Sept 2013
19. Wimax technology. http://freewimaxinfo.com/
20. Stark, H.: The Ultimate Guide to Building Your Own Smart Home in 2017. Forbes, 22 May 2017
21. Z-Wave 500 series. Aeotc.com. Accessed 30 July 2017
22. Frenzel, L.: What's the difference between bluetooth low energy and ant? Electronics Design, 29 November 2012
23. Nordic Semiconductor figures for nRF24AP1. Nordic Semiconductor. Archived from the original on 29 October 2007. Accessed 11 Dec 2007
24. Khssibi, S., et al.: Presentation and analysis of a new technology for low-power wireless sensor network. Int. J. Digit. Inf. Wirel. Commun. 3, 75 (2013)
25. Connectivity options explained. ANT+ explained, 27 October 2015
26. Grant, S.: 3GPP Low Power Wide Area Technologies - GSMA White Paper, GSMA, p. 49, 1 September 2016
27. Wang, Y.-P.E., et al.: A primer on 3GPP narrowband internet of things. IEEE Commun. Mag. 55(3), 117–123 (2017)
28. Wang, Z.J.: Unlocking the potentials of smart IoT with LPWA technologies. In: The WIOMAX Smart IoT Blog
29. LoRaWAN For Developers. www.lora-alliance.org
30. Hassan, Q.F., et al.: Internet of Things: Challenges, Advances, and Applications. Chapman & Hall/CRC Computer and Information Science Series, London (2017)
31. Dregvaite, G., Damasevicius, R. (eds.): ICIST 2016. CCIS, vol. 639. Springer, Cham (2016). https://doi.org/10.1007/978-3-319-46254-7
32. Symphony link vs LoRaWAN-difference between symphony link and LoRaWAN. Link Labs, Annapolis, MD 21401
33. TETRA - PST. PST, January 2017
34. Terrestrial trunked radio (TETRA); Release 2, ETSI TR 102 580 V1.1.1 (2007-10)

35. TETRA (Terrestrial trunked radio). Global Telecoms Inside. http://www.mobilecomms-technology.com
36. TETRA technology advantages and benefits. TETRA association, January 2016
37. LTE system overview. LTE Encyclopedia
38. LTE for critical communications. Rohill, LTEetraNode, June 2015
39. Merkel, J.: 3GPP drives GSM-R to a new track. 3GPP, August 2016
40. Bazzi, A., et al.: On the performance of IEEE 802.11p and LTE-V2 V for the cooperative awareness of connected vehicles. IEEE Trans. Veh. Technol. **66**(11), 10419–10432 (2017)
41. Masson, É., Berbineau, M.: Broadband Wireless Communications for Railway Applications. SSDC, vol. 82. Springer, Cham (2017). https://doi.org/10.1007/978-3-319-47202-7
42. Sanz, D., et al.: TGV communicant research program: from research to industrialization of onboard, broadband internet services for high-speed trains. In: 8th World Congress on Railway Research, Seoul, Korea, May 2008
43. Real-world implementation and evaluation of IEEE 802.11p for vehicular networks. CRC, Coimbra, Portugal, November 2011
44. Roy, D., et al.: Video quality assessment for inter-vehicular streaming with IEEE 802.11p, LTE, and LTE Direct networks over fading channels. Comput. Commun. **118**, 69–80 (2017)
45. Segata, M., et al.: On platooning control using IEEE 802.11p in conjunction with visible light communications. In: 12th Annual Conference on Wireless On-demand Network Systems and Services (WONS) (2016)
46. Rom, W., et al.: DEWI – wirelessly into the future. In: Euromicro Conference on Digital System Design (DSD) (2015)
47. Barkovskis, N., et al.: WSN based on accelerometer, GPS and RSSI measurements for train integrity monitoring. In: 4th International Conference on Control, Decision and Information Technologies (CoDIT) (2017)
48. Amsted Rail: IONX LLC and Havelländische Eisenbahn (HVLE) testing standards-based wireless intra-train communication system, 1 May 2017
49. Maureira, J.C.: Internet on rails. Ph.D thesis, University of Nice - Sophia-Antipolis, January 2011
50. 3INSAT – Train Integrated Safety Satellite System. European Spacial Agency, ARTES20 IAP programme
51. Safety Report Summary. France, FP7-Transport
52. Iridium next overview. https://www.iridium.com
53. Project Loon: Google. https://x.company/loon/
54. Internet Of Things: airbus defence and space and its partners to launch the MUSTANG project for global connectivity. Airbus Defence and Space, February 2015
55. A global mobile broadband revolution. Global Express, INMARSAT
56. Indra, May 2017. https://www.indracompany.com/en/noticia/indra-deploys-advanced-communications-network-improves-control-security-trains-aires-eu189
57. Siemens and Denmark's DAMM partner to offer ETCS advanced train control systems with TETRA radio communications. Siemens, November 2016
58. Project ASTRID: ASTRID TETRA Network, Belgium. http://www.mobilecomms-technology.com/projects/astrid/
59. Van den Eede, M., Davis, R.: Brussels metro communicates via TETRA, TETRA World Congress 2012. TETRA Communications Supplement

Characterization of a Wireless Train Backbone for TCMS

Juan Moreno García-Loygorri[1]([⊠]) [ID], Iñaki Val[2], Aitor Arriola[2],
and César Briso[3]

[1] Área de Ingenieria, Metro de Madrid S.A., Madrid, Spain
juan.moreno@metromadrid.es
[2] IKERLAN, Communications Department, IK4-IKERLAN,
Arrasate-Mondragón, Spain
aarriola@ikerlan.es
[3] Departamento de Teoría de la Señal y Comunicaciones, ETSIST UPM,
Madrid, Spain
cesar.briso@upm.es

Abstract. This paper presents a both narrowband and wideband measurement campaign carried out in a Metro environment in order to assess the feasibility of a wireless link for the backbone train communications network. This backbone is the part of the network that links all the vehicles in the consist (A consist is a single vehicle or a group of vehicles that cannot be uncoupled during normal operation.). All the measurements were taken using a channel sounder and also an outdoor-to-indoor link was measured in order to compare with the outdoor-to-outdoor one. The obtained results are the path-loss, power-delay-profiles (PDP), mean delay, RMS spread and also a characterization of the fading is provided.

Keywords: Subways · Measurements · Propagation · TCMS · TCN
Wireless

1 Introduction

Train communications provide added value to railways since the first tests carried out back in the 60's, but for many decades train-to-ground communications have remained as the unique link in operation. This has changed recently with some initiatives, like the Shift2Rail Initiative [1] or the 5G mobile communications. Shift2Rail is, perhaps, the most remarkable research frame in railways and one of the lines to be followed is the "development of a new-generation TCMS (Train Control Management System) to allow current bottlenecks caused by physically coupled trains". One of the ways being assessed to meet this requirement is to implement a wireless TCN (Train Communications Network) to transport the TCMS data. This is the main aim of the Roll2Rail [2] work package 2, where our research is framed. On the other hand, the development of 5G mobile will enable many railway-related use cases, like virtual coupling, remote driving and many more. This means many different links, apart from the train-to-ground, like train-to-train, intra-consist, or consist-to-consist, which is the

© Springer International Publishing AG, part of Springer Nature 2018
J. Moreno García-Loygorri et al. (Eds.): Nets4Cars 2018/Nets4Trains 2018/Nets4Aircraft 2018, LNCS 10796, pp. 92–99, 2018.
https://doi.org/10.1007/978-3-319-90371-2_10

scenario that we discuss in this paper. Therefore, the future is very promising for radio communications in railways [3].

Regarding channel models in railways, there are many for train-to-ground, in regular terrain like [4], tunnels [5], subways [6], etc. Also, the intra-train scenario has been addressed before [7] due to the popularity of IEEE 802.11 deployments in vehicles. For the near future, mmwave communications are assumed to have a significant role in many of these railway scenarios, like the intra-train [8] or the train-to-ground [9]. There are still no 5G or mmwave communication systems in operation in railways.

The structure of this article is as follows: Sect. 2 provides an overview of the different metro environment where the measurements were taken and the setup employed in the campaign; Sect. 3 presents the results and in Sect. 4 the conclusions are drawn.

2 Environment and Setup

2.1 Environment

The inter-consist or consist-to-consist link is the scenario where the consists that form a train communicate to each other (see Fig. 1, where two possibilities are shown). This is also called the backbone of the train and it is implemented on a wired basis. The main idea is to place the transmitter antenna in the roof of consist 1 and the receiver antenna in the roof of consist 2. We also placed another receiver in the passenger area of the consist 2 for comparison purposes.

We employed a train from the Metro de Madrid s8000 series manufactured by CAF and all the test were done in the same train in Line 10. The measurements carried out in this campaign involved measurements in the three different scenarios which are more likely for a train like this. These scenarios are:

- Tunnel
- Pit-like station
- Open air.

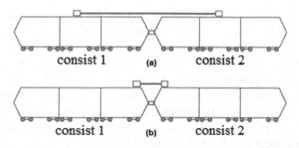

Fig. 1. Sketch of the inter-consist links. In (a) both transmitter and receiver are in the middle of the consists, whereas in (b) they are in the edges.

Car body shell of metro trains like the s8000 is usually made of aluminum but the roof is usually populated by many elements that can complicate the propagation. Among these elements we can find HVAC equipment, antennas, pantographs, etc., and most important, the fairing. In Fig. 2 a picture of the roof of the s8000 train can be seen.

Fig. 2. Installation of both the receiving and the transmitting antenna on the roof of the s8000 train.

All the measurements were taken with the train running at a very low speed (around 1 km/h) in the three environments considered: open air, tunnel and station.

2.2   Experimental Setup

To characterize the behavior of the wireless link for the train backbone, we opted for a channel sounder. Therefore, both the transmitting and the receiving antenna were placed on the roof of the train (see Fig. 2). Moreover, another receiver was placed just behind the receiving antenna but inside the train, in order to compare the difference between the backbone link (roof-to-roof) and inside the vehicle.

All the interconsist measurements for the train backbone characterization were taken at 5.2 GHz, with a 80 MHz bandwidth and an output power of 42 dBm. The channel sounder is able to work from 500 MHz up to 6 GHz and its maximum instantaneous bandwidth is limited to 80 MHz. All the antennas employed in this measurements were Mobile Mark MGRM-WHF wideband monopoles with a magnetic mount (to mount them on the train car body shell), a coaxial cable 3-m long and a SMA connector.

3 Results

We will provide two types of results: narrowband and wideband.

3.1 Narrowband

For each scenario we took several measurements, in order to characterize both the attenuation and the fading characteristics. In Fig. 3 the raw measurements are shown for the inter-consist link for tunnel, station and open air. The attenuation for the antenna placed inside the train is shown as well to emphasize the different nature of one type of link and the other. The most remarkable result is that the difference in the attenuation between the outdoor and the indoor antenna is between 34–42 dB in the three scenarios. The open air scenario shows the highest difference with 42.61 dB, whereas tunnel and (pit) station are very similar, with 35.67 dB and 34.63 dB respectively.

Regarding the absolute average attenuations, this time tunnel and open air scenarios behave similarly (37.52 dB and 37.22 dB, respectively) and station shows an extra 3 dB attenuation (40.49 dB). The most likely reason behind this behavior is that in station the number of measurements was far below than in the two others, so this measurement is less accurate. The reason for the low number of measurements in the station is that the time for the train in the station is lower than between stations.

If we look at the characterization of the fading we see two remarkably different results: an almost pure LOS channel for the outdoor-to-outdoor link and a NLOS for the outdoor-to-indoor one. In a more quantitative way, this characterization can be seen in Table 1. The outdoor-to-outdoor is a LOS link, where the direct link is significantly higher than the non-direct or multipath components. This behavior fits statistically to a Rice distribution. For the open air scenario, this LOS performance is more clear than in the two others because there are less scatters to cause multipath components and, consequently, the LOS dominates more than in the two others. The tunnel scenario shows a stronger Rician behavior than the station one. This is because in stations there are more multipath components than in tunnel.

The outdoor-to-indoor link is, by definition, non-LOS (NLOS). Therefore, the best distribution to check the fitness with is the Rayleigh. In Table 1 we can see the values for the K parameter. Station scenario shows a higher K because the contribution of the surrounding environment to the multipath is higher than in tunnels and open air.

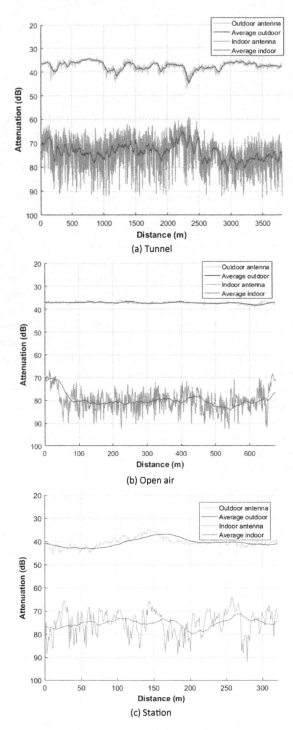

Fig. 3. Measured attenuation for the inter-consist link. Both the instantaneous received power and the moving averages (40 samples each one) are shown. Outdoor is for the receiver antenna on the roof of the train, and indoor is the receiver antenna inside the train.

Table 1. Statistical characterization of the inter-consist link

	Channel				
	Outdoor-to-outdoor			Outdoor-to-indoor	
Scenario	Distribution	K (dB)	σ	Distribution	K (dB)
Station	Rice	0.15	0.96	Rayleigh	2.64
Tunnel	Rice	9.61	0.41	Rayleigh	1.62
Open air	Rice	16.41	0.20	Rayleigh	1.79

3.2 Wideband

For the wideband characterization we will represent the power-delay-profile (PDP) in Fig. 4 and the RMS spread and the mean delay (see Table 2), for station, open air and tunnel scenarios.

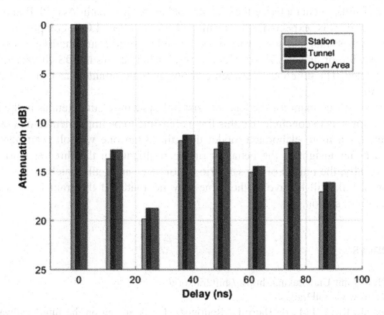

Fig. 4. Power-Delay Profile for the outdoor-to-outdoor inter-consist link in three scenarios: tunnel, station and open air.

Table 2. RMS delay spread and mean delay for the inter-consist link

Scenario	RMS delay spread (ns)	Mean delay (ns)
Tunnel	62.43	36.04
Station	61.24	31.10
Open air	61.59	34.56

The obtained PDP is based on a 8-tap channel model, with a separation between taps of 12.5 ns (receiver bandwidth is 80 MHz).

The PDP depicted on Fig. 4 highlights what we have been discussing before about the LOS characteristics of the inter-consist link when both the receiver and the transmitter antennas are placed on the roof of the train. The normalization (forcing 0 dB – 0 ns for the first ray) has been done separately for each scenario (tunnel, station and open air). We can see also that the three scenarios behave in a very similar way, but this could be a limitation of the 8-tap channel model.

4   Conclusions

We present a complete characterization of an inter-consist link (the train backbone) onboard a metro train and, more precisely, placing both the transmitter and the receiver antenna on the roof of the train. Three different setups have been compared: train inside a tunnel, on a metro station and on an outdoor track. We also have estimated the most important results to characterize the channel behavior, like path-loss, PDP and fading models. As it was expected, the results show a clear LOS component in the consist-to-consist link and some variations depending on the surrounding environment (outdoor, station or tunnel). The outdoor-to-indoor link shows NLOS characteristics as it was expected. The difference between outdoor and indoor antennas is up to 42 dB in attenuation.

The initial assessment for the inter-consist link, placing both antennas in the roof of the train, allows us to conclude that this link is feasible to be implemented on a wireless basis. Perhaps a more elaborated model than the 8-tap one we followed here could provide a better insight in the behavior of the multipath in the three scenarios considered. Finally, the impact of the scenario is nor relevant at all, which means that this inter-consist link will behave in the same way no matter if the train is on a tunnel, bridge, cutting, station, etc.

References

1. Shift2Rail Joint Undertaking. https://shift2rail.org/
2. Roll2Rail. www.roll2rail.eu/
3. Moreno, J., Riera, J.M., de Haro, L., Rodríguez, C.: A survey on the future railway radio communications services: challenges and opportunities. IEEE Commun. Mag. **53**, 62–68 (2015)
4. He, R., Ai, B., Zhong, Z., Molisch, A.F., Chen, R., Yang, Y.: A measurement-based stochastic model for high-speed railway channels. IEEE Trans. Intell. Transp. Syst. **16**(3), 1120–1135 (2015)
5. Briso-Rodríguez, C., Cruz, J.M., Alonso, J.I.: Measurements and modeling of distributed antenna systems in railway tunnels. IEEE Trans. Veh. Technol. **56**(5), 2870–2879 (2007)
6. Hrovat, A., Kandus, G., Javornik, T.: A survey of radio propagation modeling for tunnels. Commun. Surv. Tutor. **16**(2), 658–669 (2014)
7. Garcia-Loygorri, J.M., Arriola, A., Val, I., Briso, C.: 2.6 GHz intra-consist channel model for train control and management systems. IEEE Access **5**, 23052–23059 (2017)

8. Garcia-Loygorri, J.M., Briso, C., Arnedo, I., Calvo, C., Laso, M.A.G., He, D., Jiménez, F., Gonzalez-Posadas, V.: Wideband channel modeling for mm-wave inside trains for 5G-related applications. Wirel. Commun. Mob. Comput. (2018)
9. Ai, B., Cheng, X., Kürner, T., Zhong, Z.-D., Guan, K., He, R.-S., Xiong, L., Matolak, D.W., Michelson, D.G., Briso-Rodriguez, C.: Challenges toward wireless communications for high-speed railway. In: IEEE Transactions on Intelligent Transportation Systems, vol. 15, no. 5, October 2014

Narrowband Characterization
of a Train-to-Train Wireless Link at 2.6 GHz
in Metro Environments

Aitor Arriola[1(✉)] [iD], Iñaki Val[1], Juan Moreno García-Loygorri[2],
and César Briso[3]

[1] Communication Systems, Hardware Platforms and Microsystems,
IK4-IKERLAN, Arrasate-Mondragón, Spain
aarriola@ikerlan.es
[2] Engineering Area, Metro de Madrid S.A., Madrid, Spain
juan.moreno@metromadrid.es
[3] Departamento de Teoría de la Señal y Comunicaciones, ETSIST UPM,
Madrid, Spain
cesar.briso@upm.es

Abstract. A Train-to-Train (T2T) wireless link at 2.6 GHz is characterized for
three different metro environments: tunnel, station and open-field. A narrowband measurement system is used, and obtained attenuation results are analyzed
and modeled. The analysis indicates that reflections coming from the environment allow the RF signal to reach higher distances. In this sense, the station
environment is the most reflective environment, while the open-field is the
opposite situation, and the tunnel an intermediate case. Path-loss models are also
obtained for these T2T link; these models allow to estimate the behavior of the
link in each metro environment. A statistical analysis of the received signal is
also done, and a fit with a log-normal distribution is obtained.

Keywords: Train-to-Train · T2T · Channel modeling · Metro

1 Introduction

Wireless communications in railway environments have been focused traditionally on
train-to-ground links, where GSM-R has been one of the most significant examples [1].
In the last few years, other types of wireless links have been investigated for railways
[2]; this is the case of Roll2Rail project, one of the lighthouse projects of Shift2Rail
initiative, where wireless train backbone and wireless intra-car links have been characterized for metro and high-speed train environments [3, 4]. A Train-to-Train (T2T)
link has also been studied within Roll2Rail. This type of links provide an insight about
the impact of interferences when two wireless train backbones are operating in a close
environment (e.g. crossings, stations, depots, etc.), and they also allow the deployment
of novel railway applications, such as virtual coupling (i.e. a group of train consists
running together without any mechanical connection between them).

Only recently T2T channels have attracted the interest of the research community;
in [5] a T2T channel has been characterized at 5.2 GHz, and in [6] at 450 MHz. In

© Springer International Publishing AG, part of Springer Nature 2018
J. Moreno García-Loygorri et al. (Eds.): Nets4Cars 2018/Nets4Trains 2018/Nets4Aircraft 2018, LNCS 10796, pp. 100–109, 2018.
https://doi.org/10.1007/978-3-319-90371-2_11

order to cover an intermediate frequency band among those already studied, in the present work a narrowband characterization of a T2T channel has been done at 2.6 GHz in metro environments. Three specific metro environments have been selected: station, tunnel and open field (i.e. outdoors). It must be noted that the frequency of 2.6 GHz has been selected in order to obtain interference-free measurements with similar propagation properties to those in the Industrial, Scientific and Medical (ISM) band of 2.4 GHz, which is widely used in wireless communication systems.

The paper is organized as follows. First, the measurement setup is described in Sect. 2. Then, Sect. 3 presents the obtained results, including path loss modeling and statistical analyses. Finally, Sect. 4 summarizes the main results of this work.

2 Measurement Setup

In order to characterize the T2T link, a transmitting antenna has been fixed on the roof of a CAF Series 8000 metro train, and a receiving antenna on the roof of another Series 8000 train (see Fig. 1). For this purpose, Mobile Mark MGRM-WHF wideband monopole antennas have been selected [7]. This scenario with omnidirectional antennas placed on the roof has been used in order to perform a proper channel sounding of the different propagation environments.

Fig. 1. Measurement antennas installed on metro cars.

The transmitting antenna has been connected to a signal generator, transmitting a 19 dBm unmodulated carrier of 2.6 GHz, while the receiving antenna has been connected to an Ettus USRP N210 Software Defined Radio equipment acting as a receiver [8]. This measurement setup is depicted in Fig. 2.

During the measurements, the receiver equipment has recorded the received signal at a sampling frequency of 100 Hz, as one of the trains moved at a constant speed of 18 km/h, while the second train remained stopped in a nearby track; this way, the interference between two wireless train backbones during a train crossing has been simulated. It must be noted that using this measurement setup one sample every 5 cm has been obtained; this value is close to half wavelength at 2.6 GHz, which is a spatial sampling just fine enough to capture small-scale effects.

Line 10 of Metro de Madrid has been selected for these measurements, as it covers three different propagation environments: tunnels, stations and open field. As an example, Fig. 3 depicts a train crossing during measurements in an open field environment.

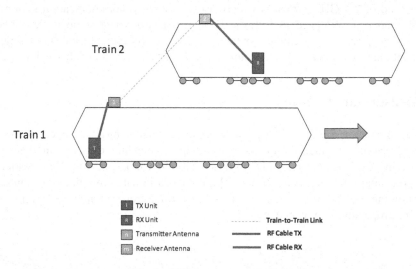

Fig. 2. T2T measurement setup.

Fig. 3. Train crossing in open field environment.

3   Measurement Results

3.1   Instantaneous and Average Attenuations

Measured attenuation values for tunnel, station and open field are shown in Figs. 4, 5 and 6, respectively. Both instantaneous and averaged data are presented. Averaged data have been obtained every 40 samples; this value has been chosen as it removes the high-frequency variations due to multipath while keeping the slow variations of the measured attenuation.

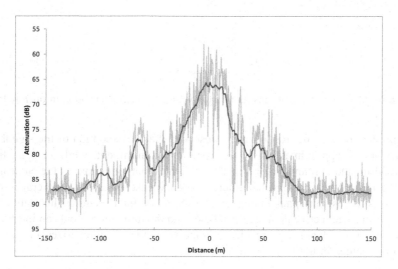

Fig. 4. Measured instantaneous (thin) and averaged (thick) attenuation in tunnel.

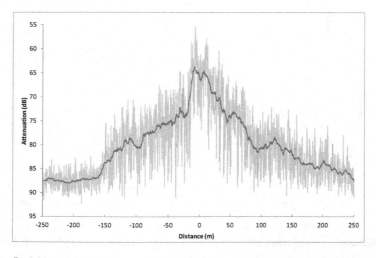

Fig. 5. Measured instantaneous (thin) and averaged (thick) attenuation in station.

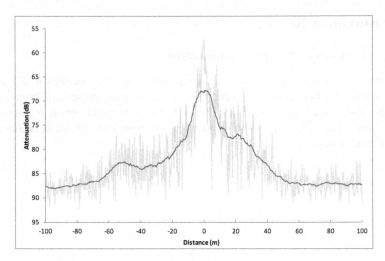

Fig. 6. Measured instantaneous (thin) and averaged (thick) attenuation in open field.

From the previous figures, it can be observed that the reception of the signal starts at a distance of approximately 250 m in station environment, while in open field it starts at 50 m, and in tunnel at 100 m. This indicates that reflections in the environment allow the radio signals to reach farther, at the expense of creating several issues in reception, such as multipath fading or Inter-Symbol Interference. The station environment is more reflective than the open field, and the tunnel represents an intermediate case. In order to obtain a more clear comparison, Fig. 7 summarizes the averaged attenuation values in the three environments.

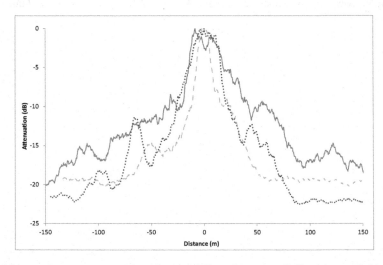

Fig. 7. Measured average attenuations in tunnel (dotted), station (full) and open field (dashed).

3.2 Path Loss Models

From the averaged attenuation results, path loss models have been obtained for each environment. Figures 8, 9 and 10 depict the averaged attenuation results together with the path loss models. In order to check the match with the models, the attenuation results for approaching and moving-away scenarios have been overlapped.

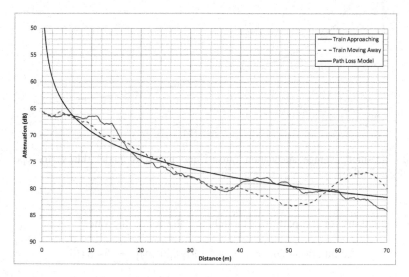

Fig. 8. Measured average attenuation (blue) and path-loss model (black) for tunnel. (Color figure online)

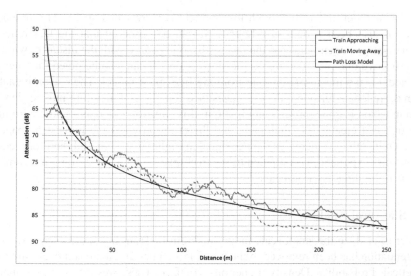

Fig. 9. Measured average attenuation (red) and path-loss model (black) for station. (Color figure online)

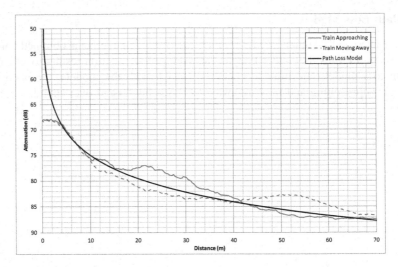

Fig. 10. Measured average attenuation (green) and path-loss model (black) for open field. (Color figure online)

The equations for the path-loss models are the following ones:

$$\text{Attenuation (Tunnel)} = 14.5 \cdot \log_{10}[d(m)] \ + \ 54.8 \,(\text{dB}) \tag{1}$$

$$\text{Attenuation (Station)} = 16.4 \cdot \log_{10}[d(m)] \ + \ 47.8 \,(\text{dB}) \tag{2}$$

$$\text{Attenuation (Open - Field)} = 15.1 \cdot \log_{10}[d(m)] \ + \ 59.9 \,(\text{dB}) \tag{3}$$

A comparison of the three path-loss models is shown in Fig. 11. The free-space model has also been added for reference. It can be observed that the less reflective environment (i.e. open field) has the fastest-decaying curve with the distance, while the most reflective one (i.e. station) has the slowest one. It can also be noted that the open field model is the most different one from the free-space model. The reason is that the antennas are located inside reflective cages (see Fig. 1), and therefore most of the T2T communication is done through multipath; in this situation, the open-field environment is the one that creates less multipath, and therefore provides the highest propagation losses. Multipath also increases the RF signal at higher distances and therefore reduces the path-loss exponent (n) compared to the free-space value (n = 2), ranging from 1.45 to 1.64 in the three environments.

3.3 Statistical Analysis

In order to analyze the small-scale fading in Train-to-Train links, the averaged part of the attenuation has been removed to the measured values and the result been fitted with theoretical Probability Density Functions (PDFs). These results are presented in

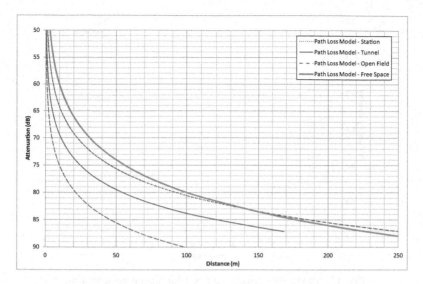

Fig. 11. Path-loss models for T2T links in metro environments.

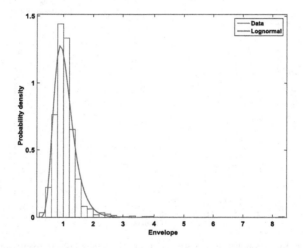

Fig. 12. Probability density function for tunnel environment.

Figs. 12, 13 and 14, and indicate that the T2T links fit statistically to a log-normal distribution in the three measured environments. This is due to the presence of moving objects between transmitting and receiving antennas, in this case the metallic structures surrounding the antennas, as depicted in Fig. 1.

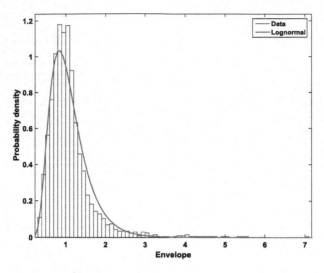

Fig. 13. Probability density function for station environment.

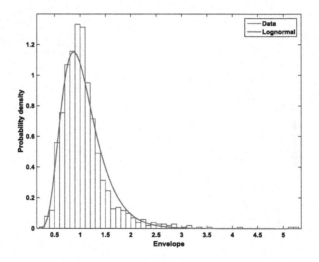

Fig. 14. Probability density function for open-field environment.

4 Conclusions

In this work a Train-to-Train wireless link has been characterized at 2.6 GHz in metro environments. Three specific environments have been covered, namely tunnel, station and open-field. Obtained results have indicated that reflections coming from the environment allow the T2T link to reach higher distances. In this sense, the station environment has been the most reflective one, therefore extending the coverage of the signal, while the open-field environment has been the least reflective one, and the tunnel an intermediate case. It must be noted that apart from extending the signal coverage, reflections also cause several issues in reception, such as multipath fading or Inter-Symbol Interference. This also needs to be studied carefully.

Path-loss models have also been obtained in this work, which allow to estimate the behavior of the T2T link in different environments. A statistical analysis of the received signal has also been done, where a fit with a log-normal distribution has been obtained.

The results of this work can be used to analyze the impact of interferences when two wireless train backbones are operating in a close area. This is what will occur during train crossings, or in crowded environments such as stations or depots.

Acknowledgments. The authors are thankful for the support of the European Commission through the Roll2Rail project, one of the lighthouse projects of Shift2Rail within the Horizon 2020 program. Roll2Rail project has received funding from the European Union's Horizon 2020 research and innovation program under Grant Agreement no. 636032.

References

1. Cellmer, J.: Le réseau GSM-R de RFF. Société de l'Électricité, de l'Électronique et des Technologies de l'Information et de la Communication (2012)
2. Unterhuber, P., Pfletschinger, S., Sand, S., Soliman, M., et al.: A survey of channel measurements and models for current and future railway communication systems. Mob. Inf. Syst. **2016**, 1–14 (2016)
3. García-Loygorri, J.M., Val, I., Arriola, A., Briso-Rodríguez, C.: 2.6 GHz intra-consist channel model for train control and management systems. IEEE Access **5**, 23052–23059 (2017)
4. Roll2Rail. www.roll2rail.eu
5. Unterhuber, P., Sand, S., Soliman, M., Siebler, B., et al.: Wide band propagation in train-to-train scenarios - measurement campaign and first results. In: 11th European Conference on   Antennas and Propagation (EUCAP) (2017)
6. Lehner, A., Strang, T., Unterhuber, P.: Train-to-train propagation at 450 MHz. In: 11th European Conference on Antennas and Propagation (EUCAP) (2017)
7. MobileMark, MGRM-WHF Heavy Duty Mag-Mount Antenna. http://www.mobilemark.com/wp-content/uploads/2015/04/antenna-spec-35-rm-whf-dm-2600.pdf
8. ETTUS, USRP N210 Datasheet. https://www.ettus.com/content/files/07495_Ettus_N200-210_DS_Flyer_HR_1.pdf

Evaluating TCMS Train-to-Ground Communication Performances Based on the LTE Technology and Discreet Event Simulations

Maha Bouaziz[1] , Ying Yan[2], Mohamed Kassab[3], José Soler[2],
and Marion Berbineau[1(✉)]

[1] University Lille Nord de France, IFSTTAR, COSYS,
Villeneuve d'Ascq 59650, France
{maha.bouaziz,marion.berbineau}@ifsttar.fr
[2] Technical University of Denmark, 2800 Kongens Lyngby, Denmark
[3] NOOCS, Sousse, Tunisia

Abstract. This paper focuses on performance evaluation of the Train to Ground traffic exchanges used to ensure safety and monitoring train functionalities carried by the Train Control Management System (TCMS). In the framework of the European project Safe4Rail from the Shift2Rail program, we try to use LTE (Long Term Evolution) network as an alternative communication technology, instead of GSM-R (Global System for Mobile communications-Railway) because of some capacity and capability limits. First step, a pure simulation is used to evaluate the network load for a high-speed scenario, when the LTE network is shared between the train and different passengers. The simulation is based on the discrete-events network simulator Riverbed Modeler. Next, second step focusses on a co-simulation testbed, to evaluate performances with real traffic based on Hardware-In-The-Loop and OpenAirInterface modules. Preliminary simulation and co-simulation results show that LTE provides good performance for the TCMS traffic exchange in terms of packet delay and data integrity.

Keywords: TCMS · Discreet event simulator · LTE · Riverbed
OpenAirInterface · Railway · Mobile Communication Gateway
Train-to-ground communication

1 Introduction

Train Control & Management System (TCMS) is a train-borne distributed control system. It provides data communications interfaces to other train-borne systems, and also telecommunications to support systems operating remotely on the wayside. TCMS is often referred to as the "brain of the train" due to its central role in coordinating control and monitoring across disparate systems [1]. The data for TCMS services can be safety-related or not. The onboard network carries operational services like CCTV (Close Circuit TeleVision), passenger information, etc. The services are also

© Springer International Publishing AG, part of Springer Nature 2018
J. Moreno García-Loygorri et al. (Eds.): Nets4Cars 2018/Nets4Trains 2018/Nets4Aircraft 2018, LNCS 10796, pp. 110–121, 2018.
https://doi.org/10.1007/978-3-319-90371-2_12

customer-oriented such as access to Internet, infotainment... In order to reduce operation and maintenance costs in the railway domain, wired communication networks are replaced by wireless systems [2, 3]. The communication between TCMS and ground systems is provided through the so-called Mobile Communication Gateway (MCG) and the Ground Communication Gateway (GCG), as specified in IEC61375 [4]. These two entities are under development in the Shift2Rail CONNECTA project [5] and they will be able to connect themselves to several types of public wireless systems such as WiFi or LTE for example. In this context, it is very important to develop various simulation/emulation tools that can allow the evaluation of the system with a "zero on site testing" approach promoted in the Shift2rail program.

As described in the EU project Safe4rail [6, 7], we are developing a hardware and software simulation platform using OpenAirInterface and Riverbed Modeler for Railway Communication that is able to evaluate TCMS performance while varying the railway environment and the use cases. Based on the test environment design in [8], we consider, in this paper, a LTE network deployed along a railway line and we present preliminary results using the hardware and software platform and the pure simulated network. We focus on the high-speed rail context.

2 Pure Simulation Platform

Several research works, in the literature, deal with field tests considering LTE signal. Several authors have also considered discrete-event simulator such as Riverbed and have evaluated performances of LTE-based train-to-ground communication in the context of Control and command with a dedicated LTE network that replace a GSM-R one or CBTC (Communication Based Train Control) [9–11].

In this Section, we consider a LTE network simulation based on a network scenario defined in [12], which uses a trajectory line covered by regular LTE Macro-cells. The TCMS traffic performances are evaluated regarding the end-to-end delay and the data loss indicators.

The test environment consists of a train and various passengers. The train is moving and exchanging TCMS traffic with ground devices (GCG) through the LTE wireless access, whereas passengers are using different applications and sharing the same network. The goal of this scenario is to evaluate the efficiency of LTE QoS management, when TCMS traffic shares the network access with other traffics. The network load is increased by different traffics from the User Equipment (UE) representing the train passengers.

2.1 Simulation Topology and Parameters

We consider the discrete-events network simulator called Riverbed Modeler (formerly OPNET Modeler ®) V.18.6.0 (Release Oct 31, 2016) to perform the proposed evaluations [13, 14]. Riverbed enables to model the network architecture of the test environment, the TCMS applications and the passenger UE applications. In addition, it is used to evaluate the interaction and the data exchanges between all network entities.

The scenario models a railway line in Denmark, between Snoghoj and Odense [12]. This line length is about 54.5 km. In the Riverbed simulation environment, the coverage of this line needs the deployment of 11 eNodeB (eNBs) in the 900 MHz band as illustrated in Fig. 1, where a train is required to perform multiple handover in moving with 300 km/h. eNBs are connected to the Evolved Packet Core (EPC) equipment, which provides the connectivity with the GCG equipment.

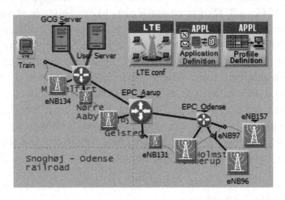

Fig. 1. Topology architecture of the Snoghoj-Odense railway trajectory

LTE Parameters. Our model is based on the Riverbed LTE model. The train and passengers are modeled as LTE User Equipments (UE). eNBs are connected to an EPC node, which models the whole LTE backbone functionalities. Then, the TCMS application servers and passenger application servers are directly connected to the EPC node. Regarding the LTE radio coverage, we propose a basic macro cell based coverage for the high-speed scenario, since macro cells are more suitable for this scenario kind [15, 16]. Table 1 summarizes the used LTE parameters.

Table 1. LTE configuration parameters [14]

Parameter	Macro cells
Frequency band	920 MHz (BW: 5 MHz)
eNB Transmission power	36 dBm
eNB antenna height	50 m
eNB antenna gain	15 dBi
UE antenna gain	1 dBi
Pathloss model	UMa[1]
Multipath channel model	ITU Pedestrian A[2]

[1]ITU-R M2135 Urban Maco (UMa). The simulation randomly chooses between Line-of-Sight and Non-Line-of-Sight cases. This parameter was chosen for a preliminary configuration.
[2]The ITU Pedestrian A multipath channel is chosen following parameters used in [12], for a preliminary configuration. This model will be changed after validation of the simulations principle.

Application Parameters. Based on the European Roll2Rail project [17], the TCMS traffic is varied following different uses cases [2]. In the Safe4Rail project, we have selected traffic types that represent the highest constraints: signaling data, video data, file date update and voice data as described in Table 2. These traffics are considered for the evaluation.

Table 2. TCMS application modeling

Application	Datagram size	Data rate
Signalling data	128 bytes	UL 8 kbps/DL 4.6 kbps
Video data	6250 bytes	UL 1 Mbps
Voice data (live)	160 bytes	UL 64 kbps
Voice data (recorded)	160 bytes	DL 64 kbps
File data	1000 bytes	UL 2 Mbps

A set of basic user profiles predefined by Riverbed Modeler models the passenger traffic. Each profile defines a set of usual LTE user applications that exchanges traffic with servers in the core network. The passenger UE profiles are presented in Table 4.

Bearer Parameters. LTE defines a class-based QoS provisioning based on the concept of bearers that are used to gather packets that have to receive a common QoS treatment. Two types of bearers are defined: Guaranteed Bit Rate (GBR) bearers and Non-GBR bearers. A bearer is associated to a QoS Class Identifier (QCI) characterized by priority level, packet delay budget and acceptable packet loss rate. In addition, a GBR bearer has a fixed UpLink (UL) and DownLink (DL) data rates. The simulated LTE architecture considers 3 bearers according to the data type [18]. The first one is a GBR bearer for TCMS Signalling data with the highest priority and scheduling priority. The second one is also a GBR bearer for TCMS Voice data with a lower priority and scheduling priority. The last one is a non-GBR bearer for TCMS Video and File data and all the Passenger UE data. Table 3 summarizes the bearers' setting.

Table 3. LTE bearer setting

EPS bearer	Signaling	Voice	Default
Application(s)	Signaling data	Voice data	Other
QoS Class Identifier (QCI)	3 (GBR)	2 (GBR)	9 (Non-GBR)
Guaranteed bitrate (uplink)	16 kbps	64 kbps	–
Guaranteed bitrate (down.)	16 kbps	64 kbps	–
Allocation retention priority	1	5	9
Scheduling priority	3	4	9
Delay budget	50 ms	150 ms	300 ms
Packet error loss rate	10^{-3}	10^{-3}	10^{-6}

The train is equipped with the MCG and moves with a high speed (300 km/s) back and forth on the defined railway trajectory. During its movement, it exchanges TCMS traffic with the GCG through its connectivity with eNBs. Besides, 8 passengers use the same LTE connectivity to send their application traffic. We use 4 MoU, 2 MuU and 2 EnU as described in Table 4.

Table 4. Passenger UE profiles and their traffics

User profile	Traffics
Mobile User (MoU)	Instant messaging, gaming, interactive content pull
Multimedia User (MuU)	VoIP and video conferencing
Engineer User (EnU)	Web browsing, email, Telnet session, file transfer

2.2 Performance Evaluation

This part focuses on evaluating whether LTE can provide the required performance in the TCMS traffic exchange between MCG and GCG. For this purpose, we evaluate the data loss and the data transfer delay for TCMS traffics.

Data Integrity. This performance allows evaluating the capacity of LTE to transfer TCMS application data between MCG and GCG, when the connection is shared with passengers. Simulation results show that LTE provides good performance. As shown in Table 5, all signaling data is successfully transmitted from the MCG to the GCG (Fig. 2), thanks to its priority among others and parameters provided from LTE such as the Guaranteed Bearer Rate (GBR) that allows transmission integrity. Besides, this traffic application is transferred through the TCP protocol following the ARQ (Automatic Repeat reQuest) scheme, which allows retransmission of lost and error data. Some fluctuations in the Voice data transmission since it uses UDP protocol without retransmission of lost packets. However, the Video application data is not well transmitted because there is no guarantee parameter used for this traffic kind, as well as the UDP protocol is used for its transferred.

Table 5. Data delivery ratio for different TCMS applications

	Signaling data	File update data	Video data	Voice data (live + recorded)
Transfer protocol	TCP	TCP	UDP	UDP
Data delivery ratio	100%	100%	62.26%	97.4%

Figure 3 shows dropped packets of the different TCMS traffic detected in the physical LTE layer during the time. At 12:13:00, an important number of data lost is detected due to the scheduling conflicts of the different data at this time that overload links and causes loss of data.

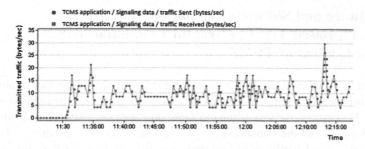

Fig. 2. Sent/received MCG signaling data

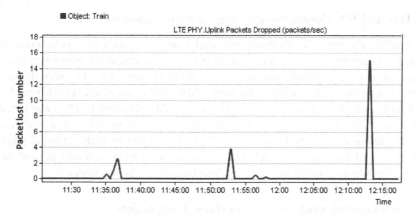

Fig. 3. Packet lost number in the LTE PHY

Data Transfer Delay. This performance allows evaluating the required delay to transfer traffic from MCG to GCG. Simulation results show that all application traffic uses a stable delay during the simulation time. Almost traffic delay is around 0.015 s, and only traffic voices take around 0.1 s (Fig. 4).

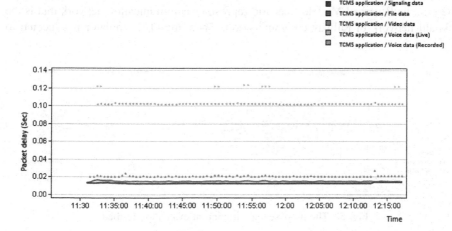

Fig. 4. Packet delay for different TCMS applications

3 Hardware and Software Evaluation Platform for LTE-Based Train-to-Ground Communication in the Context of TCMS

As previously mentioned, several authors have considered performance evaluation of LTE network based on pure simulations using Riverbed modeler as in the first part of this paper. However, these simulation tools can only measure network-level metrics for LTE applications and the transmission-level features cannot be examined. Therefore, real-time emulators have been also presented in the literature for the same purposes, e.g. Open Air Interface (OAI) [19], openLTE [20], and srs-LTE [21].

3.1 HW and SW Co-simulation Using System-in-the-Loop (SITL)

Main challenging issues in realizing co-simulation is the need of synchronization of progress or event and conversion of packets between real and simulation environments. The real-time OAI emulator operates at continuous time. On the other hand, the communication network simulator, Riverbed Modeler, is discrete-event driven. In the Safe4Rail project, we solved the problem by using SITL (System In The Loop) module in the network simulator as a gateway to connect and interact between a simulated network running in Riverbed Modeler and a test platform with the external physical hardware in real-time. In the simulation environment, a SITL gateway is used as the interface module to connect the network interface of the host computer.

3.2 Co-simulation Platform: Architecture, Components and Configurations

The co-simulation platform has been setup in order to assess the performance and reliability of the LTE network for the TCMS traffic exchange in realistic network architecture and configurations. The developed testbed consists of a real network represented by OAI setup and a simulation model in Riverbed Modeler environment. The architecture of the testbed is shown in Fig. 5.

The OAI setup is dedicated to the emulation of the LTE network behavior. Whereas, the Riverbed Modeler scenario represents communication network that is the backhaul network of railway communication. Then, the OAI emulator is expected to

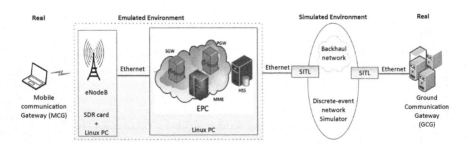

Fig. 5. The proposed co-simulation evaluation testbed

reproduce the Radio Frequency (RF) transmission features, while the communication network modelling is a discrete event-based simulation. This solution is more complex than other pure simulated system (as presented in the first part of the paper) or pure real infrastructure due to the combination. Meanwhile, it provides an opportunity to examine the data transmission from an end-to-end point of view.

A brief description of each component and configurations in the proposed framework is as following:

1. OAI LTE emulator: The methodology deployed in the OAI platform is to use the real stack to perform more realistic and reliable simulations. In OAI software implementation for eNB, it provides the entire protocol stack from physical to network layer, e.g. PHY, MAC, RLC, PDCP and RRC. Regarding the core network, the OAI implements the EPC components with the Serving Gateway (SGW), the Packet Data network Gateway (P-GW), the Mobility Management Entity (MME), the Home Subscriber Server (HSS) and the Non-Access Stratum (NAS) protocols [22, 23].
2. Riverbed Modeler network simulator: two SITL gateway modules are used at each side connecting to real network hardware. In order to run the simulation correctly and efficiently, the simulator and the SITL gateway node need to be pre-configured. For example, the real-time execution ratio property should be set, so that the simulation time in the simulator is ensured to be consistent with the real time. The SITL gateway node is assigned with the right network card. In addition, the rule for packet filtering is set appropriately in order to reduce the amount of processed data.
3. Application server: the application server is a Linux-based computer in the developed platform. It serves as the server part for TCP/UDP and video traffic.

4   Test Cases and Results

4.1   Testbed Setup

We illustrate a co-simulation platform for the evaluation of the TCMS traffic exchange between MCG and GCG using the communication technology LTE. As shown in Fig. 6, the testbed is placed in our lab environment and there is no other interfering network and disturbing of wireless signals in range during the experiment. The scenario includes an OAI-based LTE emulator connecting to a simple backhaul network model in the Riverbed Modeler via the SITL interface module. The different hardware and software deployed in this project are listed in Table 6.

The LTE emulator consists of a LTE UE, eNB and EPC. LTE eNB is a SDR base station that runs the OAI software and allows the connection of the UE and transforms the LTE frame into an Ethernet frame and vice versa. The SDR solution is based Universal Software Radio Peripheral (USRP) B210 platform, which acts as radio front-end with continuous frequency coverage from 70 MHz–6 GHz. Table 6 lists the RF properties of the LTE eNB in the measurement setup.

Fig. 6. The proposed co-simulation evaluation testbed.

Table 6. RF properties of the test setup

	LTE eNodeB properties
Frequency band	2.6 GHz, band 7
Bandwidth	10 MHz (50 DL RBs)
Duplex mode	FDD (frequency division duplex)

The aim of this setup consists in carrying out the performance test. Three different wireless transmissions are configured in the LTE emulator, from good signal strength to bad condition. Using the signal monitoring and reporting from OAI software, the LTE uplink transmission performances are observed and listed in Table 7. I/Q constellation maps out the carried uplink data to the UE on Physical Uplink Shared Channel (PUSCH), where the 16-QAM modulation scheme is used. Physical Uplink Control Channel (PUCCH) is used to transmit the uplink control information, such as Scheduling Request (SR) message. UE sends SR message to ask the network to allocate resources so that UE can transmit PUSCH.

The LTE EPC provides data communication between the LTE network and the GCG (end server). As shown in Fig. 7, the backhaul network in the testbed contains basic network architecture with a single router connecting by two SITL interfaces for packets conversion between the real and simulated environment. The router configurations are chosen such that various traffic load can be inserted in order to study the TCMS traffic shaping and scheduling effect on the received data (Table 8).

To evaluate the performance of the co-simulation platform, we carried out measurements in a single eNB LTE cellular network and a static UE. The scenario with three levels of signal conditions (from good to worse) is applied in the experiment. Traffic under test is TCP/UDP packets generated by the network testing tool IPERF [24] and video streaming packet produced by VLC Media player [25]. The results of testbed show degraded performances (such as reduced bandwidth, increased jitter, raised loss rate) along with the deterioration in signal quality.

Table 7. LTE uplink transmission performances of the test setup

	Signal level 1	Signal level 2	Signal level 3
PUSCH I/Q	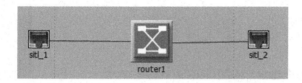		
Power PUCCH	-77/-96 dBm	-78/-96 dBm	-94/-96 dBm
SR received/total	987/50434 (diff 49447)	1103/56783 (diff 55680)	1200/61621 (diff 60421)

Fig. 7. The proposed co-simulation evaluation testbed

Table 8. Measurement results of test setup

	Signal level 1	Signal level 2	Signal level 3
TCP data			
Transfer data size	11.8 MB	2.58 MB	1.58 MB
Throughput	9.82 Mbps	1.98 bps	1.40 Mbps
UDP data with length of 1000 bytes			
Transfer data size	1.24 MB		1.24 MB
Throughput	1.04 Mbps		1.04 Mbps
Jitter	5.234 ms		55.272 ms
Lost/total	2%		69%
Video streaming			
Decoded	352 blocks	340 blocks	341 blocks
Played	808 frames	767 frames	703 frames
Lost	0 frames	5 frames	18 frames

5 Conclusion

This paper has presented two complementary strategies to evaluate the TCMS application traffic exchange between MCG and GCG through an LTE network: pure simulation platform and a software and hardware in the loop based platform. Pure simulation platform is based on the use of the discrete-event simulator Riverbed

Modeler. Preliminary simulation results for a high-speed scenario showed that LTE can be the alternative technology communication, as it allows the integrity of transferring the interesting application traffic, when passengers may use LTE simultaneously. The software and hardware in the loop based platform consists of a communication system able mutually exchanging data between real network devices and Riverbed Modeler. The interconnection between real equipment and simulation demonstrated a way to examine an endto-end network communication and quality of service assurance. The evaluation offered by both platforms will allow discussing the potential usage of wireless TCMS.

The future work will consist in a deeper study and analyze for other uses cases such as train station and existence of other trains in the parallel lines using the same LTE cell (shunting areas for example or high density lines) and also varying the environmental conditions (hilly terrain, rural, tunnels, etc.). The channel models considered in the LTE configuration will be also changed in order to be closer to railway radio channel conditions.

References

1. https://www.railengineer.uk/2015/08/11/what-is-tcms/
2. Roll2Rail Project. Deliverable 2.6: Architecture and Interface Definition for the Train to Ground Communication (2016)
3. EU. CONNECTA. D2.1: Requirements and Specification for the T2G System. Contributing to Shift2Rail's next generation of high capable and safe TCMS and brakes, CONNECTA, 9 June 2017. http://projects.shift2rail.org/s2r_ip1_n.aspx?p=CONNECTA
4. IEC Standard. IEC 61375-2-6: Electronic Railway equipment train communication network (TCN): Part 2–6: On-board to Ground Communication. IEC, 19 August 2016
5. https://shift2rail.org/projects/connecta/
6. EU. Safe4Rail. D3.2 Report on design of TCMS distributed simulation framework concept (M10), July 2017, submitted. https://safe4rail.eu/news/deliverables
7. EU. Safe4Rail. D3.3 Report on design of T2G Test Environment (M10), July 2017. https://safe4rail.eu/news/deliverables
8. Bouaziz, M., Yan, Y., Kassab, M., Soler, J., Berbineau, M.: Train-to-ground communications of a train control and monitoring systems: a simulation platform modelling approach. 7th Transport Research Arena TRA 2018, Vienna, Austria, 16–19 April 2018
9. Sniady, A., Soler, J., Kassab, M., Berbineau, M.: Ensuring long-term data integrity: ETCS data integrity requirements can be fulfilled even under unfavorable conditions with the proper LTE mechanisms. IEEE Veh. Technol. Mag. 11(2), 60–70 (2016). https://doi.org/10.1109/mvt.2015.2503882
10. Khayat, A., Kassab, M., Berbineau, M., Abid, M.A., Belghith, A.: LTE based communication system for urban guided-transport: a QoS performance study. In: Berbineau, M., et al. (eds.) Nets4Cars/Nets4Trains 2013. LNCS, vol. 7865, pp. 197–210. Springer, Heidelberg (2013). https://doi.org/10.1007/978-3-642-37974-1_16
11. Aguado, M., Jacob, E., Berbineau, M., Astorga, J., Toledo, N.: The cross layer RMPA handover: a reliable mobility pattern aware handover strategy for broadband wireless communication in a high-speed railway domain. EURASIP J. Wirel. Commun. Netw. 2012, 298 (2012). https://doi.org/10.1186/1687-1499-2012-298

12. Sniady, A., Soler, J.: Performance of LTE in high speed railway scenarios. In: Berbineau, M., et al. (eds.) Nets4Cars/Nets4Trains 2013. LNCS, vol. 7865, pp. 211–222. Springer, Heidelberg (2013). https://doi.org/10.1007/978-3-642-37974-1_17
13. Riverbed Modeler (2017). www.riverbed.com
14. Modeler Documentation Set, version 18.6, ©2016 Riverbed Technology, 30 Sept 2016
15. Sniady, A., Soler, J., Dittmann, L.: Communication technologies support to railway infrastructure and operations. Ph.D. thesis, DTU Fotonik (2015). https://doi.org/10.11581/dtu:00000010
16. Guan, K., Zhong, Z., Ai, B.: Assessment of LTE-R using high speed railway channel model. In: Proceedings of the 3rd International Conference on Communications and Mobile Computing (CMC), pp. 461–464. IEEE (2011). ISBN 978-1-61284-312-4
17. http://www.roll2rail.eu/
18. 3rd Generation Partnership Project, Technical Specification Group Services and System Aspects, Policy and charging control architecture (Release 10), March 2012
19. Nikaein, N., Knopp, R., Kaltenberger, F., Gauthier, L., Bonnet, C., Nussbaum, D., Ghaddab, R.: Demo: OpenAirInterface: an open LTE network in a PC. In: Proceedings of the 20th Annual International Conference on Mobile Computing and Networking, ser. MobiCom 2014, pp. 305–308. ACM, New York (2014)
20. Wojtowicz, B.: Open LTE, January 2017. http://openlte.sourceforge.net/
21. Gomez-Miguelez, I., Garcia-Saavedra, A., Sutton, P.D., Serrano, P., Cano, C., Leith, D.J.: srsLTE: an open-source platform for LTE evolution and experimentation. In: Proceedings of the Tenth ACM International Workshop on Wireless Network Testbeds, Experimental Evaluation, and Characterization, ser. WiNTECH 2016, pp. 25–32. ACM, New York (2016)
22. Open Air Interface Homepage. http://www.openairinterface.org. 12 Dec 2017
23. Anouar, H., Bonnet, C., Câmara, D., Filali, F., Knopp, R.: An overview of OpenAirInterface wireless network emulation methodology. ACM SIGMETRICS Perform. Eval. Rev. **36**(2), 90–94 (2008)
24. iPerf. https://iperf.fr/
25. VLC Media Player. https://www.videolan.org/vlc/index.html

Nets4Cars

A Vehicle Recognition Method Based on Adaptive Segmentation

Yusi Yang[1](✉), Yan Lai[1,2], Guanli Zhang[1], and Lan Lin[1](✉)

[1] Department of Electronic Science and Technology, Tongji University,
Shanghai 201804, China
{1732879,1631496,1433328,linlan}@tongji.edu.cn
[2] School of Telecommunication Systems Engineering,
Technical University of Madrid, Madrid 28031, Spain

Abstract. The rapid development of computer technology makes the realization of intelligent driving system possible, which provides a solution for many traffic problems today. Among them, vehicle recognition is the most crucial. Most of the previous work is based on the computer vision approach. In this work, we propose a novel method of exploring the position information to improve the target segmentation based vehicle recognition. Specifically, besides the vision clues the target position and height are also exploited adaptively in the target segmentation method, so as to get a better segmentation result. Then a multi-class classifier is adopted by using sparse autoencoder based feature extraction. The experiments are conducted on real world dataset. The experimental results show that in contrast with the state-of-the-arts, our method achieves the best performance. The dataset used for segmentation consists of 60 video sequences and the dataset used for identification contains 11173 samples. On these datasets, the proposed method has obvious improvement compared with the traditional method.

Keywords: Vehicle recognition · Segmentation · Sparse autoencoder

1 Introduction

With the development of information technology, especially in the field of image processing, assisted driving and driverless driving have become possible. In the study of smart cars [1–3], the earliest smart concept car Futurama by the United States General Motors Corporation in 1939 New York World's Fair on display. The Navlab [4] family of smart cars, developed by Carnegie Mellon in partnership with General Motors, has been in more than a dozen versions to date. Japan is an early start to study smart cars in Asian countries. Mainly Toyota, Honda, Fuji Heavy Industries and some car companies involved. Since 1988, Tsinghua University has started the development of THMR series of smart cars, in which the THMR-V smart car is loaded with sensors such as CCD cameras and laser ranging radar to achieve independent tracking of lane lines on structured roads [5]. Smart car assisted driving has been widely used, in the popularization and promotion stage at present. Among them, vehicle recognition is an indispensable part of intelligent driving system. Currently, based on monocular vision

© Springer International Publishing AG, part of Springer Nature 2018
J. Moreno García-Loygorri et al. (Eds.): Nets4Cars 2018/Nets4Trains 2018/Nets4Aircraft 2018, LNCS 10796, pp. 125–136, 2018.
https://doi.org/10.1007/978-3-319-90371-2_13

vehicle recognition methods are the following: Someone proposed method based on vehicle characteristics. For example, the bottom shadow feature first discovered by Mori and Charkari [6]. Hoffman recognizes the vehicle based on the vertical symmetry of the region of interest [7]. Guo proposed an adaptive threshold method to detect the shadow of vehicle floor [8]. Someone also proposed method based on template matching [9]. For example, Collado used the seven parameters of the vehicle's position, height, width, roof angle, windshield and bumper position to form a vehicle template [10]. Zeng proposed the establishment of a rectangular template and a U-shaped template for short-range vehicles and long-distance vehicles respectively [11]. Method based on optical flow field and machine learning based approach are also very common. However, some of these existing methods rely too much on the environment, some have strict requirements on the distance between the target and the camera, and some may have real-time problems.

This paper proposes a novel vehicle recognition method based on the target detection with adaptive segmentation. The task of vehicle recognition of intelligent driving can be divided into two steps: vehicle candidate area extraction and vehicle candidate area verification. In the extraction of vehicle candidate regions, we study common target detection algorithms and present an improved adaptive segmentation and selective search algorithm. In the validation part of the vehicle candidate area, we use the sparse autoencoder neural network to extract deep visual features and adopt the Softmax classifier for classification. Our main contribution is to exploit the target position in the procedure of adaptive segmentation to improve the vehicle recognition in the context of intelligent driving. Specifically, we first calculate and estimate the position distribution of the vehicles in the image of video sequence on a real world video corpus. According to the position distribution, an adaptive segmentation threshold is obtained to get a better segmentation result.

The experiments are conducted on a real world dataset which includes 11173 samples images with four types of vehicle: frontal, side, left bevel and right bevel, and non-vehicle samples. The experimental results show that the best average coverage of some video sequences is improved and the number of regions generated by the algorithm is also reduced, which can effectively reduce the time-consuming part of the vehicle classification and recognition. Compared with traditional HOG-based SVM multi-classifier, our method achieves higher recognition accuracy and recall rate.

2 Vehicle Target Segment Based on Improved Selective Search

2.1 Vehicle Segmenting Based on Selective Search Algorithm

Selective search algorithms include graph-based image segmentation and hierarchical clustering algorithm to fuse two parts of a small area. The Graph-Based Segmentation section is a classic image segmentation algorithm [12] proposed by Felzenszwalb. The algorithm is based on graph greedy clustering algorithm, the difference between the color differences between pixels in the image is divided into different regions, which is simple, fast and highly precise, and is a stepping stone to many algorithms.

2.2 Improved Vehicle Target Segmentation Based on Selective Search Algorithm

Based on the shortcomings of the selective algorithm in the segmentation of vehicle targets, this paper attempts to improve it to reduce the initial number of candidate boxes and improve the initial candidate box quality. The main purpose is to calculate the position of the vehicle in the video sequence and the height in the image. An adaptive segmentation threshold is obtained according to the position information and altitude information of the vehicle, so as to obtain a better segmentation result.

A Priori Analysis of Vehicle Height Information. According to the vehicle information marked in the video sequence, this paper has counted the information of 19593 cars in 50 video sequences. As shown in Fig. 1 for one of the four consecutive video images, the red box indicates the location of the vehicle, the height of the box indicates the vehicle appears in the image of the height.

(a)   (b)

(c)   (d)

Fig. 1. Vehicle in the video annotation. (Color figure online)

According to the vehicle information marked in the video sequence, this article has counted the information of 19593 cars in 50 video sequences. The 19593 car's position and height information in a 256 * 320 chart, calculated for each pixel appears on average for all vehicle height, show in Fig. 2. As the colors change from blue-yellow-red, the average height of the vehicle increases. In addition to the average height of the vehicle where there is no 0, the average pixel vehicle height of the smallest picture of 123, the largest is 785. It can be seen from the figure that the average height of the vehicles with the height and the width of the images of about 150 is relatively small. At the top and bottom of the image, the average height of the vehicles in these places is 0, because there are no vehicles due to the sky and the spatial distance between the current car and the front car respectively. The top of the image, that is, where the height is greater than 200, and the bottom of the image, that is, where the height is less than 50, are generally carts if a car appears.

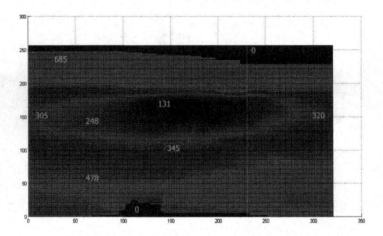

Fig. 2. Average vehicle height distribution. (Color figure online)

Based on the information obtained in the vehicle average height map, in the $123 < h < 345$ part, lower the threshold, segmentation more detailed, can car target segmentation. In the $345 < h < 785$ section, raise the threshold to prevent over-segmentation and reduce the number of area boxes. In the $h = 0$ section, the original segmentation result is maintained. Improved image segmentation guidelines are as follows:

$$Diff\left(C_i, C_j\right)$$
$$\leq \begin{cases} \min\left(\mathrm{Int}(C_i) + r(C_i),\ \mathrm{Int}(C_j) + r(C_j)\right), & h = 0 \\ \min\left(\mathrm{sigmf}(h_i) * \left(\mathrm{Int}(C_i) + r(C_i)\right),\ \mathrm{sigmf}(h_j) * \left(\mathrm{Int}(C_j) + r(C_j)\right)\right), & 123 \leq h \leq 345 \\ \min\left(\mathrm{sigmf}(h_i) * \mathrm{Int}(C_i) + r(C_i),\ \mathrm{sigmf}(h_j) * \mathrm{Int}(C_j) + r(C_j)\right), & 345 \leq h \leq 785 \end{cases}$$

$$(1)$$

where sigmf() is the Sigmoid function, h_i, h_j are the average height of the smaller point in the maximum edge of the corresponding region C_i, C_j. The Sigmoid function's graph is a continuous, smooth and strictly monotonic S-curve that is a good threshold function. Its expression is:

$$f(x) = \frac{1}{1 + e^{-x}} \tag{2}$$

To zoom in and out of this function you get:

$$f(x) = \frac{Z}{1 + e^{-a(x-c)}} \tag{3}$$

In order to get a suitable magnification reduction ratio, the article needs to set the appropriate z, a, c parameter values. Take c = 392.7, a = 0.002, z = 2.1, get the function graph shown in Fig. 3.

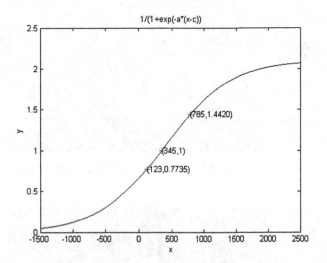

Fig. 3. Shifts the zoomed Sigmoid graph.

When h < 345, the segmentation threshold is reduced. When h = 123, the scaling factor is 0.7735. When h > 345, the segmentation threshold is enlarged. When h = 785, the magnification is 1.4420.

Improved Algorithm of Vehicle Target Segmentation and Analysis. Where k is the threshold size immediately after the initial segmentation. The color of each split area is randomly generated, representing the different regions generated by the split. The originalBoxes is the initial number of regions generated by the split.

As shown in Fig. 4, the improved algorithm can not only segment small target vehicles, but also eliminate the over-segmentation of some roads and reduce the

(a)   (b)

(c) k=45, originalBoxes=342   (d) k=45, originalBoxes=283

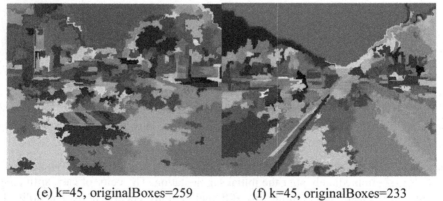

(e) k=45, originalBoxes=259   (f) k=45, originalBoxes=233

Fig. 4. Image segmentation results before and after improved algorithm.

number of candidate vehicle frames. It also helps to reduce the time for vehicle classification and recognition and improve accuracy rate.

2.3 Evaluate the Improvement Method

The method of algorithm evaluation in this paper uses the method in [13]. The average best coverage (ABO) in this method is used to measure the quality of the final vehicle candidate box.

In this paper, a total of 10 video sequences under various scenes are tested with the improved pre-algorithm and the improved algorithm respectively. Mainly records the result of ABO and the number of area boxes generated by the algorithm. The experimental results show that the candidate regions generated by the improved algorithm are significantly reduced, and the quality of the candidate regions is slightly fluctuated. The experimental comparison results are shown in the following table.

As can be seen from Table 1, the selective search algorithm is improved according to the vehicle height distribution chart and the performance statistics of the ten video sequences are improved with the improved algorithm. The final result shows that the best average coverage rate of some video sequences is improved after the improvement, and the number of regional frames generated by the algorithm is also reduced, which can effectively reduce the time-consuming part of the vehicle classification and recognition.

Table 1. Comparing results.

Video sequence	Video 1	Video 2	Video 3	Video 4	Video 5
ABO before improvement	0.510	0.551	0.501	0.510	0.615
ABO after improvement	0.540	0.547	0.530	0.505	0.616
The number of regions before improvement	623	475	561	544	491
The number of regions after improvement	382	358	396	415	384
Video sequence	Video 6	Video 7	Video 8	Video 9	Video 10
ABO before improvement	0.592	0.625	0.630	0.628	0.537
ABO after improvement	0.610	0.624	0.627	0.616	0.551
The number of regions before improvement	454	385	604	592	524
The number of regions after improvement	321	370	356	390	361

3 Vehicle Recognition Based on Multi-class Classifier

Vehicles at different angles of shooting will show different vehicle structure and shape. In this paper, the vehicles are divided into four categories according to different perspectives of the vehicle: front/rear surface, side surface, left bevel surface and right bevel surface, like Fig. 5, and the feature of the vehicle is extracted by using a sparse autoencoder neural network. According to the extracted feature data, a multi-class classifier is trained to classify the recognition vehicle and the non-vehicle. Finally, the traditional feature extraction method is compared.

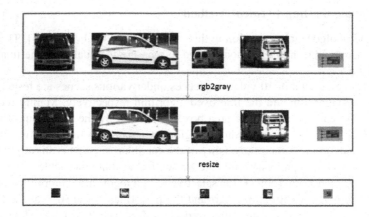

Fig. 5. Sample preparation.

3.1 Sparse Autoencoder Neural Network

Sparse autoencoder is evolved from the encoder. Automatic encoder [14] is a commonly used model in deep learning. It has similar network hierarchy with artificial neural network, including input layer, hidden layer and output layer. The difference is that an artificial neural network is a supervised learning network and an automatic encoder is an unsupervised learning network. Sparse autoencoder is added in the process of self-encoder encoding L1 regularization restrictions. In view of its good feature learning ability of input data, this paper uses sparse autoencoder combined with Softmax classifier to classify the vehicle targets.

After sparse autoencoder neural network features extracted, but also need to train the classifier. This paper selects the Softmax classifier, which is derived from the logistic dichotomous model.

In this paper, we reduce the input vehicle training sample size to 28 * 28, so the number of neurons in the input layer is input Size = 784, and hidden layer neurons are set to 196. The sparse autoencoder network with two layers and three layers of hidden layer are trained respectively. For two hidden layers, the number of iterations for training the first and second hidden layers and the number of iterations for fine-tuning the entire network were 600 and 200, respectively. For the three hidden layers, in order to make the loss function value converge, the number of iterations of training the first, second and third hidden layers and the number of iterations of fine-tuning the whole network are respectively 1000. The number of iterations when training the Softmax classifier is 400. Figures 6 and 7 show the convergence values of the loss function obtained when training the Softmax classifier and fine-tuning the whole network with two hidden layers, respectively, at 0.934 and 0.767, respectively. The sparseness parameter $\rho = 0.22$ at this time.

165	170	1.00000e+00	9.34350e-01	2.49380e-04
166	171	1.00000e+00	9.34350e-01	2.47903e-04
167	172	1.00000e+00	9.34350e-01	7.35994e-04
168	173	1.00000e+00	9.34350e-01	2.43342e-04
169	174	1.00000e+00	9.34350e-01	2.30020e-04
170	175	1.00000e+00	9.34350e-01	1.77074e-04
171	176	1.00000e+00	9.34350e-01	2.20893e-04
172	177	1.00000e+00	9.34350e-01	1.87490e-04
173	178	1.00000e+00	9.34350e-01	2.43297e-04
174	179	1.00000e+00	9.34350e-01	1.40172e-04
175	180	1.00000e+00	9.34350e-01	1.45338e-04

Function Value changing by less than Io1X

Fig. 6. Softmax classifier training results.

589	599	1.00000e+00	7.69514e-01	1.25695e+01
590	600	1.00000e+00	7.69353e-01	1.45309e+01
591	601	1.00000e+00	7.69238e-01	2.66348e+01
592	602	1.00000e+00	7.69079e-01	1.43749e+01
593	603	1.00000e+00	7.68927e-01	1.40014e+01
594	604	1.00000e+00	7.68697e-01	2.04921e+01
595	605	1.00000e+00	7.68429e-01	3.01854e+01
596	606	1.00000e+00	7.68180e-01	2.23578e+01
597	607	1.00000e+00	7.68029e-01	1.24309e+01
598	608	1.00000e+00	7.67921e-01	1.41062e+01
599	609	1.00000e+00	7.67844e-01	1.68496e+01
600	610	1.00000e+00	7.67716e-01	1.49019e+01

Exceeded Maximum Number of Iterations

Fig. 7. Fine tune network training results.

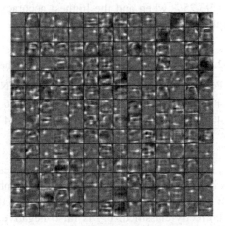

Fig. 8. The first hidden layer features.

From the training process, we can get the first 196 hidden layer neurons obtained features, each feature is 784 dimensions, the visual results as shown in Fig. 8 above. The second hidden layer neuron obtained 196 features, each feature of 196 dimensions, the visual result of which is shown in Fig. 9. It can be seen from the two feature layers that due to the decrease of hidden layer neurons and the limitation of activation, the training features become sparse and abstract.

Fig. 9. The second hidden layer features.

3.2   The Test Result of Sparse Autoencoder Neural Network Under Different Parameters

The trained sparse autoencoder neural network has different recognition accuracy under different hidden layers and different sparsity parameters. Among the two hidden layers, the highest accuracy is 93.25% when and the highest accuracy is 93.875% when for three hidden layers (Table 2).

Table 2. Table captions should be placed above the tables.

Parameter	Positive samples	Negative samples	TP	FN	TN	FP	Accuracy
Two layers +0.22	400	400	384	16	362	38	93.25%
Three layers +0.36	400	400	386	14	365	35	93.875%

TP is true positive, refers to the number of positive samples correctly classified in positive samples. FP is false positive, which means that the number of negative samples is divided into positive samples. TN is true negative, refers to the negative samples in the negative samples correctly classified. FN is false negative, refers to the positive sample is divided into negative samples of the number of samples.

Compared with SVM Multi-classifier Based on Traditional Features. On Table 3 lists the best classification results of the above two vehicle classification methods. It can be seen from the classification results that the overall classification accuracy of the sparse autoencoder network classifier in this paper is slightly higher than that of the SVM multi-class classifier based on the traditional HOG features.

Table 3. Comparison of the highest classification accuracy of the two methods.

Method	Positive samples	Negative samples	TP	FN	TN	FP	Accuracy
Hog + SVM	400	400	378	22	366	34	93.0%
Sparse autoencoder	400	400	386	14	365	35	93.875%

4 Conclusion

Vehicle recognition is an important part of intelligent driving system. Fast and accurate vehicle recognition is the premise of safe driving of smart cars. This paper summarizes the experience and achievements of predecessors in the field of intelligent vehicle driving system, studies the algorithms of image processing and machine vision, and proposes a method of vehicle recognition in intelligent driving system. This method improves the segmentation threshold of the selective search algorithm and reduces the number of frames in the candidate area of the vehicle, thus reducing the computational load of subsequent vehicle recognition. In the vehicle recognition using a multi-perspective approach, and then use the sparse autoencoder, obtained better than the traditional method results.

Acknowledgment. This work is supported by National Science Foundation of China 61373106.

References

1. Lai, Y., Wang, N., Yang, Y., Lin, L.: Traffic signs recognition and classification based on deep feature learning. In: 7th International Conference on Pattern Recognition Applications and Methods (ICPRAM), Madeira, Portugal, pp. 622–629 (2018)
2. Zhang, G., Lin, F., Lin, L.: A novel method of front vehicle recognition. In: Progress in Electromagnetic Research Symposium (PIERS), Shanghai (2016)
3. Lin, F., Lai, Y., Lin, L., Yuan, Y.: A traffic sign recognition method based on deep visual feature. In: Progress in Electromagnetic Research Symposium (PIERS), Shanghai (2016)
4. Thorpe C.E.: Vision and Navigation, vol. 93. Kluwer International (1990)
5. Zhang, F., He, K.: Multifunctional outdoor intelligent mobile robot experimental platform. Robot **24**(2), 97–101 (2002)
6. Mori, H., Charkari, N.: Shadow and rhythm as sign patterns of obstacle detection. In: 1993 Conference Proceedings of IEEE International Symposium on Industrial Electronics, ISIE 1993, Budapest (1993)
7. Hoffman, C., Dang, T., Stiller, C.: Vehicle detection fusing 2D visual features. In: Intelligent Vehicles Symposium (2004)
8. Guo, L., Li, K., Wang, J.: A feature based vehicle detection method. Automot. Eng. **28**(11), 1031–1035 (2006)
9. Tian, J., Zhen, Y.: Application of template matching in image recognition. Sens. Microsyst. **27**(1), 112–114 (2008)
10. Collado, J., Hilario, C., De, E.: Model based vehicle detection for intelligent vehicles. In: Intelligent Vehicles Symposium (2004)
11. Zeng, Z.: Lane detection and vehicle tracking in freeways. J. Autom. **29**(3), 450–456 (2003)

12. Felzenszwalb, P., Huttenlocher, D.: Efficient graph-based image segmentation. Int. J. Comput. Vis. **59**(2), 167–181 (2004)
13. Uijlings, J., Sande, K., Gevers, T.: Selective search for object recognition. Int. J. Comput. Vis. **104**(2), 154–171 (2013)
14. Bengio, Y., Courville, A.: Representation learning: a review and new perspectives. IEEE Trans. Pattern Anal. Mach. Intell. **35**(8), 1798–1828 (2014)

Traffic Signal Recognition with a Priori Analysis of Signal Position

Yingdong Yu[1(✉)], Yan Lai[1,2], Hui Wang[1], and Lan Lin[1(✉)]

[1] Department of Electronic Science and Technology,
Tongji University, Shanghai 201804, China
{yuyingdong,1631496,1336279,linlan}@tongji.edu.cn
[2] School of Telecommunication Systems Engineering,
Technical University of Madrid, 28031 Madrid, Spain

Abstract. Traffic signal recognition is one of the critical points of the technology of intelligent driving. The research on traffic signal recognition has lasted for decades and attracted more and more research attentions from the research and industry communities. Most of the previous work are based on the vision clues to deal with the problem of traffic signal recognition, while in this paper we propose a novel method which is an integration of prior signal position knowledge and the computer vision based on object detection. With prior knowledge of signal position, the detection area can be reduced and the efficiency of signal recognition is increased significantly. Experiments are conducted on the real-world dataset, and the experimental results show that compared with the previous work and the state-of-the-arts, our method achieves the best performance and satisfies the requirements of signal recognition in intelligent driving.

Keywords: Intelligent driving · Traffic signal recognition
Traffic signal tracking · Support Vector Machine

1 Introduction

With the rapid development of intelligent transportation [1], intelligent driving of vehicle has drawn more and more attentions from the research and industry communities. The automatic vision recognition is involved in many aspects of the intelligent driving, such as ground mark recognition [2], traffic sign recognition [3], vehicle recognition [4] and so on. Among them the traffic signal recognition plays the fundamental role in this task.

Traffic signal recognition is a challenging problem for decades and a lot of work has been proposed. In the early stage, most algorithms used color information directly to segment traffic light and then to detect lights by region detection. For example, Park presented circular traffic light recognition algorithm [5], and Omachi put forward a way to detect traffic light quickly [6]. The former one eliminates nonsignal light interference combined with black background and detects round traffic light by circular detection algorithm proposed by Haralick. The latter one uses Sobel edge detection operator to extract the edge information and then use the Hough transform to detect the circular

© Springer International Publishing AG, part of Springer Nature 2018
J. Moreno García-Loygorri et al. (Eds.): Nets4Cars 2018/Nets4Trains 2018/Nets4Aircraft 2018, LNCS 10796, pp. 137–148, 2018.
https://doi.org/10.1007/978-3-319-90371-2_14

traffic light area. However, these methods are usually not effective anti-interference and of poor robustness. The machine learning began to be used in traffic light recognition before long. Gong et al. proposed a method for identifying and tracking traffic lights [7]. The method uses threshold segmentation and morphological filtering to obtain candidate regions and uses machine learning to identify traffic lights. It also tracked traffic lights by Camshift algorithm [8] based on color histogram. It's proved that this method is of good adaptability and robustness. John et al. proposed the use of convolution neural networks and significant graphs into traffic light recognition methods under different light intensity [9]. They use GPS information [10] to obtain interest areas and use convolution neural networks [11] to extract and detect traffic lights. This method gets a higher accuracy rate. But due to the addition of machine learning and convolution neural networks, besides a large number of training samples, these methods are computationally more complex and less real-time.

To dealing with the problem, in this paper we present a novel traffic signal recognition method, which is an integration of prior knowledge of signal position, image analysis and object detection. Unlike traditional methods, this paper not only explore vision clues, the signal position is also exploited as prior knowledge to dealing with the problem. Specifically, the location of the traffic lights is applied to establish the positional relationship between the captured image and the traffic signal to estimate the probability density of a traffic signal position distribution in images. According to the signal position distribution, the areas of the image with smaller probability will be skipped for detection and this position map is also employed in the object detection.

The experimental videos and images are obtained from driving recorder. The accuracy of this method is apparently higher than traditional machine learning methods, but it's more complicated in data processing. Experiments show that the prior analysis based on the location information can effectively filter out the interference area and area like shade, car taillights and so on, which greatly reduces the amount of calculation and increases the accuracy rate. On the other hand, it also reduces the operation time and enhance real-time.

2 Traffic Light Recognition System

2.1 Overall Structure

The overall structure of the traffic light detection system in this paper is shown in Fig. 1. First of all, we filter target area using location information. Then we conduct image processing including threshold segmentation, morphological processing and so on. In this way, we can extract the target areas and use the trained SVM [12] classifier to classify them. At last we use the KCF [13] to track the traffic lights in successive images.

2.2 Priori Analysis Based on Location Information

The traditional traffic light recognition mainly gets both the use of digital image processing and machine learning. Image processing is applied to the detection and

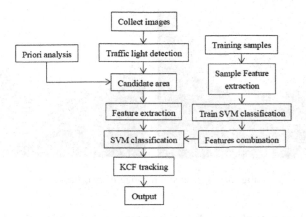

Fig. 1. Traffic light experiment algorithm

extraction of candidate blocks of traffic lights. Machine learning is used to analyze and judge the extracted classifiers. In addition to the above two aspects, this paper adds a priori analysis based on the position information of traffic light into the recognition system.

Height Estimation of the Detection Area. We establish a monocular visual geometric model to estimate the height of the traffic light detection area, as shown in Fig. 2. The height of the traffic light H is known. According to the national standard, the vertical column is over 3 m and the cantilever is between 5.5 and 7 m. f is the lens focal length parameter, L is the distance from the intersection of the vehicle.

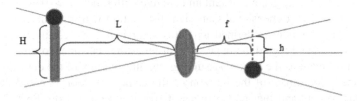

Fig. 2. Monocular visual geometric model

The height of traffic lights is fixed and known, and the traffic lights are useless when traffic lights are too far or too close. Therefore, when the distance changes, the position of traffic lights in the image will change. According to the actual observation, when the distance between the vehicle camera and the signal lamp is between 100 m and 10 m, the light emitting part of the traffic light is located on the upper part of the optical axis.

Therefore, the height of the optical axis of the camera on the image plane of the camera is taken as the lower limit of signal detection. When the distance is 10 m, the projection height of the signal light emitting area on the image plane is taken as the upper limit of the signal detection as shown in Fig. 3.

Fig. 3. The detection range of two images

Stochastic process model. In order to be able to detect traffic lights better, a random model is constructed on a frame-by-frame basis to provide a priori probability of detection of each frame of image. Detection range shown in Fig. 3, the upper limit is 100 m between the camera and the traffic light while the lower limit is 10.

The model defines that the random variables within the range shown in Fig. 3 meet the two-dimensional Gaussian distribution. And as time t changes, the traffic light image height and peak geometric height will change. Two-dimensional Gaussian distribution is as follows:

$$f(x,y,t) = \frac{1}{2ps_1s_2\sqrt{1-r^2}}\exp\left(-\frac{1}{2(1-r^2)}\left[\frac{(x-m_1)^2}{s_1^2} - 2r\frac{(x-m_1)(y-m_2(t))}{2s_1s_2} + \frac{(y-m_2(t))^2}{s_2^2}\right]\right)$$

(1)

Among them, $\sigma_1, \sigma_2, \mu_1, \rho$ are constant and change with time. $\sigma_1 > 0, \sigma_2 > 0, |\rho| < 1$. (X, Y) obeys the two-dimensional Gaussian distribution with parameter at time t.

The law of the model is defined as follows: In Fig. 2 we establish a rectangular coordinate system and regard the upper left corner as the coordinate origin, the width as the x-axis, the height as the y-axis. Assuming that the height y of the detection height is top_line, the y-coordinate of the horizon of the camera is floor_line and the distance between the vehicle and the intersection is L (t), it is known from Sect. 2.1 that the height of the traffic light from the lens is h = fH/L, $5 \le L(t) \le 50$, so $\mu_2(t)$ satisfied:

$$\mu_2(t) = \text{floor\_line} - \text{top\_line} - \frac{f}{L(t)}H$$

(2)

The model has a large value in the peak area and changes as the distance between the vehicle camera and the intersection traffic lights changes. Then, to ensure that the traffic light is near the peak of the test, there should have a greater weight in the vicinity. With this weight based on location information, we set up a detection threshold so that areas with low probability of traffic light such as image edges can be directly filtered and greatly reduce the amount of computation and improve the accuracy of SVM classification.

2.3   The Detection of Lights

The Process of Traffic Light Detection. In this paper, we analyze traffic lights by HSV [14] and YCbCr [15]. The signal of red and green color is divided by Cr channel. The V-channel and Tophat image enhancement algorithm are used to segment the signal light brightness information. Then we get candidate segmentation area combined with the color and brightness information. At last we set the size of the light emitting area of the signal and the aspect ratio of the external rectangle to obtain the final candidate area.

Traffic Light Image Segmentation. In this paper, we use the YCbCr color space to binarize the image, and then set the red and green thresholds to segment the traffic lights in the image.

We calculate the color distribution histogram of 50 different traffic light image and gain their mean value. The red light was mainly distributed in the interval [150, 240] and the green light was [25, 100]. Therefore, this paper selects the red threshold TL_red = 150, TH_red = 240; green threshold TL_green = 25, TH_green = 100. The effect of binary image after the color threshold segmentation is shown in Fig. 4.

Fig. 4. The effect of binary image (Color figure online)

As we can notice from the figure above, the image after the color threshold segmentation also retains many areas that are similar to the traffic light, such as traffic signs, tree shade and pedestrian clothes. It is obvious that the traffic lights are brighter than these areas, so we can filter out these areas based on it. Therefore, we use the Tophat algorithm to morphologically filter the image before binarizing the image. This algorithm is useful to obtain dark pixel regions in brighter backgrounds and bright pixel regions in darker ones.

After color threshold segmentation, we further use the brightness value segmentation. V in HSV color space represents the brightness value. After counting the gray histograms of 100 traffic lights under the V channel, we set the gray value of the V channel in the interval [145, 255]. Combine color and brightness information, we can gain the final segmentation area of traffic lights. The result is shown in Fig. 5.

Fig. 5. The result after color threshold and brightness value segmentation

For some other disturbances, we use the shape characteristics of traffic lights for further filtering. Select the size of 100 m for the lower limit, TL_area = 50.0 m area size for the upper limit, TH_area = 500. The aspect ratio is set to TL_region = 0.8 and TH_region = 1.2. The effect is shown in Fig. 6.

Fig. 6. Left one: based on area size; Right one: based on aspect ratio

SVM signal recognition based on location information. In Sect. 2.2 we establish a stochastic process model using the location information. This model obtains the probability of traffic lights at different positions in each picture according to the distance between the camera and the traffic lights and the image plane distribution. Then, according to a large amount of data statistics, we can get a threshold τ which can be used to reduce the amount of complexity and the amount of calculation. When the probability that the detection area in the image is greater than τ, we determine the area to be detected. Otherwise, no detection is performed. Then we get a classification result by a SVM classifier which detect the areas picked out by the stochastic process model.

Figure 7 is a frame of a video. If we do not combine the location information for prior analysis, we will get four traffic light candidate areas shown in the figure. According to the stochastic process model established by the location information, the probability of the central locations of the four traffic light candidate regions of the frame image can be obtained as [5.36e−07, 0.4825, 0.4807, 1.02 e−10], τ = 0.3. Thus, the area 2 and area 3 are selected. Then we use SVM classifier to classify them and get the result that they are traffic lights. In this way, we don't need to classify area 1 and area 4 which reduce the amount of calculation.

Fig. 7. An example of candidate areas of traffic light

2.4   Traffic Lights Recognition

Before target feature extraction, we will make basic pre-processing on sample images: the image grayscale and make the image size become 80 * 34.

Determine feature types and weighting algorithms. In this paper, we use the SVM to classify the traffic lights and the cross-validation for the parameter selection. First, we choose the initial parameter value to test the training samples with cross-validation, and then adjust the parameters according to the step size and test again until we get the best result. The result is that the classification model established for the HSV statistical histogram, the HOG, the EOH and the SIFT_BoW feature can obtain higher accuracy. In this way, the color, edge and feature point can indicate the visual characteristics of traffic light better.

Because several features can express the visual characteristics of traffic lights well, in order to maintain a good accuracy, we select the above three features combined with look-up table method and adaptive weight method to make up the classifier.

In this paper, the classification of traffic lights is a dichotomous problem. Setting the positive sample label as 1 and the negative sample label as −1, we can get the feature lookup table composed of 1 and −1. By analyzing the classification results of the three classifiers, if the classification result is all 1 or two are 1, it is judged to be traffic light. When all the classification results are −1, it is judged as the background target. In other cases, we use adaptive weight method to decide (Table 1).

The adaptive weight rule is based on HOG, HSV and SIFT_BoW. The three features constitute three classifiers and set the weight according to the accuracy of test and output result combing the results of the three classifiers. In this paper, two methods will be combined to classify the samples. The process is shown in Fig. 8.

Table 1. Inquiry table Traffic lights

	Traffic lights	Font size and style
HOG	1, 1, 1	
	1, 1, −1	−1, −1, −1
HSV	1, −1, 1	
SIFT_BoW	−1, 1, 1	

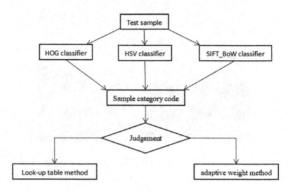

Fig. 8. Traffic light classification

3   Experiment and Analysis

3.1   Traffic Light Recognition

We choose Pike F-100C industrial camera and collect traffic video in Shanghai. And the video image resolution is 1032 * 776. The test environment is on the 3.2 GHz Core i5 CPU, 4 GB of memory and achieve the above algorithm on Matlab platform.

According to the test data, the HOG, HSV and SIFT_BoW feature weights of red light samples are 0.44, 0.37 and 0.19, and 0.41, 0.41 and 0.18 for green light.

The multi-feature combination classification method is compared with the three single-feature classification results of HOG, HSV and SIFT_BoW. The specific test results are shown in Table 2.

Table 2. Comparing results

	HOG	HSV	SIFT_BoW	Multi-feature
Red light accuracy	97.73%	95.45%	89.09%	98.55%
Green light accuracy	96.36%	96.36%	87.73%	98.09%

In addition to the use of traffic light pictures for identification, we also conducted a video-based traffic light recognition experiment. The video is collected in the natural environment, including circular lights and arrow lights. Four different video sequences are selected to verify the accuracy of this method. The definition accuracy is as follows;

1. Only based on multi-feature, the results shown in Table 3.

Table 3. The results based on multi-feature combination

Video	Total number of frames	False inspection frames	Missed inspection frames	Accuracy
1	467	28	24	88.87%
2	503	37	16	89.46%
3	580	29	22	91.21%
4	487	20	9	94.05%

2. Based on location information and multi-feature, the results shown in Table 4.

Table 4. The results based on position information and multi-feature combination

Video	Total number of frames	False inspection frames	Missed inspection frames	Accuracy
1	467	13	24	92.08%
2	503	25	16	91.85%
3	580	19	27	92.07%
4	487	14	9	95.28%

3.2 Traffic Light Tracking

The KCF algorithm is a tracking-detection kernel-dependent filter tracking method. The basic idea is to use the tracking target as a positive sample and the environment around the target as a negative sample to design a classifier. By extracting the HOG characteristic data of the tracking region, KCF algorithm builds a tracking sample and then uses the kernel function to calculate the similarity between the candidate region and the regard the target with high similarity as a new tracking target. In the previous section, we found that HOG is the best classification feature, so using the KCF algorithm to track also can get high accuracy.

The flow is shown in Fig. 9, where n indicates that the NO.n frame starts to be detected, and k indicates the number of skipped frames.

Thus, we use KCF to track traffic lights in different videos. Figure 10 shows a frame tracking image of the four selected videos.

Figure 11 shows the accuracy of traffic light tracking in a video using KCF. We can notice that when the distance with center up to 15 pixels, the accuracy of tracking is almost 100%.

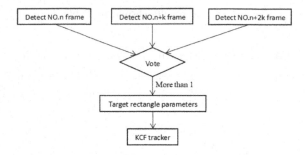

Fig. 9. The process of traffic light tracking

Fig. 10. Tracking images

3.3 Experimental Analysis

The comparison of Tables 3 and 4 shows that difference between the pure SVM algorithm and the combination of location information and SVM identification algorithm:

1. Only in video 3, the number of missed frames has increased. Because the undetected factor is that the traffic light target area is not located in the detection phase, a part of the video 3 image is incorrectly determined as the background target based on the location information, which results in an increase of missed frames.

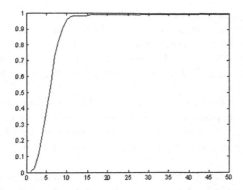

Fig. 11. The accuracy of tracking while the distance with center changes

2. False detected frames are all reduced. Combined with the location information, we can filter out many areas that are similar to the traffic light, such as traffic signs, tree shade and pedestrian clothes. In this way, we can improve the recognition accuracy of traffic lights.
3. We can see from the Figs. 10 and 11 that the effect of traffic light tracking by KCF algorithm is great. It's based on the good effect of traffic light recognition. Therefore, the combination of the two sections is excellent.

4   Conclusion

This paper summarizes the existing traffic signal recognition methods and proposes a traffic signal recognition method combined with location information, multi-feature fusion and target tracking. A priori analysis of the position of the traffic lights is used to estimate the statistical distribution of the location of the traffic lights and the k-nearest neighbor method is used to detect the traffic light based on the location features. Combining look-up table method and adaptive weight method to combine multiple feature classifiers to improve the recognition accuracy. The KCF algorithm is applied to the traffic lights tracking stage to improve the real-time detection. Experiments show that the method proposed in this paper has a good effect on the detection and tracking of traffic lights, meeting the detection requirements for traffic lights in intelligent traffic.

Acknowledgement. This work is supported by National Science Foundation of China 61373106.

References

1. Goetz, J., Zittlau, D., Happe, J.: Advanced driver assistance systems—enhancement of safety and comfort. Autotechnology **6**(6), 34–38 (2006)
2. Lin, F., Lai, Y., Lin, L., Yuan, Y.: A traffic sign recognition method based on deep visual feature. In: 2016 Progress in Electromagnetic Research Symposium (PIERS), Shanghai, 8–11 August, pp. 2247–2250 (2016)

3. Lai, Y., Wang, N., Yang, Y., Lin, L.: Traffic signs recognition and classification based on deep feature learning. In: 7th International Conference on Pattern Recognition Applications and Methods (ICPRAM), Madeira, Portugal, 16–18 January, pp. 622–629 (2018)
4. Zhang, G., Lin, F., Lin, L.: A novel method of front vehicle recognition. In: 2016 Progress in Electromagnetic Research Symposium (PIERS), Shanghai, 8–11 August, pp. 2126–2130 (2016)
5. Park, J.H., Jeong, C.: Real-time signal light detection. In: 2nd International Conference on Future Generation Communication and Networking Symposia, pp. 139–142. IEEE (2008)
6. Omachi, M., Omachi, S.: Traffic light detection with color and edge information. In: 2nd International Conference on Computer Science and Information Technology, pp. 284–287. IEEE (2009)
7. Gong, J., Jiang, Y., Xiong, G., et al.: The recognition and tracking of traffic lights based on color segmentation and Camshift for intelligent vehicles. In: Intelligent Vehicles Symposium (IV), pp. 431–435, IEEE (2010)
8. Bradski, G.R.: Computer vision face tracking for use in a perceptual user interface. Intel Technol. J. **Q2**, 214–219 (1998)
9. John, V., Yoneda, K., Qi, B., et al.: Traffic light recognition in varying illumination using deep learning and saliency map. In: 17th International Conference on Intelligent Transportation Systems (ITSC), pp. 2286–2291. IEEE (2014)
10. Fairfield, N., Urmson, C.: Traffic light mapping and detection. In: International Conference on Robotics and Automation (ICRA), pp. 5421–5426. IEEE (2011)
11. Krizhevsky, A., Sutskever, I., Hinton, G.E.: ImageNet classification with deep convolutional neural networks. In: Advances in Neural Information Processing Systems, pp. 1097–1105 (2012)
12. Cristianini, N., Shawe-Taylor, J.: An Introduction to Support Vector Machines and Other Kernel-Based Learning Methods. Cambridge University Press, Cambridge (2000)
13. Henriques, J.F., Caseiro, R., Martins, P., et al.: High-speed tracking with kernelized correlation filters. IEEE Trans. Pattern Anal. Mach. Intell. **37**(3), 583–596 (2015)
14. Su, C.H., Chiu, H.S., Hsieh, T.M.: An efficient image retrieval based on HSV color space. In: 2011 International Conference on Electrical and Control Engineering (ICECE), pp. 5746–5749. IEEE (2011)
15. Recky, M., Leberl, F.: Windows detection using k-means in CIE-lab color space. In: 20th International Conference on Pattern Recognition (ICPR), pp. 356–359. IEEE (2010)

Standardizing IT Systems on Public Transport: An Eco-Driving Assistance System Case Study

Joshua Puerta[1,2(✉)], Alfonso Brazález[1,2], Angel Suescun[1,2],
Olatz Iparraguirre[1,2], and Unai Atutxa[1,2]

[1] Ceit, Manuel Lardizabal 15, 20018 Donostia/San Sebastián, Spain
{jpuerta,abrazalez,asuescun,
oiparraguirre,uatutxa}@ceit.es
[2] Universidad de Navarra, Tecnun, Manuel Lardizabal 13,
20018 Donostia/San Sebastián, Spain

Abstract. As urbanization increases, mobility becomes more complex and supposes a major challenge for public transportation authorities. An approach to tackle this problem is to introduce systems that ease vehicle operation and monitoring. However, these systems are hard to maintain and integrate. On this paper, a new information technology (IT) architecture is introduced. Developed by the ITxPT association, the architecture aims to improve the cost-effective implementation of the IT modules in public transport fleets. This architecture has capitalized the work of several European projects to create a solid standard ready to test on field. Finally, a use case of the introduction of an eco-driving assistance system that employs this architecture in real operation is presented.

Keywords: ITS · IT architecture · Public transportation
Service oriented architecture

1 Introduction

According to the UN, latest research on world urbanization suggests that we are aiming for an urban world, with prospections of a 67% of world population living in cities by 2050 [1]. Such growth will imply a huge technological and management challenge and will force people to rethink how mobility inside urban areas should be understood. The aim is to provide better services for more people on more complex cities while reducing energy use [2, 3]. Several European projects aspire to achieve these goals through investing in public transport systems and vehicles [4, 5].

In order to travel efficiently between destinations, citizens share city buses, light rails and trains. The downsides of the public transport are the inconvenience and uncertainty associated with the limited frequency, stops number and capacity of these transportation means. A suitable option to overcome these issues is introducing Information Technology (IT) solutions to improve vehicles' energy efficiency, increase punctuality and empower citizens to choose the best mobility option according to their needs.

© Springer International Publishing AG, part of Springer Nature 2018
J. Moreno García-Loygorri et al. (Eds.): Nets4Cars 2018/Nets4Trains 2018/Nets4Aircraft 2018, LNCS 10796, pp. 149–158, 2018.
https://doi.org/10.1007/978-3-319-90371-2_15

Nowadays, vehicles from the fleets of the Public Transport Operators (PTO) contain first generation IT systems. These systems are functional but are hard to maintain, scale and substitute because of installation spots, difficult maintenance access, *ad-hoc* interfaces, redundancies and use of multi-connectors. This fact occurred due to the lack of standards that specify how the IT systems should blend with their surrounding ecosystem. Currently, the option taken by the manufacturers is to develop proprietary solutions that are non-trivial to configure and integrate.

This complexity involves direct negative consequences for the PTOs such as more expensive IT modules, high maintenance costs and slower technology adoption. Automatic Vehicle Monitoring Systems (AVMS), Automatic Passenger Counting (APC), eco-driving or ticketing, for example, are IT modules based on technologies that are evolving exponentially, introducing innovations and demanding more resources, such as processing power and connectivity. Keeping with technological trends lead to better quality of service and user acceptation, which is beneficial for public transport stakeholders.

In order to face the upcoming mobility challenges, public transportation must prepare to introduce plug-and-play robust IT systems. To improve technological adoption speed and reduce costs, the IT systems should be interoperable, easily configurable, monitorable, flexible and scalable. To achieve these characteristics, the International Association of Public Transport (UITP), vehicle manufacturers and PTOs consolidated the Information Technology for Public Transport (ITxPT) initiative. The initiative, which is based on several European projects, generates standards that define the guidelines and rules to develop IT systems that support the needs of the industry.

2   ITxPT

The ITxPT is an association that aims to promote the implementation of standards that allow the application of plug-and-play interoperable IT systems in the public transport context [6]. To achieve this goal, the ITxPT initiative defines an optimized IT architecture to handle different functionalities. ITxPT also provides support for the deployment of guidelines, and offers a technical platform to test and validate a complete installation.

Figure 1 shows the difference between a common architecture and the ITxPT architecture for an urban bus. On the upper image, a common IT architecture is shown. Each IT module is connected to the vehicle data line (Bus-FMS), has a specific driver screen and a unique antenna, convoluting the architecture with unnecessary redundancies. In the lower figure, the architecture suggested by ITxPT shows a reorganization of the functionalities provided by each IT module. Each module is connected to the IP network, were all the functionalities are shared through services. There is a module that bridges the vehicle data line with the IP network (FMS to IP), a display module (*Multi Application Driver Terminal* - MADT) and a single antenna. This architecture provides simplicity through the organization of functionalities as services and by providing a common communication layer.

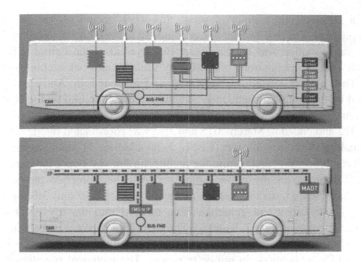

Fig. 1. Upper: common IT architecture on vehicle. Lower: ITxPT suggested IT architecture. Courtesy of the ITxPT association.

3 Architecture and Standards

The main goal of the architecture is to provide interoperability. In this context, interoperability describes the ability of an IT module to fully interact with another IT module of the system without explicit configurations or excessive use of resources. To achieve this feature, the architecture is divided in the following three layers:

- **Physical layer**: this layer contains the specifications for the IP-communication networks onboard PT vehicles and are collected in the technical specification TS13149-8 [9]. Some of the topics covered by this standard are energy efficiency through power modes, specific connectors for each type of used physical interface (power, audio, antenna, auxiliary, bus-FMS, and Ethernet backbone) and enclosure dimensioning. From an OSI model point of view, this layer includes enough specifications to define the OSI physical layer.

- **Communication protocol layer**: it defines the network and system architecture for onboard modules for communication and resource sharing. The main feature is the mandatory use of IP based networks to interconnect the vehicle, the IT modules and the back office. This layer stablishes addressing policies and the handling of service publication, subscription and discovery. The technical specification englobing this layer is the TS13149-7 [8]. This specification includes information to implement the data link, network, transport, session, presentation and application layers of the OSI model.

- **Service layer**: this layer describes the structure of the services and categorizes them in mandatory and custom services. This layer is also related with the application layer of the OSI model. Mandatory services must be implemented to obtain a full ITxPT compliance on the vehicle. An example of mandatory service is the module inventory service. The technical specification detailing this layer is the TS13149-9.

From a standardization point of view, this work capitalizes the results of three European projects. The first project that recognized the need for a common IT platform on public transportation was the European Bus System of the Future (EBSF) project [12], which laid the foundations of ITxPT by drafting an open architecture based on services. This project started in September 2008, ended in April 2013, and was coordinated by the UITP. Subsequently, the 3iBS project focused on the deployment of guidelines and building of a test bench for the IT systems [11]. This project started on October 2012 and ended in March 2015 and also was coordinated by the UITP. Finally, the continuation of the first project (EBSF_2) handled the IT standard introduction in existing fleets, retrofitting and testing the architecture in real operation conditions [10].

Figure 2 summarizes the relationships between the European projects that feed ITxPT for the research, documentation and validation. EBSF and 3iBS projects generated the specifications and guidelines that merged into the EN13149 standard as technical specifications (parts 7, 8 and 9). The CEN TC278 WG3 is realizing this work, which is a work group from the European Committee for Standardization (CEN) concerned with ITS applications in public transport. The technical specifications include rules for data communication inside public transport vehicles. Inside this standard, there are several parts, which correspond with the architecture layers: physical, communication protocol and service layer respectively. To complete the standardization, the EBSF_2 project provides context to test the IT architecture on real operation conditions, which validates the whole system [10].

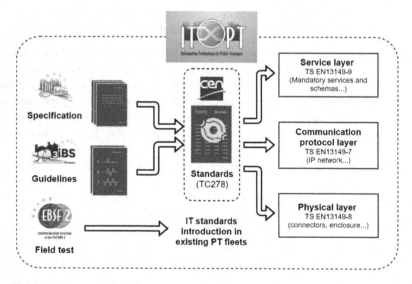

Fig. 2. Interconnection between core European projects and generated standards

4 Physical and Logical Implementations

In this section, details of the architecture implementation are provided. Apart from the architecture layers, there are three communication networks, which manage the information transmission from the onboard IT modules to the back office. These networks have a specific domain and range. The onboard IP networks include the backbone IP network, where all the IT modules are connected; and the public IP network, which provide internet access to the passengers. The back-office IP networks contain all the networks that are not in the vehicle such as PT operator network and PT authority network. To merge the onboard and back-office domains, the onboard to back office IP link includes specific subsystems that handle the communication between the two parts, such as the gateway and Over-the-Air modules.

As stated in the introduction, one of the objectives of the IT architecture is to implement interoperability through plug-and-play onboard IT systems. To achieve interoperability at network level, zero-configuration networking (*zeroconf*) technologies are suggested as one of the results of the research done in the EBSF project [12]. *Zeroconf* aims to provide plug-and-play networking by handling addressing, automatic distribution and resolution of hostnames and automatic location of network services.

An IT module can offer several services and must be available over the network. For this reason, IT modules must implement service publication, subscription and discovery utilities. Using the *zeroconf* perspective, the chosen technology to implement these utilities is Domain Name System – Service Discovery (DNS-SD).

Domain Name System (DNS) is an application layer protocol that matches addresses with names in a hierarchical and decentralized approach. DNS-SD exploits DNS protocol to program interfaces that discovers the services published on the network and their resolution to hostnames [7]. The name of a service must contain a definition of the service and a location. By using this technology, it is possible to decentralize services in different IT modules and interact with them just by knowing their domain name. A service record (SRV record) gives the location of the service so it can be located on the network. The Fig. 3 below shows the structure of a SRV record.

SRV Record structure

<modulename>._<service name>._<type>._<protocol>.<domain>
TTL class priority weight port target

Example: nonvis._inventory._itxpt_socket._tcp.local
3600 IN SRV 0 0 9 nonvis.local.

Fig. 3. SRV record structure with the inventory use case as example

To publish the SRV records, multicast DNS (mDNS) is used, which resolves the host names into IP addresses without using a local name server. Summarizing, by using mDNS/DNS-SD, an IT module plugged into the network will be automatically configured and discoverable by other services.

For the implementation of these protocols in IT modules, ITxPT promotes the use of open technologies. Taking into account the kind of embedded system contained in the onboard devices, there are different implementation options for *Zeroconf*. If the embedded processor runs an operative system, there are several open software packages like *Bonjour*, *Avahi* and *jmDNS*. If a *bare metal* or real-time operative system (RTOS) approach is taken, there are less implementation options. For instance, a specific compilation for the target processor of one of the mentioned packages or a custom implementation of the protocol stack might be the only solutions.

Leaving the physical network and topology aside, to handle interoperability from a logical perspective, Service oriented Architecture (SoA) is employed. SoA stablishes strict separation of concerns between the members of the network. This perspective enforces the encapsulation of the implementation and focuses on robust interfaces. In the case of introducing a new module or replacing an old one, the only requirement is to keep the interface. Service interface implementation depends on which type of interface is chosen (i.e.: sockets and http). Most common services focus on receiving and sending information containing module data, which is structured. To handle this kind of data sharing, XML schemas are used. Summarizing, SoA is what grants to the architecture a high scalability and time reduction of integrating new utilities into the vehicle and back-office.

5   Use Case: Retrofitting an Eco-Driving Assistance System

The EBSF_2 project aims to develop the new generation of urban bus system by improving energy efficiency and the appearance of the bus to attract a higher number of users [10]. The project attempts six key areas for innovation approximately, including green driver assistance system and vehicle design. The key areas are materialized through technological innovations witch take place in 12 European cities, where public transport organizations lend their infrastructures to run the trials. Further details of the technological innovations are on Table 1. In the framework of the EBSF_2 project, one of the main objectives is the introduction of IT standards in existing fleets, so the suggested IT architecture is tested in several demonstration sites.

Table 1. EBSF_2 demonstration sites

City	Priority topics
Barcelona	Energy strategy, driver assistance, IT standard introduction
Dresden	Vehicle design
Gothenburg	Energy strategy, vehicle design, urban infrastructure
Helsinki	Energy strategy, driver assistance
London	IT standard introduction
Lyon	Energy strategy, driver assistance, ZEV mode for hybrid bus
Madrid	Driver assistance
Paris	Intelligent garage and predictive maintenance, urban infrastructure
Paris Area	IT standard introduction, intelligent garage and predictive maintenance
Ravenna	IT standard introduction, intelligent garage and predictive maintenance
San Sebastian	Driver assistance, vehicle design, IT standard introduction, intelligent garage and predictive maintenance
Stuttgart	Energy strategy

One of the demonstration sites was San Sebastian [13], which has run four technological innovations: two of them centered in eco-driving assistance systems: one focused on vehicle design; and the last one focused on introducing intelligent garage and predictive maintenance. The demonstration, which was organized by ceit-IK4 and the involved PTO was DBUS, lasted for 4 months (April 2017–July 2017) where several indicators were measured to evaluate the driver's acceptance and operational aspects of the system.

The studied use case focuses on a non-visual eco-driving assistance system (NONVIS) which aims to provide information to the drivers about their eco-driving performance by using auditory and haptic stimulation. The NONVIS IT module consists on an on-board unit with peripherals to handle sound and vibrations.

NONVIS processes information about the vehicle status, operation data and eco-driving inputs, therefore, the module has to interact with other devices. Taking advantage of the project context where IT architectures were to be implemented, ITxPT architecture was chosen as the way of connecting systems. As there were not full ITxPT compliant vehicles on the DBUS fleet, a subset of the IT architecture was used, specifically the features including IP networking and service orientation.

The legacy module that provided data to NONVIS is called EKOBUS and it was retrofitted into the architecture. Figure 4 drafts a global view of the implementation. In simple terms, the two IT modules are connected to the IP network automatically and interact by publishing and subscribing to hosted services.

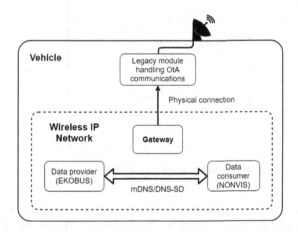

Fig. 4. Network schematic of a vehicle containing NONVIS

Regarding to the network, stablishing a physical backbone IP network was unrealizable due to incompatibilities of legacy modules with the Ethernet physical layer, so a wireless local IP network was stablished through the standard IEEE 802.11 (Wi-Fi). To protect the network, several security protocols were adopted such as WPA2. The network elements were the following ones: a gateway that generated the wireless backbone IP network and interfaced with outside systems, EKOBUS module that provided other modules with vehicle data and the NONVIS module that transformed driving information into non-visual stimuli. The EKOBUS module was retrofitted to couple with the ITxPT architecture.

From the service orientation point of view, EKOBUS module published SRV registers that broadcasted the service over the network. Due to the use of mDNS/DNS-SD, the service was discoverable in the network and the address could be resolved.

Figure 5 explains the communication sequence. To retrieve the data from EKO-BUS, the NONVIS module must send an XML schema subscribing to the service. This subscription schema contains several fields that confirm the identity and integrity of the subscriber. If the subscribing module has permission to access, the data EKOBUS starts the data stream to the subscribed module in XML format synchronously. Inside each XML, there are fields that include vehicle state data such as speed and RPMs, route and driver information and eco-driving alerts.

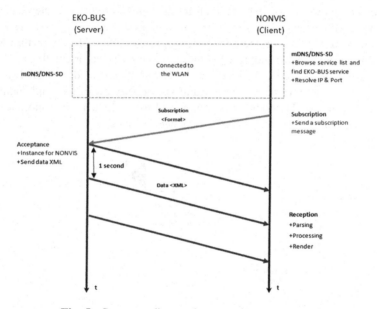

Fig. 5. Sequence diagram between the two systems

After the data acquisition, NONVIS processes the received input and renders the stimuli corresponding to the eco-driving performance. When the NONVIS module reach an ending state, it sends another XML schema to unsubscribe from the service, so it lets the EKOBUS module know when the communication instance can be closed.

6 Conclusions

As mentioned before, for the last years, the ITxPT initiative has participated in different projects to provide a standardized method to build IT systems through the development of an architecture that has been tested in simulators and field tests. By creating an architecture that focuses on interoperability and modularity, maintenance cost reduction and simple up-to-date services are achieved.

The NONVIS demonstration in San Sebastian further proved that the ITxPT architecture for in-vehicle IT module communication is effective and is ready for operation. Even though the retrofit of the legacy modules was complicated, implementing the architecture lead to quickly replaceable modules with shorter maintenance times. Regarding the module development phase, the adoption of the architecture simplified testing and prototyping due its ubiquitous characteristics. Figures and results on collected data are yet to come on final deliverables but from field observations, the subscriptions and data streams worked robustly, providing of high rate of transaction success and low latency. Moreover, using Wi-Fi as a substitute of physical IP network for retrofitting purposes was proved as a practical and efficient solution, but several aspects such security must be improved to allow out-of-demo retrofit deployments. For instance, using WPA3 protocol with signal limitations might be an interesting starting point.

In the context of EBSF_2 project, other demo sites implemented more technological innovations using the discussed IT architecture. In the case of London, their ITxPT architecture implementation included a complex multi-supplier environment, including key IT systems such as AVMS and back-office communications. Specifically, the London demo goal was tracking four buses equipped with an AVMS system provided by different manufacturers [14]. The London demo proves that the architecture can handle multiple IT systems providers, giving coherent information to the back office at the same time.

Summarizing, the EBSF_2 project confirmed that the architecture is suitable for real operation, which helped to involve more stakeholders to the development of the standard. From a technological penetration perspective, in less than a year several vehicles and modules have acquired the ITxPT label [15], qualifying them as full compliant systems.

Acknowledgements. This work is part of EBSF_2, a 3-year European research project to develop the new generation of urban buses under the H2020 framework. The authors would like to thank to the UITP, ITxPT association, DBUS and DATIK for their support on the development of this project.

References

1. United Nations Population Division: Department of Economic and Social Affairs, "World Urbanization Prospects" (2014)
2. Mobility 4 EU consortium: "Societal needs and requirements for future transportation and mobility as well as opportunities and challenges of current solutions" (2017)
3. Van Audenhove, F.-J., Koriichuk, O., Dauby, L., Pourbarx, J.: The Future of Urban Mobility 2.0: Imperatives to Shape Extended Mobility Ecosystems of Tomorrow (2014)
4. Tozzi, M., Bousse, Y., Karlsson, M., Guida, U.: A European initiative for more efficient and attractive bus systems: the EBSF-2 project. Transp. Res. Procedia **14**, 2640–2648 (2016)
5. Glotz-Richter, M., Koch, H.: Electrification of public transport in cities (horizon 2020 ELIPTIC project). Transp. Res. Procedia **14**, 2614–2619 (2016)

6. ITxPT association: ITxPT Wiki - General information. http://wiki.itxpt.org/index.php?title= ITxPT_Wiki. Accessed 30 Jan 2018
7. Gulbrandsen, A., Vixie, P.: A DNS RR for specifying the location of services (DNS SRV) (1996). https://www.rfc-editor.org/info/rfc2052
8. EPL 278: CEN/TS 13149-7:2015, "Public transport. Road vehicle scheduling and control systems. System and Network Architecture". BSI (2015)
9. EPL 278: CEN/TS 13149-8:2013, "Public transport. Road vehicle scheduling and control systems. Physical layer for IP communication". BSI (2013)
10. UITP: "About EBSF_2 | ebsf2.eu". http://ebsf2.eu/about-ebsf2. Accessed 3 Mar 2018
11. UITP: "About 3iBS—3iBS - intelligent, innovative, integrated Bus System". http://www. 3ibs.eu/en/about-3ibs. Accessed 3 Mar 2018
12. UITP: "EBSF - European Bus System of the Future". http://www.uitp.org/ebsf-european-bus-system-future. Accessed 3 Mar 2018
13. UITP: "San Sebastian | ebsf2.eu". http://ebsf2.eu/demonstration-sites/san_sebastian. Accessed 3 Mar 2018
14. UITP: "London | ebsf2.eu". http://ebsf2.eu/demonstration-sites/london. Accessed 3 Mar 2018
15. ITxPT association: "ITxPT labels the first on-board device for Public Transport vehicles". http://itxpt.org/en/news/itxpt-labels-the-first-on-board-device-for-public-transport-vehicles. Accessed 3 Mar 2018

Fading Characterization of 73 GHz Millimeter-Wave V2V Channel Based on Real Measurements

Hui Wang[1], Xuefeng Yin[1,2(✉)], Xuesong Cai[1], Haowen Wang[3],
Ziming Yu[4], and Juyul Lee[5]

[1] College of Electronics and Information Engineering, Tongji University,
Shanghai, China
{1252759,yinxuefeng,caixuesong}@tongji.edu.cn
[2] National Computer and Information Technology Practical Education
Demonstration Center, Tongji University, Shanghai, China
[3] Shanghai Research Center for Wireless Communications (WiCo),
Shanghai, China
haowen.wang@wico.sh
[4] 5G Research Department, Huawei Technologies Corporation, Chengdu, China
yuziming@huawei.com
[5] Electronics and Telecommunications Research Institute (ETRI),
Daejeon, South Korea
juyul@etri.re.kr

Abstract. In this work, a recently conducted measurement campaign for millimeter wave (mm-wave) vehicle to vehicle (V2V) propagation channel characterization is introduced. Two vehicles carrying a transmitter (Tx) and a receiver (Rx) respectively were driven towards each other at an average speed of 60 km/h in an urban area of Jiading District, Shanghai, China. The measurement was conducted with 409.6 MHz bandwidth at center frequency 73 GHz. The parameters investigated include the large-scale fading and small-scale fading coefficients. Specifically, a 2-slope path-loss model was proposed. Six kinds of distributions of analytical expressions were used to fit the fast fading distribution. The results show that the fast fading distribution changes from Rician to Nakagami, finally to lognormal with the distance between the Tx and the Rx increases.

Keywords: Vehicle to vehicle communication · Channel measurement
Millimeter-wave · Channel fading characterization

1 Introduction

Mm-wave communications are going to be used for V2V communications [1]. Recently, the mm-wave V2V communications have been paid a tremendous attention. This is due to the fact that the mm-wave communication is expected to enable gigabyte per second data transmission for the future intelligent transportation systems. In such systems, a large amount of sensors are going to be deployed in the vehicles.

© Springer International Publishing AG, part of Springer Nature 2018
J. Moreno García-Loygorri et al. (Eds.): Nets4Cars 2018/Nets4Trains 2018/Nets4Aircraft 2018, LNCS 10796, pp. 159–168, 2018.
https://doi.org/10.1007/978-3-319-90371-2_16

Furthermore, in order to realize unmanned manoeuvered vehicle technologies, big data needs to be exchanged between terminals and the cloud. For these applications, it is important to develop V2V mm-wave communication systems and techniques. As a fundamental research, the channel characterization for the mm-wave frequency bands is important for understanding the wave propagation in a variety of vehicular scenarios.

The reasons to investigate the propagation channel characteristics for mm-wave channels are as follows: Assuming that mm-wave propagation occurs along straight rays, this ray-alike propagation and the high attenuation of the mm-wave may jointly lead to the effect that the propagation does not involve multiple bounces. For the outdoor V2V scenario, it can be expected that there are not many multipath components existing in the channel, mainly resulting from the high attenuation and the directionality of antennas [2–4]. Meanwhile, the rapidly varying environment can introduce non-stationarity into the channel. Therefore, how to maintain a stable connection between the Tx and the Rx that are installed in different vehicles is of great importance for the design and performance evaluation of V2V communication systems.

V2V communications have been a hot-spot for research and industry as the rapid development of unmanned technologies. Channel models established so far can be divided into two classes: the simulation-based models and the measurement-based models. In the former category, the so-called geometrical scattering models are widely investigated. Most of them based on the assumption that scatterers are distributed either regularly, e.g. on one-ring, two-rings, elliptical ring, cylinder, ellipsoid, and etc., or irregularly [5, 6]. With the ideal assumptions of scatterer distributions, channel characteristics are derived which constitute a series of geometry-based stochastic models [7–15]. In the measurement based category, most V2V measurements are conducted at sub-6 GHz band [16–21]. Only few researchers conducted the mm-wave V2V channel measurements. For instance, the impact of interference from side lanes was studied in [22]. The time varying K-factor under the influence of velocity, vibrations and road quality was illustrated in [23]. The blockage characteristics including delay, angular spread and blockage loss was investigated in [24]. These studies facilitate evaluating system performance analytically and alleviate the difficulties in designing communication techniques. However, as far as we concerned, the fading characterization of V2V channel at 73 GHz has not been experimentally investigated based on measurements due to the expensive cost of equipments and the difficulties of conducting measurements.

In our work, a road measurement of V2V channel at center frequency of 73 GHz was carried out. The large-scale channel parameters such as path loss and the small-scale channel parameters e.g. fast fading coefficients are investigated. Furthermore, a 2-slope path loss model was proposed in the work and the statistical characteristics of shadowing and fast fading are investigated. Six types of distribution functions are used to find the best-fit for fast fading coefficients. Rician K-factor and m-parameter of Nakagami are calculated for modelling and in-depth analysis.

The rest of the work is organized as follows: In Sect. 2, we introduce the measurement equipments and scenarios. In Sect. 3, the measurement results are analysed. Finally, the conclusive remarks are presented in Sect. 4.

2 Measurement Equipment and Scenarios

In the measurement campaign, the WiCo mm-wave channel sounder was adopted. A PN sequence modulated with QPSK and raised-cosine pulse-shaped was exploited to sound the channel at the center frequency of 73 GHz. The sequence length was 4095 chips. The bandwidth was 409.6 MHz. Two rubidium clocks were used to synchronize the Tx and the Rx. GPS devices were used to record position information which can be used for location mapping. Two identical antennas with 10° Half-Power-Bandwidth (HPBW) and gains of 25 dBi were adopted as Tx and Rx. The front view of sounder, the side view of horn antenna are shown in Fig. 1. As illustrated in Fig. 2, two sets of devices were placed into two 7-passenger cars separately. In order to obtain better signal-to-noise ratio (SNR), the Tx and Rx antennas were mounted on the car roof, which aims to avoid the car penetration loss. The heights of both antennas were around 1.5 m. Figure 3 shows the satellite map of the measurement area. The yellow line denotes the route of measurement. Two cars accelerated from 0 to 60 km/h and then were driven toward each other at a stable speed. The measurement campaign was

(a) The front view of WiCo sounder   (b) The side view of horn antenna used in measurement campaign

Fig. 1. Pictures of measurement devices

(a)   (b)

Fig. 2. Photographs taken when the equipments are placed in car.

conducted in the urban area of Jiading district, Shanghai. The route is adjacent to an underground station and business buildings. Hence, the traffic was busy during the measurements. The whole route is about 1.05 km. The route contains four lanes among where no obstacles lie. The maximum speed of the car is 60 km/h. Some of the measurement specifications are listed in Table 1.

Fig. 3. Satellite map of driving route (Color figure online)

Table 1. Measurement specifications

Center frequency	73 GHz	Sounding signal	PN sequence
Bandwidth	409.6 MHz	Sequence length	4095
Antenna height	1.5 m	Antenna type	Horn antenna
Antenna gain	25 dBi	Average speed	60 km/h
HPBW of antenna	10°	Total distance	1.05 km

3 Measurement Results

3.1 Large-Scale Fading

Figure 4 shows the power gain of the narrowband channel after averaging out the fast fading. The black curve represents the results obtained through the measurements, and

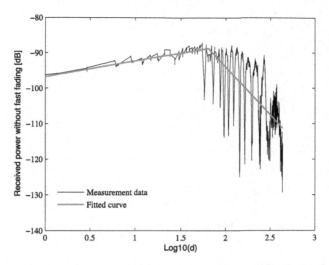

Fig. 4. Narrow-band power after removing fast fading and its fitted curve (Color figure online)

the red curve with analytical expressions is fitted to the black curve in terms of the least-mean-square sense. The expression of the fitted curve is:

$$PL(d) = \begin{cases} 4.4 \cdot \log(d) - 96.8 & 0 < d < 63 \text{ m} \\ -27.0 \cdot \log(d) - 40.0 & 63 \text{ m} < d < 437 \text{ m} \end{cases} \qquad (1)$$

Obviously, the fitted curve can be divided into 2 parts. It should be noted that in the first part, the power increases as the distance enlarges. This is of course not the exact characteristics of pure propagation channels, since the HPBW of horn antenna is only 10° which creates a strong directional selectivity. Furthermore, two cars were driven in different lanes, which leads to the occasions that the Rx and Tx are not aligned when two cars are close to each other. In those cases, an obviously lower received power is observed due to the misalignment. In the second part of the fitted curve, it can be observed that the received power declines with significant fluctuations as the Tx-Rx distance increases. This severe variation behavior is mainly caused by the influence of vehicles existing nearby. The obstruction from cars was randomly present. Hence, the shadowing caused by vehicles was also random, which leads to the fluctuation of received power. Figure 5 demonstrates the cumulative distribution function (CDF) of the shadowing existing in the 2 parts respectively. It can be clearly observed that the shadowing in the second part is much larger than the first one. This is reasonable since the shadowing is mainly caused by obstruction, and the obstruction due to cars in the later portion of the curve happens more frequently in our measurement campaign.

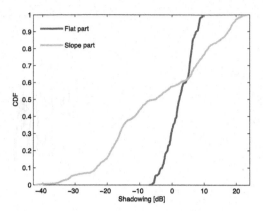

Fig. 5. CDFs of shadowing

3.2 Small-Scale Fading

Small-scale fading is also termed as the fast fading or multi-path fading in literature [25]. In our work, we adopted a distance window with the length of 40 wavelengths to study the statistics of a group of fast fading samples observed through the window. The Kolmogorov-Smirnov (K-S) test is used to find the best fitted distribution for the fast fading coefficients [26]. Six distribution functions of known expressions, i.e., Nakagami, Lognormal, Rician, Rayleigh, Gamma and Weibull are applied. The distribution with minimum K-S statistics is regarded the best-fitted among these options. Figure 6 illustrates the best-fitted distribution for the fast fading at different distances. It can be observed that in the measurements considered here, the best-fitted distribution of fast fading varies when the Tx-Rx distance changes. Figure 7 illustrates the Probability Density Function (PDF) of best fitted distribution. Most groups of fast fading follow lognormal distributions. In addition, most lognormal distributions are found when the

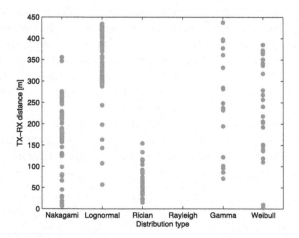

Fig. 6. Distributions of fast fading vs Tx-Rx distance

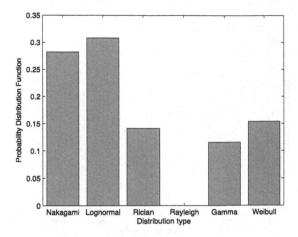

Fig. 7. The PDF of fast fading coefficients

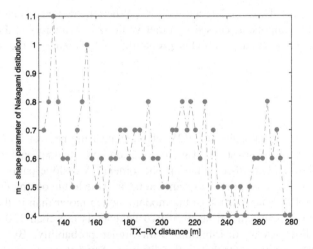

Fig. 8. Nakagami m-factor vs Tx-Rx distance

Tx- Rx distance is larger than 288 m. When the Tx-Rx distance is between 120 m and 288 m, most groups of fast fading follow Nakagami distributions. The m-parameter of Nakagami distribution is reported in Fig. 8. It can be observed from Fig. 8 that the values of m decrease as the Tx-Rx distance increases. This implies that the fast fading becomes severer when two vehicles move away from each other. The fast fading is regarded worse than Rayleigh, since almost all m-parameters are less than 1 [27]. When the distance is less than 120 m, most groups of fast fading follow Rician distribution. Figure 9 demonstrates the Rician K-factor versus the Tx-Rx distance. It is interesting to find that the Rician K-factor increases firstly and then decreases. The breaking point is about 50 m. Two possible reasons are postulated as follows. One is that the car surfaces cause lots of multi-path components when the two cars are close to each other. The

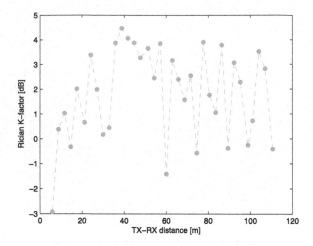

Fig. 9. Rician K-factor vs Tx-Rx distance

other one is because Tx is not aligned with Rx. When the distance is larger than 50 m, more multi-path components caused by other vehicles or scatterers in the scenario can be captured by the antenna with higher probability, which leads to the decrease of the Rician K-factor.

4   Conclusions

A road measurement campaign of V2V channel measurement at 73 GHz was conducted in this work. The study was focused on the channel fading in terms of large-scale fading and small-scale fading phenomena. A 2-slope path-loss model was proposed and the breaking point was found at 63 m. Due to the obstruction of vehicles, the shadowing of the later portion of the model is much larger than in the first part. As for the fast fading, when the distance of two vehicles is less than 120 m, fast fading coefficients follow Rician distributions with higher probability. By computing the Rician K-factors, we can infer that as the distance of two vehicles increases, the LOS component become stronger first and then weaker during this distance range. Here, the breaking point is observed to be about 50 m. When the distance is between 120 and 288 m, the fast fading follows Nakagami distributions. By observing the m-parameter of Nakagami distribution, it can be known that the multi-path fading from cars nearby is insignificant as two cars are close to each other. When the distance is larger than 288 m, most samples of fast fading follow lognormal distributions. These findings can be adopted for generating time-variant channel realizations for evaluating mm-wave V2V communication systems and technologies.

Acknowledgment. The authors wish to express their thanks to Mr. Jianguo Xie, Mr. Kai Tu and Mr. Jingxiang Hong for conducting the measurement. This work was jointly supported by National Natural Science Foundation of China (NSFC) (Grant No. 61471268), the Key Project "5G Ka frequency bands and higher and lower frequency band cooperative trail system research and development" under Grant 2016ZX03001015 of China Ministry of Industry and Information Technology, the HongKong, Macao and Taiwan Science & Technology Cooperation Program of China under Grant 2014DFT10290, and Institute for Information & communications Technology Promotion (IITP) grant funded by the Korean government (MSIT) ["Development of time-space based spectrum engineering technologies for the preemptive using of frequency"].

References

1. Giordani, M., Zanella, A., Zorzi, M.: Millimeter wave communication in vehicular networks: challenges and opportunities. In: International Conference on Modern Circuits and Systems Technologies, pp. 1–6 (2017)
2. Viriyasitavat, W., Boban, M., Tsai, H.M., Vasilakos, A.: Vehicular communications: survey and challenges of channel and propagation models. IEEE Veh. Technol. Mag. **10**(2), 55–66 (2015)
3. Cheng, X., Yang, L., Shen, X.: D2D for intelligent transportation systems: a feasibility study. IEEE Trans. Intell. Transp. Syst. **16**(4), 1784–1793 (2015)
4. Fallgren, M., Timus, B.: Scenarios, requirements and KPIs for 5G mobile and wireless system (2013)
5. Yin, X., Cheng, X.: Propagation Channel Characterization, Parameter Estimation, and Modeling for Wireless Communications. Wiley-IEEE Press (2014)
6. Cheng, X., Wang, C.X., Laurenson, D.I., Salous, S., Vasilakos, A.V.: An adaptive geometry-based stochastic model for non-isotropic MIMO mobile to mobile channels. IEEE Trans. Wirel. Commun. **8**(9), 4824–4835 (2009)
7. Patzold, M., Hogstad, B.O., Youssef, N.: Modeling, analysis, and simulation of MIMO mobile to mobile fading channels. IEEE Trans. Wirel. Commun. **7**(2), 510–520 (2008)
8. Liang, X., Zhao, X., Li, S., Wang, Q., Lu, W.: A 3D geometry-based scattering model for vehicle to vehicle wideband MIMO relay-based cooperative channels, vol. 13, no. 10, pp. 1–10 (2016)
9. Cheng, X., Yao, Q., Wen, M., Wang, C.X., Song, L.Y., Jiao, B.L.: Wideband channel modeling and intercarrier interference cancellation for vehicle-to-vehicle communication systems. IEEE J. Sel. Areas Commun. **31**(9), 434–448 (2013)
10. Zhao, X., Liang, X., Li, S., Ai, B.: Two-cylinder and multi-ring GBSSM for realizing and modeling of vehicle-to-vehicle wideband MIMO channels. IEEE Trans. Intell. Transp. Syst. **17**(10), 2787–2799 (2016)
11. Li, Y., He, R., Lin, S., Guan, K., He, D., Wang, Q., Zhong, Z.: Cluster-based non- stationary channel modeling for vehicle-to-vehicle communications. IEEE Antennas Wirel. Propagation Lett. **PP**(99), 1 (2016)
12. Yuan, Y., Wang, C.X., He, Y., Alwakeel, M.M., Aggoune, E.H.M.: 3D wideband non-stationary geometry-based stochastic models for non-isotropic MIMO vehicle to vehicle channels. IEEE Trans. Wirel. Commun. **14**(12), 6883–6895 (2015)
13. Guan, K., Ai, B., Nicolas, M.L., Geise, R., Muller, A., Zhong, Z., Kurner, T.: On the influence of scattering from traffic signs in vehicle-to-x communications. IEEE Trans. Veh. Technol. **65**(8), 5835–5849 (2016)
14. Ghazal, A., Yuan, Y., Wang, C.X., Zhang, Y., Yao, Q., Zhou, H., Duan, W.: A non-stationary IMT-advanced MIMO channel model for high-mobility wireless communication systems (2017)

15. Azpilicueta, L., Aguirre, E., Falcone, F., Lopez-Iturri, P., Alejos, A.V.: Radio channel characterization of vehicle-to-infrastructure communications at 60 GHz. In: International Conference on Electromagnetics in Advanced Applications (2015)
16. He, R., Renaudin, O., Kolmonen, V.M., Haneda, K., Zhong, Z., Ai, B., Oestges, C.: A dynamic wideband directional channel model for vehicle to vehicle communications. IEEE Trans. Industr. Electron. **62**(12), 7870–7882 (2015)
17. Ibdah, Y., Ding, Y.: Mobile-to-mobile channel measurements at 1.85 GHz in suburban environments. IEEE Trans. Commun. **63**(2), 466–475 (2015)
18. Cheng, L., Henty, B.E., Stancil, D.D., Bai, F., Mudalige, P.: Mobile vehicle-to-vehicle narrow-band channel measurement and characterization of the 5.9 GHz dedicated short range communication (DSRC) frequency band. IEEE J. Sel. Areas Commun. **25**(8), 1501–1516 (2007)
19. Walter, M., Fiebig, U.C., Zajic, A.: Experimental verification of the non-stationary statistical model for V2V scatter channels. In: Vehicular Technology Conference, pp. 1–5 (2014)
20. Shemshaki, M., Lasser, G., Ekiz, L., Mecklenbrauker, C.: Empirical path loss model fit from measurements from a vehicle-to-infrastructure network in Munich at 5.9 GHz. In: IEEE International Symposium on Personal, Indoor, and Mobile Radio Communications, pp. 181–185 (2015)
21. He, R., Molisch, A.F., Tufvesson, F., Wang, R., Zhang, T., Li, Z., Zhong, Z., Ai, B.: Measurement-based analysis of relaying performance for Vehicle-to-Vehicle communications with large vehicle obstructions. In: Vehicular Technology Conference, pp. 1–6 (2017)
22. Petrov, V., Kokkoniemi, J., Moltchanov, D., Lehtomaki, J., Juntti, M., Koucheryavy, Y.: The impact of interference from the side lanes on mmwave/THz band V2V communication systems with directional antennas. IEEE Trans. Veh. Technol. **PP**(99), 1 (2018)
23. Blumenstein, J., Prokes, A., Vychodil, J., Pospisil, M., Mikulasek, T.: Time-varying k factor of the mm-wave vehicular channel: velocity, vibrations and the road quality influence. In: 2017 IEEE 28th Annual International Symposium on Personal, Indoor, and Mobile Radio Communications (PIMRC), pp. 1–5, October 2017
24. Park, J.J., Lee, J., Liang, J., Kim, K.W., Lee, K.C., Kim, M.D.: Millimeter wave vehicular blockage characteristics based on 28 GHz measurements. In: 2017 IEEE 86th Vehicular Technology Conference (VTC-Fall), pp. 1–5, September 2017
25. Cai, X., Peng, B., Yin, X., Perez, A.: Hough-transform-based cluster identification and modeling for V2V channels based on measurements. IEEE Trans. Veh. Technol. **PP**(99), 1 (2017)
26. Millard, J., Kurz, L.: The Kolmogorov-Smirnov tests in signal detection (corresp.). IEEE Trans. Inf. Theory **13**(2), 341–342 (1967)
27. Goldsmith, A.: Wireless Communications (2007)

A Flexible TDMA Overlay Protocol
for Vehicles Platooning

Aqsa Aslam[1,3](✉) ⓘ, Luis Almeida[1,2,3] ⓘ, and Frederico Santos[1,4] ⓘ

[1] IT - Instituto de Telecomunicações, Porto, Portugal
engr.aqsa.tl@gmail.com, lda@fe.up.pt, fred@isec.pt
[2] CISTER - Centro de Inv. em Sistemas de Tempo-Real, Porto, Portugal
[3] FEUP - Universidade do Porto, Porto, Portugal
[4] ISEC - Instituto Politécnico de Coimbra, Coimbra, Portugal

Abstract. Vehicular Ad-hoc Networks (VANETs) can enable a wide range of vehicle coordination applications such as platooning. A good use of the communication channel is paramount for an adequate quality of service. Currently, IEEE 802.11p is the standard used in VANETS and relies on CSMA/CA, which is prone to collisions that degrade the channel quality. This has led to recent proposals for TDMA-based overlay protocols that synchronize vehicles beacons to prevent or reduce collisions. In this paper, we propose RA-TDMAp that puts together properties of two previous works. On one hand, it allows the nodes in one platoon to remain synchronized even in the presence of interfering traffic, e.g. from other vehicles, by adapting the phase of the TDMA round to escape periodic interference. On the other hand, it reduces channel occupation by having just the leader transmitting with high power, to reach all the platoon at once, while the followers transmit with low power. The order of transmission is such that the leader gathers information from the whole platoon in just one round. We simulated RA-TDMAp in realistic conditions using the PLEXE simulation framework. We show the phase adaptation of the TDMA round and we compare RA-TDMAp to state of the art protocols tailored for platooning, with three networking metrics: channel busy ratio, collisions and safe time ratio, all of which confirm the superiority of RA-TDMAp.

Keywords: VANETs · MAC protocol · TDMA · CSMA/CA

1 Introduction

Vehicular Ad-hoc Networks (VANETs) are an important component of an Intelligent Transportation System (ITS) enabling communication among vehicles for collaborative applications, both safety-oriented, e.g., platooning, and non-safety ones, e.g., infotainment.

Safety applications are particularly demanding concerning the communication channel reliability, requiring less packet drops, e.g., caused by access collisions, and lower latency. Existing standards, namely WAVE in the US and ITS-G5 in Europe, use the IEEE 802.11p DSRC (Dedicated Short-Range Communication) protocol [1] that relies on CSMA/CA distributed access arbitration with different enhancements. For example, ITS-G5 adds Distributed Congestion Control (DCC) which acts on certain

J. Moreno García-Loygorri et al. (Eds.): Nets4Cars 2018/Nets4Trains 2018/Nets4Aircraft 2018, LNCS 10796, pp. 169–180, 2018.
https://doi.org/10.1007/978-3-319-90371-2_17

MAC parameters (e.g., transmission frequencies, data rate and power levels) to reduce channel occupation. However, CSMA/CA does not preclude collisions and the channel quality can degrade insignificant under intense traffic [1, 2].

In this paper, we focus on the specific case of vehicles platooning applications. We investigate the use of the RA-TDMA framework [3] on top of IEEE 802.11p to combine the benefits of both TDMA and CSMA/CA paradigms, namely collisions reduction through synchronization of beacons and efficient bandwidth usage with asynchronous access. This framework is particularly effective in this scope in which most communications are periodic and with similar period. It allows synchronizing the beacons of the vehicles engaged in each platoon independently, thus avoiding global TDMA schemes that synchronize all vehicles in range. Then, the adaptive feature of the framework detects the delays caused by interference from other vehicles outside the platoon and shifts correspondingly the TDMA round, escaping that periodic interference.

However, the original RA-TDMA protocol was developed for teams of robots operating in a WiFi infrastructured area. This is not compatible with vehicle platooning where minimizing the channel occupation requires a judicious use of transmission power. Thus, we take inspiration from the technique used in [4] in which the leader of each platoon, only, transmits its beacons at high power while the other platoon members use lower power beacons and forward information of each other in a multi-hop scheme. We combine this technique with the adaptive feature of RA-TDMA and we propose the new RA-TDMAp protocol, which is tailored for platooning applications. We use the PLEXE/ Veins/ OMNeT++ simulation framework [5] to compare both approaches under similar platooning operational conditions, as well as with the native CSMA/CA mechanism of IEEE 802.11p. We can see that our adaptive approach brings a clear improvement of the channel quality with a near one order of magnitude reduction in collisions and busy time ratio, and a visible increase in the safe time ratio.

The remainder of the paper starts by presenting state of the art TDMA based protocols for Vehicle-to-vehicle communications, highlighting the fact that avoiding collisions at the MAC layer in an efficient way is still open. Then Sect. 3 presents the PLEXE simulation framework while our approach using RA-TDMAp is presented in Sect. 4. Section 5 presents simulation results under different traffic conditions and Sect. 6 concludes the paper.

2   Related Work

The literature on MAC protocols for VANETs is vast. These protocols need to deal with highly dynamic topologies, aiming, at the same time, at providing equal access to the channel for all vehicles, improving the reliability of the communication channel and increasing the efficiency of channel utilization [6, 7].

ITS-G5 proposes Cooperative Awareness Messages (CAMs) broadcast at fixed intervals in the range of 0.1 s to 1 s for cooperative applications, e.g., platooning [8]. These messages contain vehicle state information such as speed, position, and heading, enabling neighbor vehicles to share their states. CAMs are also typically known as beacons in the vehicular networks domain, i.e., periodic messages broadcast to all one-hop neighbors [9].

One of the problems of the CSMA/CA native arbitration of IEEE 802.11p that supports ITS-G5 and WAVE is a potential excess of collisions and channel degradation in dense traffic scenarios. To alleviate this problem several TDMA-based MAC protocols and general information dissemination protocols [9] have been proposed for VANETs that synchronize beacons to reduce collisions and channel congestion. Here we present just the main features of some representative protocols in that class that address certain issues in specific scenarios. A longer discussion and a possible taxonomy can be found in [10].

VeMAC [11] is a contention-free multi-channel protocol for VANETs aiming at structured highway scenarios and using the Control Channel (CCH) of IEEE 802.11p. It targets reducing access and merging collisions caused by vehicle mobility, assigning disjoint sets of time slots to vehicles moving in opposite directions and to the roadside unit (RSU). VeSOMAC [12] also aims at highways but does not rely on infrastructure (RSUs) or leader vehicles in platoons. It uses an in-band signalling scheme that carries information about allocated slots supporting fast slot reconfiguration following topology changes, e.g., when platoons merge. DMMAC [13] is an alternative to IEEE 802.11p that provides an adaptive broadcasting mechanism designed to provide collision-free and delay-bounded transmissions. STDMA [14] provides a decentralized dynamic slot assignment mechanism aiming at real-time communication. DTMAC [15] is based on VeMAC (and IEEE 802.11p) but it is infrastructure-free (no RSUs) and uses vehicular location information to improve channel reuse and increase scalability. Another distributed and infrastructure-free approach for platoons is proposed in [4], built on top of IEEE 802.11p, in which the beacons of vehicles are synchronized within each platoon, only, with potential collisions with external vehicles, including from different platoons, being sorted out by the native CSMA/CA arbitration of IEEE 802.11p.

Among the previous approaches we can find two groups, those that add an overlay TDMA layer on top of IEEE 802.11p, and those that propose alternatives to that MAC layer. The second ones are typically collision-free but also intolerant to collisions, being more sensitive to synchronization precision thus requiring tight synchronization. Moreover, they consider the communication channel as a global entity that is partitioned in time slots in different ways, potentially allowing slots reuse. Such a global approach raises a scalability issue depending on the range of the communications, limiting the number of vehicles that can engage the VANET or increasing the number of slots complicating synchronization and efficient bandwidth usage.

With respect to the first group (TDMA overlay over IEEE 802.11p), the approach of Segata et al. [4] deserves a special reference for bearing similarities with RA-TDMAp and being directly comparable. It is tailored for platooning, considering the requirements of the formation control and the reliability of communications under different traffic conditions. It does not require tight synchronization and tolerates collisions with external traffic using the underlying CSMA/CA of IEEE 802.11p. The beacons of all vehicles in the platoon are equally spaced along the beacon interval, creating a cycle. The leader vehicle transmits first with higher power, reaching the whole platoon in one-hop and setting the start of a cycle. All follower vehicles compute their offset with respect to the leader beacon, starting from the one closest to the leader down to the last vehicle in the platoon, and transmit at their assigned time with lower power. Each follower retransmits relevant control information received from its followers in the direction of the leader. Since it is implemented in the PLEXE simulation framework, which we describe next, we will refer to it as "PLEXE-Slotted" approach.

3   Simulation Framework

To analyse the RA-TDMAp protocol under different network and road traffic conditions we decided to use PLEXE[1] [5], which is an Open Source extension to the well known and widely used Veins[2] [16] simulation framework that builds on SUMO[3] for road traffic simulation and on the discrete event simulator OMNeT++[4]. The Veins simulation framework provides a simulation environment able to test real-world scenarios, considering high mobility, high-level application protocols, together with communication and networking protocols with the full stack of IEEE 802.11p/IEEE 1609.4 standards. In turn, OMNeT++ sets the environment to define the applications and protocols logic, allowing to collect operational data for performance analysis.

PLEXE is the current state-of-the art system level platooning simulator, incorporating mobility tightly-coupled with automatic control and communications. It allows defining highway scenarios, effective application, and protocols as well as analyzing network metrics such as collisions and packet delivery ratio etc. Figure 1 shows a snapshot of the PLEXE graphical front-end with a platoon (red cars) together with other external traffic (blue cars).

Fig. 1. Screenshot of the PLEXE (Color figure online)

4   RA-TDMAp for Vehicle Platoons

RA-TDMAp is an instantiation of RA-TDMA [3] to vehicle platoons that use transmission power control. It is a thin layer inserted just above the IEEE 802.11p MAC protocol that controls the transmission instants, being transparent for the applications that run on top (Fig. 2).

---

[1] http://plexe.car2x.org/ .

[2] http://veins.car2x.org/ .

[3] http://sumo.sourceforge.net/ .

[4] https://www.omnetpp.org/ .

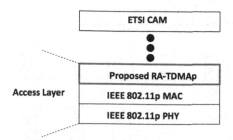

Fig. 2. Modified ITS-G5 architecture

The power management approach is that of [4] (PLEXE-Slotted) in which the leader transmits with high power so that it reaches all platoon members and serves as a synchronization mark setting the start of a round (Fig. 3). The follower vehicles transmit with low power equally spaced in the beacon interval (round period). Low power transmissions allow reducing significantly the channel occupation increasing scalability of the protocol. However, RA-TDMAp differs from [4] in two main aspects, the leader adjusts its transmission instants according to the delays suffered by the platoon members in the previous round and the order of transmissions of the followers is inverted, starting from the last vehicle, which transmits after the leader, up to the first follower that transmits at the end of the cycle, before the next leader beacon.

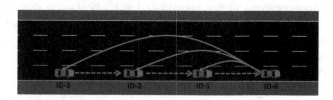

Fig. 3. Synchronization in a platoon, with up-stream multi-hop communication

In the presence of interfering traffic from other vehicles, the native IEEE 802.11p arbitration serializes contending transmitters generating delays that can affect the beacons of platoon members. These delays can be observed by the neighboring platoon members that log them in a Delay vector. This vector is piggybacked in the beacons and forwarded up the line topology, reaching the leader in a single TDMA round. The leader uses the maximum of these delays to delay its next transmission, thus delaying the following TDMA round (Fig. 4). This allows, in the following rounds, escaping the periodic interference that caused the delays, effectively reducing the chance of recurrent collisions that would otherwise occur. Figure 4 also shows the assignment of logical IDs to vehicles according to their position in the platoon, starting with the leader that is node 0, followed by the last vehicle, 3 in this case, then 2 and then 1, the closest to the leader. This position-based rule can rely on GPS, on a topology tracking method or on both.

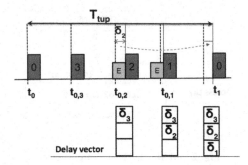

Fig. 4. Adaptive synchronization in RA-TDMAp, with interference and delays measurement and propagation.

The beacon interval in RA-TDMAp, interchangeably called TDMA round period, is represented by *Ttup*. It is divided by *N* vehicles currently engaged in the platoon creating a target separation between consecutive platoon beacons equal to *Txwin* = *Ttup/N*. If in the nth round the leader transmits at time $t_{n,0}$, the follower $i > 0$ in that round is expected to transmit at time $t_{n,i}$ (Eq. 1).

$$t_{n,i} = t_{n,0} + T_{xwin} \times (N - i) \tag{1}$$

Once vehicle 1 transmits, the leader becomes aware of all delays that may have affected the platoon beacons in that round (δ_i, i = 1...N−1) and uses the maximum value, if within a tolerable limit (Δ), to delay its next beacon transmission. Using Δ allows bounding the maximum delay that can affect the leader beacon, which is normally a fraction of the beacons separation Txwin.

This is formalized in Eq. 2. Note that δ_i is the delay between the effective and expected reception instants of the preceding vehicle(s).

$$t_{n+1} = t_n + T_{tup} + \min(\Delta, \min_{i=1...N-1}(\delta_i)) \tag{2}$$

In the presence of packet losses, if the leader does not receive information from the delays that affected the followers, it considers them as null and transmits one beacon interval after the previous transmission. Similarly, if a follower misses the leader beacon it transmits its own beacon one beacon interval after its previous transmission. This makes the protocol very robust to varying channel conditions.

5   Evaluation of the Protocol

In this section we analyse the performance of the proposed RA-TDMAp protocol in demanding traffic conditions resorting to the PLEXE simulation framework (Sect. 3). We first show the simulation setup including the used models and scenarios, after we validate the adaptive feature of RA-TDMAp in platooning, and then we compare RA-TDMAp with two other state of the art protocols, namely PLEXE-Slotted and

IEEE 802.11p (CSMA/CA). For the comparison we use two typical network metrics, similarly to [4], which are the channel busy ratio and the collisions rate. Finally, we include another comparison using the so-called safe time ratio, which represents how well the protocols meet specified application timing requirements.

5.1   Simulation Setup

We used the PHY and MAC models of IEEE 802.11p proposed in [17], using a bitrate of 6 Mbit/s, which is suited for demanding safety related applications [18]. We configured the transmission power of the leader to 100mW (high power) as it needs to reach all the cars in the platoon. For the followers we used three different power values (low power), namely 0.05 mW, 0.5 mW and 1 mW, since they only need to communicate with the car in front. Furthermore, we did not enable the switching between Control Channel (CCH) and Service Channel (SCH), using only the CCH, and all beacons use the same Access Category (AC). Table 1 summarizes all communication related parameters.

Table 1. PHY and MAC parameters

Parameter	Values
PHY/MAC model	IEEE 802.11p/1609.4 only (CCH)
Channel	5.89 GHz
Bitrate	6 Mbit/s
MSDU size	200 B
Leader's Tx power	100 mW
Follower's Tx power	0.05 mW, 0.5 mW and 1 mW

To investigate the proposed protocol performance, we carried out a set of simulations in a moderately dense traffic environment. We specifically simulated a realistic case with a stretch of a 4-lane highway filled with 160 cars organized in platoons of 10 vehicles, plus 10 external cars that create extra communication interference. Other relevant parameters are the distance between vehicles inside the platoon (gap), set to 5 m, and the speed of all the platoons, set to 100 km/h. The summary of the simulation parameters is shown in Table 2.

Table 2. Scenario configurations

Parameter	Values
Number of cars	160
Platoon size	10 cars
External cars	10
Inter-vehicle gap	5 m
Controller	ACC

5.2   Validating RA-TDMAp Adaptation to Interference Delays

The distinctive feature of RA-TDMAp is its capacity to shift the TDMA round made of the beacons in the platoon to avoid other transmissions that were causing interference delays. If the interference is periodic and with similar period, shifting the round removes the interference. If further delays subsist, the protocol continues shifting the round. Thus, given its relevance, we show here a validation of this adaptive feature of the protocol before moving to the comparisons. For the sake of simplicity of representation, we use a platoon with just 4 vehicles in the same simulation scenario and we log the respective transmission instants.

Figure 5 shows the evolution of the offsets of the transmissions of the platoon members with respect to the leader transmission in each cycle. Each trace corresponds to the offset of one member (1 to 3 starting from below), except for the upper trace that represents the next leader transmission with respect to its previous one, thus it shows how much the leader has delayed the next TDMA round (or cycle). Without interference from external vehicles the offsets would be constant as given by Eq. 1. However, the figure shows there are in fact interferences, which are then accommodated by the leader in the following cycle (upper trace) according to Eq. 2. This behavior is clear in the figure with the upper trace containing the variations of the lower traces. However, it has more variations than these, since the leader transmissions also suffer direct interference. Finally, the tall spikes that sporadically affect the upper trace represent leader beacon losses, doubling the difference between consecutive leader beacons.

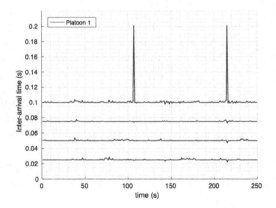

Fig. 5. Adaptation mechanism of RA-TDMAp

5.3   Comparison of Protocols

We ran the simulation for 30 s of simulated time and gathered traces in the scenario referred in Table 2 using the three protocols, namely RA-TDMAp, PLEXE-Slotted and CSMA/CA. The first metric we use for comparison is the channel busy time ratio or busy time ratio. This is a physical layer metric that indicates the percentage of times each node tried to access the channel and the channel was busy. This metric is described with more detail in [9].

Figure 6 shows the results for the three followers transmission power levels. We can see that while PLEXE-Slotted and CSMA/CA perform approximately similarly, RA-TDMAp shows a 4 to 5 times reduction for all the three cases. This is a direct consequence of the adaptation feature of the protocol that quickly moves the platoon transmissions away from the interferences. Concerning the followers' transmission power, we can see that as it increases it causes the busy time ratio to increase approximately similarly for all approaches. This is expected as higher power reduces channel spatial reuse and increases interference.

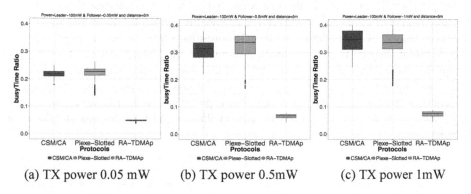

(a) TX power 0.05 mW   (b) TX power 0.5mW   (c) TX power 1mW

Fig. 6. Busy time ratio for given scenario under 5 m and three follower's TX powers

The second metric is the collisions rate, i.e., the average number of collisions per second. The simulator determines collisions as the frames that were not correctly decoded due to interference. More details can also be found in [9].

The results are shown in Fig. 7. PLEXE-Slotted exhibits some benefit when compared to CSMA/CA because of synchronizing the beacons inside each platoon. However, the benefit is small. A much larger benefit is achieved by RA-TDMAp, from near one order of magnitude for very low power to around 7 times for intermediate and 5 times for high followers' transmission power. Again, this is due to the adaptive

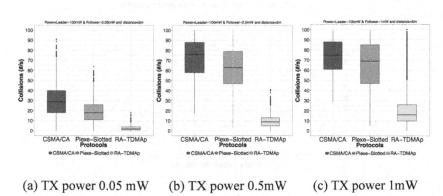

(a) TX power 0.05 mW   (b) TX power 0.5mW   (c) TX power 1mW

Fig. 7. Collisions rate for given scenario with 5 m gap and three follower's TX powers

feature of the protocol that, upon interference, pulls the platoon away from it from one cycle to the next. Thus, periodic interferences will not persist interfering as opposed to the other cases. Similarly to the previous metric, the relative performance of the three protocols is kept as the followers' transmission power increases, since the corresponding larger range leads to increasing collisions.

Beyond properties of the communication channel, it is also relevant to assess how well the channel meets application requirements. Thus, we use the metric proposed in [4] called safe time ratio that aims at distributed feedback control in the context of vehicle platooning. This metric captures how much time a platoon is in safe state during the simulation time. A safe state occurs when the communication delay affecting the platoon controller is below a given requirement for which the controller was tuned. Longer delays are considered unsafe. The results show, again, a superiority of RA-TDMAp, being the only protocol, among PLEXE-Slotted and CSMA/CA, that keeps the platoons in safe state above 99% of the time for delay requirements down to 0.2 s and for all tested power levels of the platoons' followers. The advantage is specially noticeable for very low transmission power and tighter delay requirements, e.g., 99% for 0.2 s with RA-TDMAp against 95% for PLEXE-Slotted and 90% for CSMA/CA.

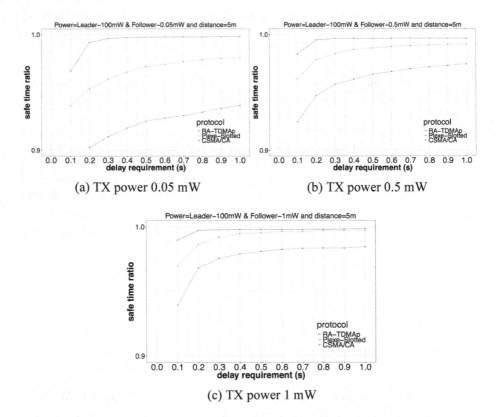

(a) TX power 0.05 mW

(b) TX power 0.5 mW

(c) TX power 1 mW

Fig. 8. Safe time ratio for all approaches under three followers' transmit power levels

6 Conclusion

Vehicular networks are growingly important as the level of vehicles driving automation is increasing. In particular, collaborative applications such as platooning can improve vehicle and users safety as well as fuel efficiency. However, the effectiveness of these applications relies on the quality of the channel. In this paper we proposed the RA-TDMAp protocol that is deployed on top of IEEE 802.11p, which is the state-of-the-art standard for vehicular networks and which relies on CSMA/CA arbitration. RA-TDMAp organizes the vehicle beacons in each platoon in a TDMA round, separately, and shifts this round to escape from periodic interference from other vehicles. We carried out simulations in realistic scenarios using the PLEXE-Veins-SUMO-OMNeT++ frame-work and we assessed RA-TDMAp against two state-of-the-art alternatives, CSMA/CA from native IEEE 802.11p and PLEXE-Slotted, which was proposed within PLEXE and works similarly to RA-TDMAp but without the capacity to shift the TDMA round. The results show a clear benefit of using RA-TDMAp, with nearly one order of magnitude reduction in collisions rate, a factor of 4 to 5 reduction in channel occupation and a significant improvement in safe time ratio, a communications-related control metric. Future work will extend the RA-TDMAp assessment to more scenarios and more protocols. Moreover, we are also building upon the current experience with plain IEEE 802.11 technology to assess the applicability of our proposed approach to a concept of bicycles, to allow multimedia communication among groups of users in an urban mobility concept.

Acknowledgement. This article is a result of the project Generation.Mobi, reference POCI-01-0247-FEDER-017369, supported by European Regional Development Fund (FEDER), through Operational Program Competitiveness and Internationalization (POCI).

References

1. ETSI EN 302 663 (V1.2.1): Intelligent Transport Systems (ITS), Access layer specification for Intelligent Transport Systems operating in the 5 GHz frequency band, vol. 5, November 2012
2. Eckhoff, D., Sofra, N., German, R.: A performance study of cooperative awareness in ETSI ITS G5 and IEEE WAVE. In: 10th Annual Conference on Wireless On-demand Network Systems and Services (WONS), pp. 196–200. March 2013
3. Santos, F., Almeida, L., Lopes, L.S.: Self-configuration of an adaptive TDMA wireless communication protocol for teams of mobile robots. In: IEEE International Conference on Emerging Technologies and Factory Automation, 2008. ETFA 2008, pp. 1197–1204. IEEE (2008)
4. Segata, M., Bloessl, B., Joerer, S., Sommer, C., Gerla, M., Cigno, R.L., Dressler, F.: Towards inter-vehicle communication strategies for platooning support. In: 7th International Workshop on Communication Technologies for Vehicles (Nets4Cars-Fall), pp. 1–6. IEEE (2014)
5. Segata, M., Joerer, S., Bloessl, B., Sommer, C., Dressler, F., Lo Cigno, R.: PLEXE: a platooning extension for veins. In: 6th IEEE Vehicular Networking Conference (VNC 2014). Paderborn, Germany, pp. 53–60. IEEE. December 2014

6. Autolitano, A., Campolo, C., Molinaro, A., Scopigno, R., Vesco, A.: An insight into decentralized congestion control techniques for VANETs from ETSI TS 102 687 V1.1.1. In: Wireless Days (WD), 2013 IFIP, pp. 1–6. Nov 2013
7. Hadded, M., Muhlethaler, P., Laouiti, A., Zagrouba, R., Saidane, L.A.: TDMA-based MAC protocols for vehicular ad hoc networks: A survey, qualitative analysis, and open research issues. IEEE Commun. Surv. Tutor. **17**(4), 2461–2492 (2015)
8. Lyamin, N., Vinel, A., Jonsson, M., Bellalta, B.: Cooperative awareness in VANETs: on ETSI EN 302 637-2 performance. IEEE Trans. Veh. Technol. **67**, 17–28 (2017)
9. Sommer, C., Joerer, S., Segata, M., Tonguz, O.K., Cigno, R.L., Dressler, F.: How shadowing hurts vehicular communications and how dynamic beaconing can help. IEEE Trans. Mob. Comput. **14**(7), 1411–1421 (2015)
10. Aslam, A., Almeida, L., Santos, F.: Using RA-TDMA to support concurrent collaborative applications in VANETs. In: IEEE EUROCON 2017-17th International Conference on Smart Technologies, pp. 896–901. IEEE (2017)
11. Omar, H., Zhuang, W., Li, L.: VeMAC: a TDMA-based MAC protocol for reliable broadcast in VANETs. IEEE Trans. Mob. Comput. **12**(9), 1724–1736 (2013)
12. Yu, F., Biswas, S.: A self-organizing MAC protocol for DSRC based vehicular ad hoc networks. In: 27th International Conference on Distributed Computing Systems Workshops, 2007. ICDCSW 2007, p. 88. IEEE (2007)
13. Lu, N., Ji, Y., Liu, F., Wang, X.: A dedicated multi-channel mac protocol design for VANET with adaptive broadcasting. In: 2010 IEEE Wireless Communication and Networking Conference, pp. 1–6. IEEE (2010)
14. Alonso, A., Sjöberg, K., Uhlemann, E., Ström, E., Mecklenbräuker, C.: Challenging vehicular scenarios for self-organizing time division multiple access. Eur. Coop. Field Sci. Tech. Res. (2011)
15. Hadded, M., Laouiti, A., Zagrouba, R., Muhlethaler, P., Saidane, L.A.: A fully distributed TDMA based mac protocol for vehicular ad hoc networks. In: International Conference on Performance Evaluation and Modeling in Wired and Wireless networks PEMWN 2015 (2015)
16. Sommer, C., German, R., Dressler, F.: Bidirectionally coupled network and road traffic simulation for improved IVC analysis. IEEE Trans. Mob. Comput. **10**(1), 3–15 (2011)
17. Eckhoff, D., Sommer, C.: A multi-channel IEEE 1609.4 and 802.11p EDCA model for the veins framework. In: 5th ACM/ICST International Conference on Simulation Tools and Techniques for Communications, Networks and Systems (SIMUTools 2012): 5th ACM/ICST International Workshop on OMNeT++ (OMNeT++ 2012), Poster Session. Desenzano, Italy: ACM, March 2012
18. Jiang, D., Chen, Q., Delgrossi, L.: Optimal data rate selection for vehicle safety communications. In: Proceedings of the Fifth ACM International Workshop on Vehicular Inter-NETworking, pp. 30–38. ACM (2008)

Abstract of Invited Talks

Demo for Channel Sounding in the Air-to-Ground Link

Cesar Briso[✉]

Departamento de Teoría de la Señal y Comunicaciones,
ETSIST UPM, Madrid, Spain
cesar.briso@upm.es

Air-to-ground channels are one of the most relevant in the field of Intelligent Transportation Systems (ITS). To properly control the UAV and to carry one the several applications that are useful in this medium (real-time video streaming, telemetry, etc.) is more than convenient to have a proper estimation if the most important channel parameters. Using a medium-size high-performance UAV with the channel sounder transmitter installed on board, measurements of propagation, path-loss and delay spread, will be made for several different heights for the UAV in a short range of distances (0–40 m). The receiver of the channel sounder will be installed on a laboratory in the ground with an external antenna.

© Springer International Publishing AG, part of Springer Nature 2018
J. Moreno García-Loygorri et al. (Eds.): Nets4Cars 2018/Nets4Trains 2018/Nets4Aircraft 2018, LNCS 10796, p. 183, 2018.
https://doi.org/10.1007/978-3-319-90371-2

Software Demonstration for Millimeter-Wave Railway Communications

Ke Guan[1,2,3](✉)

[1] Beijing Jiaotong University, Beijing, China
ke.guan.bjtu@qq.com
[2] Technische Universität Braunschweig, Braunschweig, Germany
[3] Electronics and Telecommunications Research Institute, Daejeon, South Korea

In the vision of "smart rail mobility", a seamless high-data-rate wireless connectivity with several GHz bandwidth will be required. This forms a strong motivation for exploring the underutilized millimeter wave (mm Wave) band. In this software, the link-level performance of a typical high-data rate railway communication system – the mobile hotspot network enhanced (MHN-E) system at 25 GHz band – is demonstrated. The dynamic line of sight, reflected rays and scattered rays in a typical high-speed railway outdoor scenario are generated by the high-performance ray-tracing simulation platform jointly developed by Beijing Jiaotong University, China and Technische Universität Braunschweig, Germany. With the realistic ray-tracing results, the time-variant channel impulse response and channel transfer function can be obtained. Based on this channel information, the link-level simulator developed by Electronics and Telecommunications Research Institute, Korea, can calculate the corresponding signal-to-noise ratio (SNR), throughput and the other key performance indicators. The MHN-E system has been hardware demonstrated at PyeongChang 2018 Olympics achieving up to 5 Gbps data rate at the speed of 60 km/h and software demonstrated for the performance at the real high speed up to 500 km/h.

© Springer International Publishing AG, part of Springer Nature 2018
J. Moreno García-Loygorri et al. (Eds.): Nets4Cars 2018/Nets4Trains 2018/Nets4Aircraft 2018, LNCS 10796, p. 184, 2018.
https://doi.org/10.1007/978-3-319-90371-2

Author Index

Printed in the United States
By Bookmasters